AMERICA GOES TO THE MOVIES:
THE 1990s

By Wes Laurie

Introduction

Hello. My name is Wes Laurie and I grew up to be a screenwriter in the business of motion pictures. Of course, if you have a static picture and five bucks I'm willing to write that for you too. Most of what I write and have sold to folks is never seen or heard of again and as of this writing most of what has been produced is Indie horror movies that you may have a hard time finding. Seek them out if you want to get weird I suppose.

I was born in the 1980s but hit puberty in the 1990s. The 80s for me involved a lot of movies featuring puppets and the 90s, well, the 90s was a real smorgasbord of creativity. In the 90s we got to have Summer blockbusters, but Indie movies were getting their fair share of theater time as well. Money was being invested into low budget Indies at a rate that, as an adult still making his way up from the bottom of the industry, I am quite envious of. The diversity of films in the 90s planted and spread the seeds of creativity for many a future filmmaker, and while superhero movies seem to choke the Hollywood pipeline of product these days, there are still quite a few flashes of creative spirit to catch sight of. In the craft of filmmaking the past is an undeniably strong authority in terms of inspiration and education, regardless of how new technologies reshape the business.

As one revisits a decade and basks in the nostalgia, it is also inevitable that they will see the shortcomings of expression on display as well.

There are many things that were acceptable in the 90s that are not politically correct with our civilized advances today. For example, I tried watching the television show *Friends* and couldn't help but think someone not of that generation might watch the same show and be offended by all of jokes circling around being homophobic and sexist. Of course, all you have to do is go online and play some video games to realize the same non-pc rhetoric and slurs are alive and well within the latest generation. Maybe I should write an entire book exploring the negative connotations of such things within art, whether expressed intentionally or not?   Not today. Nostalgia trip!

Let's take a trip back to the 1990s. It's not a big leap backwards for me, pretty sure I was existing in the 90s just yesterday. Now I feel old. Bear with your old man narrator if you will and we shall explore the movies that were at the top of the box office earnings in North America for each year of the decade that was the 1990s.

1990

10. *Kindergarten Cop* - directed by Ivan Reitman, screenplay by Murray Salem, Herschel Weingrod, and Timothy Harris. Domestic Box Office: $91,457,688

An elderly woman with a Mr. Burns-ish build, my kindergarten teacher was comparable to a strict and freaky cop. She had to have been in her 80s while presiding over the expansion of young minds, mostly by handing out coloring pages, in that classroom. Personally, I think I was a well-behaved student, but she liked to crack down if she got the slightest whiff of rebellion.

The end of the day ritual for exiting class involved a chant about how we would miss her and how we loved her, topped off with us having to blow her a kiss. Then we'd line up single file and she would reward us with stickers as we went out the door. The blowing her a kiss portion of the proceedings never sat well with me and I would often decline to participate. My refusal to bestow air kisses upon the teacher sometimes led to me not getting a sticker. It made me sad because I really liked stickers. Specifically, I recall one day when the boy in front of me got a rad motorcycle sticker and I got none. A motorcycle sticker would have looked awesome in my sticker album; insert pouty-face emoji here. Anyway, that's the plot to *Kindergarten Cop.*

Okay, the real plot follows an undercover cop that ends up having to pose as a kindergarten teacher to try and figure out which student is the son of a

2

murderous drug dealer cooling his heels in jail. He wants to find the kid in order to find the kid's mother in order to get her to testify against said drug dealer. The rough and tough cop gets in touch with his softer side, growing fond of his new job and the kids of his class, while falling in love with the woman he has been seeking for the previously mentioned legal reasons. Spoiler alert: the bad guy gets released from jail and the cop, John Kimble, has to save the day.

Kindergarten Cop came out when I was around eight years old. My movie diet by this time had already expanded beyond children's fare and into movies featuring action stars. Jean-Claude Van Damme and Steven Seagal were superstars with Arnold Schwarzenegger and Sylvester Stallone also pumping up my playtime adrenaline levels, along with a sprinkling of inspirational offerings from Patrick Swayze, Harrison Ford, Bruce Willis, and later in the 90s Wesley Snipes. When it came down to Van Damme or Seagal I chose to be a Seagal fan and in the Schwarzenegger vs Stallone debates I sided with Arnie. Therefore, *Kindergarten Cop* starring Arnold Schwarzenegger was a no-brainer choice for viewing entertainment.

The movie works as an interesting bridge between family style movies and action movies. John Kimble is an action movie character but placed within a family safe comedy scenario. The movie did not pull back all the way on punches when it came to presenting the crime and action elements, giving those aspects of the movie the darkness that satiated my childhood appetite for adult violence. At the age of eight I was not all that far removed from kindergarten myself and could appreciate the overall scenario involving kids my age in peril, therefore, I am saying the blend of light-hearted comedy with a dose of action worked for a broad audience and hit the movie market at exactly the right time to be an interesting genre splitting success. The movie was released in theaters in December of 1990, but eventually became a popular VHS rental for me. I could watch *Follow That Bird*, then *Kindergarten Cop*, and complete the triple feature experience with Marked *For Death*. Of course, when I spent the weekend at my grandma's we rented way more than three movies, a kid can sit through a lot of action, skipping sleep, when pumped up on Doritos and Mountain Dew.

Out of all of the 90s action stars Arnold Schwarzenegger is the one that did the best job of branding catchphrases. *Kindergarten Cop* was not an exception to that formula. The movie is chock-full of lines made hilariously memorable in equal parts due to Schwarzenegger's accent and then the fact that he is often yelling them at small children. Specifically, the moment when John Kimble states that he has a headache and a child suggests that it might be a tumor and Kimble replies "It's not a tumor," is very quotable thanks to the fun way "tumor" sounds with Arnold's accent. Quotes from *Kindergarten Cop* have been a popular choice for Internet soundboards used in making prank phone calls. I'm not sure it will ever get old hearing people answer the phone to John Kimble suggesting they play the game "Who is my daddy and what does he do."

Arnold Schwarzenegger may have been at the head of the class, but *Kindergarten Cop* wasn't just a one man show. John Kimble wasn't supposed to be teaching kindergarten and only lands in that spot due to his partner, played by actress Pamela Reed, getting sick. Actress Pamela Reed would later team up with both Schwarzenegger and director Ivan Reitman for the male pregnancy movie *Junior*.

On the action movie side (or more twisted family side) the main antagonist of the movie is played by actor Richard Tyson with support from his nefarious mother played by Carroll Baker. However, on the family movie side of things Oscar winner Linda Hunt plays the suspicious school principal who disapproves of Kimble's methods, yet by the end is won over as a friend. Linda Hunt won her Oscar for Best Supporting Actress due to her part in the film *The Year Of Living Dangerously*. She was the first person to win an Oscar for a role portraying the opposite sex. Her winning role was her playing a male dwarf named Billy Kwan. Hunt is generally listed as being four foot nine, give or take.

The woman John Kimble searches for, Joyce, is a role that Penelope Ann Miller filled. Movie fans of my age, the younger spectrum of the target audience, may have recognized Miller from her roles in *Big Top Pee-Wee* and *Adventures In Babysitting*. She also plays Gail, opposite Al Pacino, in the gangster thriller *Carlito's Way*. I like *Carlito's Way*.

Little kids are known to say some funny things and the children featured in the movie really shine at being cute while angling for chuckles. Among the child actors a young Odette Annable, also known as Odette Yustman, made her acting debut. Adam Wylie was present and has also gone on to have a lengthy acting career of note. Also, Ross Malinger has a *Kindergarten Cop* credit, though the pinnacle of his child acting for many might have been as Tom Hanks' kid in *Sleepless in Seattle*. Director Ivan Reitman's son Mr. Jason Reitman played "Kissing Boy," in the movie. The younger Reitman is a known director himself these days with projects such as *Thank You For Smoking, Juno, Up In The Air, Young Adult, Labor Day, Tully*, and I'm sure the list will go on and on. However, the lead child of interest, the spawn of the murderous drug dealer Crisp and sweet Joyce, Dominic, was played by twins Joseph and Christian Cousins. The Cousins brothers would go on to the prestige of acting in *Critters 3* and the reoccurring role of Bobby Ewing on the soap opera *Knots Landing*.

Some of the scenes in *Kindergarten Cop* were filmed in California, including work at Universal Studios. However, the bulk of the shoot took place in Astoria, Oregon. This is a fun fact mainly due to the popular adventure film *The Goonies* was set there as well. Other movies that have commenced with production within Astoria, Oregon include *Short Circuit, The Black Stallion*, two *Free Willy* movies, the third Ninja Turtles movie, a Benji flick, and *The Ring Two*.

A sequel, *Kindergarten Cop 2*, came out in 2016 starring Dolph Lundgren. I will admit that I have not, nor do I plan on watching that follow up effort. Really, as far as the first *Kindergarten Cop* goes, I enjoy the nostalgia of thinking about the movie, but as an adult, I have a hard time sitting through it again.

9. *Dick Tracy* - directed by Warren Beatty, screenplay by Jim Cash and Jack Epps Jr. Domestic Box Office: $103,738,726

The character Dick Tracy got his start in the funny papers with the comic strip going to newspaper print in 1931. Chester Gould is the name of Tracy's creator, though many others have taken control of the detective and his adventures over the decades.

Aside from being a comic in the 1930s the property was also turned into a radio program and then it was a serial film series from Republic Pictures. In the 1940s RKO Radio Pictures produced four Dick Tracy movies. In the 1950s Ralph Byrd starred as the character for a television series, however, his death in 1952 ended the continuation of that production. Skip ahead to the 60s and Dick Tracy made it on television as an animated series and there was a pilot shot for a non-cartoon version starring Ray MacDonnell as the lead. The 60s live-action variation was not picked up by the networks.

Dick Tracy kept chugging along solving crimes in comic syndication and the character must have meant a lot to Warren Beatty because he supposedly didn't want the gap between the 60s and the 90s to have been void of new Dick Tracy movies. It is said that he championed the material starting in 1975, but due to someone else holding the rights couldn't make headway.

Beatty wasn't alone in his admiration for the comic detective as many a producer, director, and actor cycled in and out of various incarnations of new Dick Tracy projects that never went into full production. At one point Warren Beatty was attached to star with Walter Hill directing. The project went far enough that sets were built, however, Hill and Beatty were said to have disagreed on the tone of the film. Beatty wished to stay true to the comic strip and Hill wanted to stamp it with grittier violence. It is also said that Beatty made some financial demands that the studio balked at, but in the game that is Hollywood negotiations who is to say what is greed and what is strategy, because after the collapse of the project Warren Beatty ended up getting to stay true to his vision for the property. When the rights were available for option once again in 1985 Warren Beatty put his money where his passion was and snatched them up himself.

Maybe I made Warren Beatty sound very artistic and noble there with the buying of the rights. I am as jaded as the next person when it comes to believing in the truth of magic in Hollywood. I concede that for all I know he fleeced someone else out of the money and used that to buy the rights. Either scenario or a mixture of the two could be true. Take note: rule number one in movie producing is spend other people's money not your own.

The story in 1990's *Dick Tracy* centers around the detective, as played by Warren Beatty, and his attempts to stop gangster Big Boy Caprice, played by Al Pacino, from taking over and proliferating all crime in the city. Other areas of focus for the story involve Dick Tracy taking a Kid, played by Charlie Korsmo, under his wing and then a sort of love triangle between Dick Tracy, Tess Trueheart, and Breathless Mahoney. Glenne Headly played Trueheart and pop singer Madonna played Mahoney.

The rest of the cast is populated with names such as: Dustin Hoffman, Paul Sorvino, Dick Van Dyke, Mandy Patinkin, William Forsythe, Kathy Bates, Catherine O'Hara, James Caan, and many other notables that get left off of this list because I am tired of name-dropping.

Cracking into the top ten earning films of 1990, *Dick Tracy* did earn its budget back, along with the massive advertising expenditures deployed by Disney, though that was after combining theater ticket and then home video sales. Ideally a studio would love to recoup at a faster rate and the success of the film is something that divides people in debate when thinking of the film in terms of accolades, earnings, and critical reception. No one rushed to make a sequel.

As a kid I bought Dick Tracy trading cards and got excited about the Dick Tracy collectible plastic cups that arrived at McDonalds. Those cups at McDonalds were a big thing for kids my age when it came to movie promotional items. I would wager to say those cups were even better than the toys that came in Happy Meals, though I hoarded plenty of those as well.

The advertising gimmicks and the collectibles, those were fun. When it came time to enjoy the hyped up movie, however, I did not get converted into a Dick Tracy fan at all. The movie bored me.

The movie was marketed to children, but I don't think it played to that audience exactly right. Dick Tracy was an icon to older men such as Warren Beatty and in trying to stay true to the source material *Dick Tracy* failed to capture the modern audience. When Tim Burton made *Batman*, he paid some homage to Batman's past, the movie does have campy aspects, but he also included more gritty aspects that made it feel like an end of the 80s film, not complete revisit of the Adam West and 60s era Batman. We fell in love, hook, line, and sinker for our new version of *Batman*. *Dick Tracy* did not arrive feeling like it wanted to become one with our generation in that same manner, even with the technological wonder that went into the process.

In retrospect, *Dick Tracy* did not need to cater to my generation or audiences of 1990. I am just pointing out some of the "at the time" thinking that may have driven my childhood brain away from embracing the movie. As an adult, the technical accolades and production efforts that went into the movie are more understandable and the meaning and style of the movie far more intriguing. *Dick Tracy* is impressive as a feat of filmmaking. After saying that, however, I'm still not saying I adore *Dick Tracy* the movie. You can check it out for historical or cinephile purposes, but at the end of the day I'd sooner re-watch *Batman*. Or *Who Framed Roger Rabbit?* Or *Sin City*. Or *Boogie Nights*.

Unlike many comic hero movies, *Dick Tracy* doesn't waste much time schooling the audience with origin story material. Perhaps this was another notch against it in terms of capturing the imaginations of a new era; not familiarizing them with how things were going to go or were supposed to be. For those who think the movie started off too much "already in the thick of things," there is actually some movie tie-in comic books, with the likeness of Warren Beatty included, that were published to try and provide more backstory for the events of the film.

Dick Tracy acquired six Academy Award Nominations, falling short in the categories of Best Sound, Best Costume Design, Best Cinematography, and no trophy for Al Pacino as Best Actor in a Supporting Role. However, three golden Oscar statues did go home with people involved in the categories of Best Art Direction-Set Direction, Best Makeup, and Best Music, Original Song went to Stephen Sondheim for the track *Sooner or Later* (*I Always Get My Man*.) The song was performed by Madonna.

Along with the songs created by Stephen Sondheim, legendary composer Danny Elfman handled the orchestral music of the film. Dick Tracy is considered to be the first movie to use digital audio, which is something Danny Elfman has vocalized some negative opinion on in terms of how it is used in filmmaking and the potential for the life music brings to a film being overshadowed by the sound effects.

The extensive and award winning makeup work on the film makes most of the gangsters look like they've been mutated; disfigured faces and heads are par for the course. There are many theories as to why that style was chosen in terms of representing the characters, aside from staying true to the comic source material. Personally, I just assume it is an exaggeration on gangster nicknames. Gangsters of that bygone era were always sporting fun nicknames like Babyface, Scarface, or Three-fingers Fat Face, and in the *Dick Tracy* movie, like the original comic, nicknames are taken a step farther in literality with extreme visual representation. One would think that such quirky details would have made *Dick Tracy* a smash hit with kids resulting in a Saturday morning cartoon or something for the 90s. Coming out of the 80s I know I was ingrained with appreciation for puppets and practical effects, but while this helped make me a hardcore Teenage Mutant Ninja Turtle fan, it never translated to me backing *Dick Tracy*.

The sets and set pieces were a blended wonder of paintings and practical effects, including the usage of miniatures, that stand the test of time in terms of being interesting within an industry ruled by CGI. Over 57 matte paintings, on glass, were said to have been created for the production, helping try to bring the city to life when combined with the action elements of the actors at work. All in all, the results are a comic strip based movie that gets pretty close to looking like a comic strip.

The colors used in the movie were limited and chosen to mimic the comic. Maybe kids had a hard time finding Dick Tracy's yellow clothes all that cool, but as an adult it is cool to see them sticking to detail with regard to the origins. Yet, I will point out that when I think of a man dressed in all yellow I first think of the man from *Curious George*.

One actor that specifically benefited from the colors and lighting of the movie in my opinion is Madonna. She's not someone I equate with A-list acting and while I might be able to hum along with a few of her pop tunes I've never been all that attracted to her artistry or sex symbol imagery. However, in *Dick Tracy* her pale skin is given a new glow of life that is very becoming, and she fills the shoes of sexpot Breathless Mahoney quite well. Madonna joined the marketing push for the movie by promoting Dick Tracy on stage during her *Blond Ambition* tour. Offscreen she and Warren Beatty also dated one another.

The character and tales of Dick Tracy will surely get more movie treatments at some point, but as I write this in the year 2018, I'd wager it is a head-scratcher to studio executives trying to figure out how to best approach the subject matter. Will it need some modern flair, or should it remain strictly tethered to its old school roots? A gritty reboot sounds just as silly as a man in all yellow fighting off villains with enlarged heads, and yet, there is something magical about imagining that potential ridiculousness. It's a more confusing property in terms of trying to form a broad audience bridge between youth and adult movie fans, more so than say *The Transformers*, where big budget spectacle translated mostly with ease. Perhaps you are reading this in the distant future, however, and *Dick Tracy* is already a box office puzzle solved. I don't know, I can only see into the future after it has already happened and by then I am usually too late to make good predictions.

8. *Die Hard 2* - directed by Renny Harlin, screenplay by Steven E. de Souza and Doug Richardson. Domestic Box Office: $117,540,947

The first *Die Hard* is still the best out of the action series, but *Die Hard 2*, in which they tried to DIE HARDER, is a serviceable sequel. The first film saw NYPD detective John McClane saving his wife and other hostages from a terrorist infested skyscraper. In *Die Hard 2: Die Harder* John McClane is sort of placed into the same plot only this time at an airport. His wife is on a plane and when terrorists take over the airport systems, effectively controlling the fates of the passengers on all flights, her life is once again in danger along with many others. All of this takes place on Christmas Eve, once again, and is due to villains wishing to free their favorite Central American General drug lord from United States custody. McClane must go rogue and save the day!

When I say that the film is serviceable, my opinion is that it does the trick in continuing the series, validates that the series can be sustainable in terms of sequels being a draw, and if you're in the mood is entertaining. The *Die Hard* series lives and dies on John McClane's attitude, including the one-liners, as well as the action set pieces he is thrown in to. *Die Hard 2* checks the boxes. It is perhaps best as a "turn your brain off" style of movie, too easy to pick at critically if you have your mind too focused on logistics and reality. Also, after you have seen the movie once, subsequent beholding may give it a "going through the motions" vibe and really, I have found it to be an easy movie to turn on and fall asleep to.

Bruce Willis commands the role of John McClane and if one were to point out what made Bruce Willis a movie star, I'd reckon the *Die Hard* movies are what launched him up there as bankable blockbuster talent through the 90s. In the first movie of the series McClane went to battle against the villain Hans Gruber, made quite memorable by actor Alan Rickman. In the sequel the main antagonist role is Stuart as played by actor William Sadler. Sadler's villain is a more traditional style of "bad guy" and while he is solid in his performance, for me Alan Rickman's Hans Gruber really twinkled with a lot more Hollywood magic.

Bonnie Bedelia reprises her role of Holly McClane and finds herself stuck on a plane with Richard Thornberg, played by William Atherton, a reporter from the first film that the McClanes are not too fond of. Reginald VelJohnson has a bit in the movie as Al Powell, a crucial ally to McClane in the first *Die Hard*. Reginald VelJohnson is blessed with a fabulous name, but his acting career may have been cursed by the television show *Family Matters*. Every time I see this actor in something my brain immediately points out: there is Uncle Carl! And from Carl Winslow the brain quickly boots up an image of his nephew Steve Urkel and then cues Urkel's annoying voice delivering the catchphrase: "Did I do that?" Of course, I then hear that followed up in Urkel's nasally tone by: "I've fallen and I can't get up!"

Some other names to round out the cast of Die Hard 2 are Dennis Franz, Art Evans, Franco Nero, Sheila McCarthy, Fred Thompson, John Amos, John Leguizamo, and Tom Bower. Robert Patrick, Vondie Curtis-Hall, Colm Meaney, and Mark Boone Junior are also in there, along with Don Harvey and many more.

The story for *Die Hard 2* is based off of the novel *58 Minutes* written by Walter Wager. Other films adapted from Walter Wager novels include: *Twilight's Last Gleaming* starring Burt Lancaster, *Telefon* starring Charles Bronson, and *Raw Deal* starring Arnold Schwarzenegger.

While *Dick Tracy*, the ninth highest grossing film of 1990, used matte paintings in a notable way, *Die Hard 2* is credited with a first with regard to usage of a matte painting. The production utilized a matte painting that had been photographed and then scanned into a computer. This painting was then digitally composited with live-action footage for the last runway scene within the movie.

Finland born director Renny Harland had a second movie released in 1990 as well. This was *The Adventures of Ford Fairlane* starring Andrew Dice Clay. Harland's directing career has been mostly involved with the action genre, though he has bounced into horror films a time or two. He directed *A Nightmare On Elm Street 4: The Dream Master* prior to *Die Hard 2*. Then he went on to direct another big action name in Sylvester Stallone with *Cliffhanger*. *Cutthroat Island*, *Deep Blue Sea*, *Driven*, *Exorcist: The Beginning*, and *12 Rounds* are also Renny Harland directed movies. However, as of this writing my favorite work of his is probably the 1996 action flick *The Long Kiss Goodnight* starring Harland's then wife Geena Davis along with Samuel L. Jackson. It's a fun one with a Shane Black script.

The *Die Hard 2* production had to chase the weather when it came to locations. The airport setting is not a single airport, many locations were used in an attempt to keep snow on the ground. The production team kept running into warm weather and fake snow was eventually utilized. In the end, the chase was probably worth it as *Die Hard 2* not only became the eighth highest box office earner of 1990, but financially outperformed the original *Die Hard*. Of course, giving credit where it is due, the success of the first film lobbed the audience over to the second film for the slam dunk.

7. *Total Recall* - directed by Paul Verhoeven, screenplay by Ronald Shusett, Dan O'Bannon, and Gary Goldman. Domestic Box Office: $119,394,840

Arnold Schwarzenegger flexed his star power in 1990 with *Total Recall* being his second film to land in the top ten of box office earners. In case you skimmed past the first movie listed for 1990 it was *Kindergarten Cop* also starring Schwarzenegger.

Total Recall is a science fiction and action film following the character Douglas Quaid, a construction worker, who dreams of visiting Mars, which at this future date is a colonized planet. He goes to a place known as "Rekall" and takes them up on their virtual vacation offer to implant a Mars experience into his mind. The procedure goes wrong and Douglas Quaid realizes that his virtual vacation might have touched into real memories about Mars and being a spy on the run. Who is he on the run from? The people who want to kill him! The question is up in the air and caught in a hail of bullets as to whether or not Quaid's construction worker life was fake or if his journey as a spy is fake. He does his best to survive and find the answers. And there is an alien woman with three boobs.

Yes. The lady with three boobs thing has to be gotten out of the way first. Why? Because in the 90s when *Total Recall* came out so too did the news that there was a lady with three boobs in it and myself and every boy I knew had to see that for himself. It was a big deal. I had barely gotten to where I would peek through my fingers during movie scenes of nudity and already I was going to be shown three boobs, all at once, on one lady! Magical.

Now that I've expressed how excited three boobies made some young boys, let me break the bad news. The actress that showed off those boobs did not enjoy the experience. Actress Lycia Neff has been quoted as saying that the moment embarrassed her immensely and she was holding back tears during the shoot. However, she also made it be known that Arnold didn't try to feel her up or anything. His eyes were creepy looking to her in a general creepy sense, but he was a professional and mostly ignored her during the moment.

If you think I have been too immature making a big deal out of the three breasted woman of *Total Recall*, well, when they did the 2012 remake they made sure to include a three-breasted woman. It must have been an important detail that needed to carry over. In the remake Kaitlyn Leeb has the character credit of: Three-Breasted Woman.

As is the case with many a movie, *Total Recall* took a long time to get all of the right pieces fit together for movie realization. The original screenplay by Dan O'Bannon and Ronald Shusett, already established with their work on the *Alien* franchise, was based on the Philip K. Dick short story *We Can Remember It for You Wholesale*. This writing duo spent some time holding on to the rights and searching for backers. Eventually producer Dino De Laurentiis championed the project and then the carousel of actors and directors attached to the project began.

In the acting department someone at certain points envisioned either Richard Dreyfuss or Patrick Swayze in the lead. Wouldn't it have been awesome if they had gone with both Dreyfuss and Swayze as three-boobed, that's six total boobs, conjoined twins? However, when director David Cronenberg became attached he personally wished for William Hurt to lead the cast. Cronenberg spent a year preparing and working on aspects of the script. Ultimately his time was spent in vain and his vision did not woo the producers or original writers. It is said that some of the creative elements that ended up in the final script were indeed creations of Cronenberg even though he did not garner a movie credit.

In the meantime, Dino De Laurentiis's company went bankrupt and that is when it is said Mr. Arnold Schwarzenegger seized the opportunity and charmed the production company Carolco into picking up the rights in order to reshape the project to star himself. Carolco is a company that has its own fun story of going from Hollywood success to bankruptcy, but at this point and time they were reaping the benefits of both Schwarzenegger and Sylvester Stallone's star powers; Carolco had their first major hit with *First Blood* ala Rambo.

Arnold Schwarzenegger's deal supposedly allowed him an impressive amount of control over the production of the movie. Once upon a time the actor had lobbied to get himself into the costume for *Robocop*. Schwarzenegger didn't fit into the Robocop suit, but he seemed to remain a fan of the project and its director Paul Verhoeven, personally requesting the Dutch director for *Total Recall* duties.

Paul Verhoeven has a bit of an interesting MPAA legacy. The MPAA are responsible for assigning the rating to a movie and it seems that time and again Mr. Verhoeven's films are said to get tagged with an X or NC-17 ratings. *Total Recall* is said to have originally earned an X rating, not due to the flash of a three-boobed lady, but because of the violence. Verhoeven's previous film *Robocop* also had a hard time with grisly imagery and the ratings board.

Then Verhoeven followed *Total Recall* up with the infamously steamy *Basic Instinct*, and then followed that up with *Showgirls* which actually went to theaters with the curse of an NC-17 rating. *Showgirls* is such a melodramatic and goofy movie that the adult rating worked well as hype and advertising in my opinion, got people to take enough notice that even if they did not support it at theaters they helped it reach cult status on home video.

Paul Verhoeven also had to re-cut some violent scenes in his movie *Starship Troopers* in order to get an R rating. In the year 2000 the MPAA finally blessed a Paul Verhoeven film with an out of the gate R for the Kevin Bacon starring horror/ thriller *Hollow Man*.

Sharon Stone plays the wife character of Lori within *Total Recall*. It's obvious that she made an impression on the director as he cast her in *Basic Instinct*. Most film buffs probably think of Sharon Stone uncrossing her legs in *Basic Instinct* when they think of steamy cinema, as opposed to the three-boobed lady in *Total Recall*. *Basic Instinct* really launched Sharon Stone into another stratosphere of fame for quite some time. An amusing observation often attributed to Paul Verhoeven with regard to Sharon Stone and his casting of her for *Basic Instinct* is that he saw how she went from timid to diabolical so believably in *Total Recall that he knew she would fit the twisted part in his follow up film. The addendum to this is that he also says this is true of Stone as a person offscreen as well.*

Sharon Stone spring boarded off of *Total Recall* into household recognition. Rachel Ticotin plays the "good guy" female lead of Melina in the film, yet her career trajectory did not go up into the Hollywood lights in the same fashion. In my movie watching experience she is a face I recognize without being able to put the name to it. I remember the guard character of Sally Bishop from the Nicolas Cage action movie *Con Air*. However, in my mind I never connected the dots that Sally Bishop was the same woman that starred in *Total Recall* nor would I at the snap of the fingers be able to recite her real name.

Aside from keeping busy in the movie industry Rachel Ticotin has also had a successful television career. She has had roles in major shows such as *Law & Order L.A.* and *Grey's Anatomy*. She married, had a child with, and divorced famous television star David Caruso before marrying actor Peter Strauss. Her name also gets swirled around whenever people bring up the extramarital affairs of Arnold Schwarzenegger; if you're a fan of those types of "stories" perhaps you were more familiar with her name than I. Supposedly she and Arnold had an affair during the shooting of *Total Recall*. By typing that am I spreading scandalous albeit dated gossip or just reporting what I've heard? And as such an apparent horn-dog, how did the filming of *Total Recall* get by without behind the scenes footage leaking of Schwarzenegger motorboating the three-boobed lady? (Have you turned my coverage of *Total Recall* into a drinking game yet? Take a shot every time I manage to work the alien with the extra boob into this!)

The entire cast and crew of *Total Recall* had their strength tested during the movie shoot, which took place in Mexico. All movie shoots can be trying, but this production is known, not for Arnie trying to grope everyone, but specifically for having been devastated by the spread of food poisoning. Also, sickness was onset by the poor air quality at the time in Mexico City with at least one production member being transported to the hospital via helicopter after taking ill. Yet, through the trying times and the complicated process that making a large scale action/ science fiction film indeed is, the creators of *Total Recall* pulled off an end product that earned well at the box office.

Total Recall is an Oscar winning film. Nominated for, and not winning, in the categories of Best Sound and Best Sound Effects Editing, the golden statue actually won by the movie came before the main show with a Special Achievement Award for Visual Effects. Of course, outside of the Oscars, the Saturn Award for Best Science Fiction Film of the year was indeed bestowed upon *Total Recall*. Now all we need is a spinoff movie about the Three-Breasted Woman.

Total Recall for me remains a decent enough watch for just kicking back and being entertained. The technology featured in the film doesn't hold up

100% and overall the film is a bit corny, you can make a game out of pausing it to capture the many weird faces Arnold pulls throughout his performance, but, indeed, entertaining.

6. *The Hunt for Red October* - directed by John McTiernan, screenplay by Larry Ferguson and Donald E. Stewart. Domestic Box Office: $122,012,643

The 1988 action film *Die Hard* was popular enough to spawn a sequel, *Die Hard 2 Die Harder* which you may have noticed on this list of movies that ruled ticket sales in 1990. (If you did not, maybe it was my fault. I'll admit I didn't write volumes about *Die Hard 2* because I was chomping at the bit to write about the Three-Breasted woman in *Total Recall*.) The director of the first *Die Hard* did not direct the sequel because he, John McTiernan, was busy directing another movie that cracked 1990's list of top earners, while also surpassing the tickets sales of the aforementioned sequel, and that movie was *The Hunt for Red October*.

The Hunt For Red October is based off of the Tom Clancy novel of the same name. It was Clancy's first major novel published and the film became the first not only based off of one Clancy's books, but also to feature his reoccurring hero character Jack Ryan. Alec Baldwin is the first actor to become Jack Ryan, a role in later features that would be played by Harrison Ford, Ben Affleck, Chris Pine, and as of this writing a television show starring

John Kransinski is in the works. Even though *The Hunt For Red October* and Baldwin's version of Jack Ryan came out first, it is Harrison Ford that my mind first associates with the role due to *Patriot Games* and *Clear and Present Danger*.

When it comes to thinking of *The Hunt For Red October*, instead of Alec Baldwin as Jack Ryan, my mind immediately associates the movie with the Scottish actor playing a Russian character ala Sean Connery as Marko Ramius.

If you want men, *The Hunt For Red October*'s cast has got men for you! For the price of admission alongside Baldwin and Connery a theater goer also got some Scott Glenn, James Earl Jones, Sam Neill, Tim Curry, Richard Jordan, Stellan Skarsgard, Peter Firth, Joss Ackland, Fred Dalton Thomas, and the guy everyone knows as "that sex offender that was in *Beetlejuice*" Mr. Jeffrey Jones. You cram a lot of testosterone into a submarine and darn right you're going to get some movie tension!

Trekkies may notice that Gates McFadden appears as Jack Ryan's wife Caroline Ryan.

The Hunt For Red October is no Village People song when it comes to naval shenanigans. The plot revolves around a state-of-the-art Russian nuclear submarine gone rogue. The mutinous Russian Marko Ramius has taken control of the submarine as it travels toward the United States. The CIA is tasked with figuring out his intentions: defecting or attacking? Either way, they seek out the location of the submarine so that they can either ask some questions or blow it up. Another Russian sub gets involved, there's killing and sinister cloak and dagger subterfuge, it's not just men looking at beeping radar screens.

Now, let's get back to the real legacy of *The Hunt For Red October*, Sean Connery's hair! Many people like to make fun of his stab at a Scottish-Russian accent, but the other Hollywood story that circulates around this film and actor is that his hair for the movie cost $20,000! The story behind the story with regard to that claim is not that his wig work cost literally $20,000, but that due to Sean Connery showing up to work with a ponytail, that he insisted on keeping, the production filmed some scenes with said hair style. However, as the hair choice became a big onset joke, Connery changed his mind, to the relief of the director, and allowed them to fit a different hairpiece to his head. The hair did not cost $20,000, but the re-shooting of those scenes proved to be costly.

In defense of Sean Connery and some of his initial creative choices as well as his overall performance, if one is indeed critical of such things, is the fact that he is said to have stepped into the job, like a pro, at the last minute. Actor Klaus Maria Brandauer was initially cast in the role and bowed out after production was already well underway. John McTiernan rewarded Connery by casting him along with the ponytail in his 1992 film *Medicine Man*.

All jokes aside, the United States military took to aiding the production seriously. The Tom Cruise starring movie *Top Gun* is credited with getting the military's production support because after the success of that movie recruits signing up for the air force increased. *The Hunt For Red October* was seen as a potential recruiting tool for the Navy.

The Oscars took *The Hunt For Red October* seriously enough come awards season. The film was nominated for three golden statues: Best Film Editing, Best Sound, and then winning one Oscar for Best Sound Effects Editing. Hmm. Okay, maybe the movie was actually all about those radar pings!

As with most film adaptations of novels, there are notable differences in the products. I always find if I read a book first and then see the movie that the movie is not as good. Therefore, if you are a new Tom Clancy fan and for some reason have not read *The Hunt For Red October* or seen the movie, perhaps consider what order you want to consume them in. The movie actually does try to address and correct some technical aspects of the book that were thought to be improvements in a scientific manner. Spoiler: the submarine location off of the coast of the U.S. is changed due to the location in the book being considered not realistic enough due to the shallows of the water in that region.

If you are a gamer perhaps the name Tom Clancy doesn't even make you think of books or movies for his material has inspired many a video game experience as well. *The Hunt For Red October* got a few video game iterations of its own. A 1987 submarine simulator for computers came out based on the book and the movie inspired a 1990 computer release as well. Then a 1991 video game followed that was released for the Nintendo Entertainment System ala the NES console, followed by ports for the Super NES and Gameboy. I would wager the side-scrolling adventure for Nintendo is the most remembered of those video game ventures.

Tom Clancy's literature expanded out strong into the other entertainment formats. Even though the author died in 2013 the brand name will live on and if you're a fan of any of the products bearing his name, maybe going back to the beginning with *The Hunt For Red October* is a worthwhile activity.

5. *Teenage Mutant Ninja Turtle*s - directed by Steve Barron, screenplay by Todd W. Langen and Bobby Herbek. Domestic Box Office: $135,265,915

If you asked me what my favorite food was when I was a small child, for the longest time my answer would have been: tacos. Tacos were forgotten when the Teenage Mutant Ninja Turtles took over pop culture devouring as much pizza as they could get their hands on. Pizza became my favorite food as well. Heck, you can make taco pizza if you want! I guess you could cram pizza into a taco shell as well, but now I am getting sidetracked and don't want my mind to get lost in that black hole that is full of thoughts like: "Why are there so many foods with different names when a lot of them are really just the same ingredients? Whoa, dude."

The Ninja Turtles hit the scene defining what was "cool" for kids my age. They didn't do it by trying to force us into eating pizza, but just by letting it all hang out and being their fun-loving selves while having action adventures. He-Man and G.I. Joe before them were far stuffier when it came to tackling their daily moral conundrums. The turtles did pause for serious reflection, with wisdom provided via Master Splinter, but they never let their responsibilities and issues stop them from yelling "Cowabunga!"

Before the turtles came along I would say that I was prone to finding the villains of children's programming to be the coolest characters. When I played with my toys the good guys still got to win, but I always made sure that the villain's sendoff was spectacular and well-earned with tones of tragedy in a "this man in black was just too cool for the world and its rules," sort of way. The Ninja Turtles, however, swept in with four lead personalities that really gave every kid someone to follow in a hero's journey. Leonardo had the more solemn leader qualities, Raphael got to be the headstrong turtle, Donatello was the science brainiac, and Michelangelo was the wild-child jokester. While they all had different personality traits to a degree, they still came together when it came time to either have fun or kick butt. They showed off working as a team while being an individual and they made it cooler by far to be the good guy.

The plot of the live-action *Teenage Mutant Ninja Turtles* follows the teen turtles as they come out of hiding in the sewers to take on the criminal ninja network known as the Foot Clan. The battle to protect the city ends up taking the turtles and their master on a journey of team and self-discovery, confronting an enemy from Splinter's past, the leader of the Foot Clan Oruku Saki better known as The Shredder.

The Ninja Turtles for pop culture consumption were first born as a comic book created by Kevin Eastman and Peter Laird. After naming each turtle after a famous Renaissance artist, the ninja adventures began as a one-shot comic meant to parody other comic book heroes. However, it didn't take too long for their commercial potential to catch on and the toy and television industry came-a-calling.

My brother and I were into action figure toys, fully invested in He-man and other character lines, however, when it came to Teenage Mutant Ninja Turtle toys, we never really built up a similar collection. I'm not sure why we only had a few of the Turtle figures, but it's possible that they were costlier compared to the other toys we would circle in the Christmas catalog for Grandma, err, Santa Clause to buy. The same goes for the comic books. I recall only owning one Ninja Turtle comic book. However, the cartoon was a program that I indeed tuned into and I fully bought into the first movie with excitement. I was not disappointed.

Teenage Mutant Ninja Turtles the movie was grittier than the cartoon by far. Ultimately, I think that helped sell the transition from animation to live-action. There is no way I would go to school and admit to liking He-man, Sesame Street, or any of the other "kid" products out there. However, the extra little pinch of violence and adult tone given to the Ninja Turtles film made it something that we could publicly discuss and support without feeling too childish. Kids want to be cool like adults and get to watch adult things. The creators of that first movie knew what they were doing. It's sort of the same approach, less nefarious, as cigarette companies knowing how to appeal to youth in order to take advantage of nice lungs for a longer period of time.

Even with how dark *Teenage Mutant Ninja Turtles* sort of turned out, it might have been even darker as imagined by its director. According to some sources the director did not get final cut over the movie and was booted out of forming the end product.

The violence and dark look of *Teenage Mutant Ninja Turtles* did not sit well with many parents, however. I recall it took some convincing of the adults around me that the word "mutant" wasn't something to fear. Literally, the initial pause there was in my consuming of all things Ninja Turtles was

32

the word mutant and what perversions that might imply.

After the first movie, the parents won the battle against the darker tone and violence. The sequels to the initial *Teenage Mutant Ninja Turtles* movie were purposefully made to be more kid friendly for concerned adults. Subsequently, even though I saw both of them in the theater upon release, neither one made quite the impression on me as the original. Of course, the soundtrack to *Teenage Mutant Ninja Turtles II: The Secret of the Ooze* is a different story. I owned the cassette and blasted Vanilla Ice *Ninja Rap* into my brain as often as possible. We were so cool in the 90s.

In the realm of movies *Teenage Mutant Ninja Turtles* is a franchise that got a reboot in 2014 by Michael Bay's production company. As an adult I did not get into the new reincarnation, preferring to think back fondly on the first movie only. As a franchise, however, I think that *Teenage Mutant Ninja Turtles* is going to always remain viable as source material for new movie and series reboots and I find nothing to hate about that. My first exposure to the turtles was through the cartoon and the movie was very different from the cartoon, yet that was never an issue to me. The Ninja Turtles as a property in my mind is so wide open in terms of how the material can be approached, the already "out there" canon of mutated turtles fighting crime or aliens or what-have-you doesn't have a set of rules that I as a fan of the earliest projects feel creators must adhere to.

The one thing that I can say that I do hate involving the Ninja Turtles, a bad memory that will forever haunt me, is the Teenage Mutant Ninja Turtle Pies. These were deep fried, glazed and green, Hostess products pumped full of vanilla pudding. It is my own fault that my memory of these is one of horror because I ate way too many in one sitting. The mass intake of pies led to me vomiting, one of the most memorable to me vomit sessions of my life. No turtle pies for me, ever again, thanks, but no thanks.

The animatronic turtles in the movie were state of the art productions created by Jim Henson's company. The puppet master Henson is said to have been critical of the film's tone himself, however, it is also said that he provided his services as part of being a standup guy helping a friend that maybe he owed a favor. Director Steve Barron at the time was mainly known for his music video work but directed several episodes of Jim Henson's show *The Storyteller*. I don't think many would doubt that having Jim Henson involved helped Barron achieve blockbuster success. *Teenage Mutant Ninja Turtles* was one of the last movies that Jim Henson worked on before his death in May of 1990.

Inside of the turtles were David Forman, Lief Tilden, Michelan Sisti, and Josh Pias. However, the actors shouldering the physical burdens of the costumes were not also responsible for the voices. Josh Pias alone acted inside of the costume and provided the voice ala playing Rapheal. The other three turtles were voiced by Corey Feldman as Donatello, Brian Tochi as Leonardo, and Robbie Rist as Michelangelo. In that regard, the voice actors may have benefited from more of the acting glory when it comes to people remembering the turtles as characters. Each actor did get to come out of the shell for cameos, however. The man inside of Michelangelo played a pizza delivery man, Leonardo got a Gang Member credit, Donatello also played a Foot Messenger, and Raphael is the passenger in the same taxi cab that his turtle form goes on to the hood of. Of the four actors only Robbie Rist and Brian Tochi returned for voice work on the sequels. As a kid, I specifically remember the fact that Donatello no longer sounded like Corey Feldman and that did count against the production in said child mind.

The role of Master Splinter is the same man who brought Elmo on Sesame Street to life for many years: Kevin Clash. The man behind Elmo and Splinter would go on to face some sexual abuse charges that tarnished his reputation. The news really went all out to report those charges against Elmo, the headlines didn't seem to pronounce the news as loud when the courts cleared Clash of all charges. Of course, critics can point out that they were dismissed due to statute of limitations technicalities, so, Master Splinter not being as wise and morally strong as he seemed, and Elmo was a pervert are more than likely going to be the pop culture legacy.

Judith Hoag, Elias Koteas, James Saito, Michael Turney, and many others, obviously, filled out the rest of the *Teenage Mutant Ninja Turtle* cast. A cast trivia fact that I find fun is that Oscar winning actor Sam Rockwell can be seen as a member of the Foot Clan accredited as Head Thug.

Another fun fact is that Sally Menke edited *Teenage Mutant Ninja Turtles*. She went on to become the editor of all of Quentin Tarantino's films up until the time of her death in 2010. *Reservoir Dogs, Pulp Fiction, Jackie Brown, Kill Bill 1 & 2, Death Proof*, and *Inglorious Basterds* were all visions that Menke helped shape.

4. *Pretty Woman* - directed by Garry Marshall, screenplay by J.F. Lawton. Domestic Box Office: $178,406,268

Random musing: I want to write a screenplay about a disgruntled hooker that travels to Hollywood hellbent on killing Garry Marshall because she is offended by his call girl fairy tale *Pretty Woman*. Of course director Garry Marshall died in 2016, but I guess the protagonist and would-be assassin doesn't need to be aware of that.

The story of *Pretty Woman* follows a prostitute that is hired by a wealthy corporate raider to be his date over an extended period of time, escorting him to various social functions as he plots the takeover of someone's business. Eventually he not only falls in love with the woman but changes his cutthroat business attitude thanks to her positive influence. Richard Gere plays the lead of Edward Lewis opposite the lead of Julia Roberts as Vivian Ward.

While *Pretty Woman* is noted as the final film performance of actor Ralph Bellamy before his death, it is another supporting cast member that I actually find most interesting to take note of. The television show *Seinfeld* rose to prominence with one of the main characters being the neurotic George as played by actor Jason Alexander. I'm not sure Jason Alexander can ever do another role without someone thinking: it's George! *Pretty Woman* may just be the last time he got away with being an actor not overshadowed by his "must-see-tv" character. Jason Alexander plays the loathsome Philip Stuckey in *Pretty Woman*.

Richard Gere ranked right up there with Patrick Swayze when it came to my Grandma's preferred movie hunks. Therefore, on the weekends at her house, when I got to twenty-four hour binge watch movies, *Pretty Woman* is one I ended up seeing just about as many times as *Dirty Dancing*. I never complained or wandered off really, even as a teen boy I found the movie charming and with elements of interest to my budding mind. To this day, and I am not blaming *Pretty Woman*, I am for some reason a fan of developing "hooker with a heart of gold" stories. While much seedier and eccentric, *Breath Of Hate*, later named by someone at a distribution company as *The Last House*, marked my screenwriting credit debut and blends a call girl in love with a client, daydreaming of a better life plot with the ole "one last job that goes wrong" angle.

Pretty Woman is a production that started out with a script that was much darker than the end product. Elements such as drug addiction for Vivian were axed and the sweet, "dreamy" romance was able to take shape. The chemistry between Richard Gere and Julia Roberts placed them into the arena of America's Movie Sweethearts with Hollywood eventually getting them to re-team for the romantic comedy *The Runaway Bride*. However, I think Tom Hanks and Meg Ryan still won and hold the America's Sweethearts title for their turns in *Joe Versus the Volcano*, *Sleepless In Seattle*, and *You've Got Mail*.

If *Pretty Woman* had stuck with the darker tone I don't think Gere and Roberts would have gotten the same genre spotlight and fan adoration as they did after *Pretty Woman* was released. As I write this I wonder if any other couple will ever get that type of marketing push. Romance and romantic comedies aren't really being made in the lighthearted mold of the 90s.

Back on the term America's Sweethearts, oddly enough Julia Roberts does star in an actual movie titled *America's Sweethearts*. It's about a couple of actors, that were once a couple, constantly cast in movies together because America is in love with their love. John Cusack and Catherine Zeta-Jones star as the fictional estranged sweethearts in that

2001 picture. I personally don't recommend it as something to watch, but I also wouldn't fully trust me as a movie critic.

As an onscreen couple, perchance Richard Gere and Julia Roberts did not surpass the magic of Tom Hanks and Meg Ryan, but Julia Roberts herself went on to become quite the in-demand actress for romantic movies in the 90s. Meg Ryan, by the way, is said to have been one of the actors to have turned down the lead role in *Pretty Woman*. She didn't pass up the romantic *When Harry Met Sally* though which premiered a year earlier and landed in eleventh place in terms of 1989 box office earnings.

The casting process for *Pretty Woman* explored many different talents for the lead roles. Julia Roberts tells a tale in interviews about how after she became attached to the movie she talked Richard Gere into participating. Apparently Gere did not want the role, turned it down several times, did not plan to be talked into it, but Roberts wooed him over dinner. The duo hung out with one another and at one point Garry Marshall called Gere to see how things were going and to see if Gere had interest in coming onboard to work with Roberts. At that exact moment that Gere was on the phone with the director, possibly preparing to decline, Julia Roberts slid over a Post-It note to him that said, "Please say yes." Richard Gere found her note too sweet to say anything other than yes.

In 1964 Roy Orbison released the song *Oh, Pretty Woman* and that tune enjoyed three weeks at number one on the Billboard Hot 100 music chart. In 1990 the movie *Pretty Woman* not only derived its name from the song, but also featured it on its soundtrack. As a kid I am sure that I had heard *Oh, Pretty Woman* prior to the movie, old school acts in both rock and country were familiar listening to me alongside my collection of Weird Al albums, however, I do recall the release of the movie bringing about a popular resurgence of the song. Fun fact: I am going to quit writing about *Pretty Woman* and go listen to Roy Orbison music. This will undoubtedly segue into listening to The Traveling Wilburys and I may never finish writing this listicle book.

3. *Dances with Wolves* - directed by Kevin Costner, screenplay by Michael Blake. Domestic Box Office: $184,208,848

Dances with Wolves stars Kevin Costner as Lieutenant Dunbar, a soldier sent to man a remote outpost. It is set in the 1800s. Dunbar soon encounters his Native American neighbors and begins to visit them, learning of their ways and realizing his misconceptions about them as a people. This leads to him fighting for the tribe, them fighting for him, and love is fallen into by Dunbar and the white woman that was adopted by the tribe that lives amongst them as Stands With Fists; Mary McDonnell portrays this character.

Also, when killing time, Dunbar tries to make pals with a wolf. Despite what the title suggests, an elaborate man and beast ballroom dance competition never takes place.

Holy moly, what an epic venture to make for your directorial debut! Kevin Costner is said to have pumped at least three million of his own cash into the production of *Dances With Wolves* as the budget soared with all of the epic set pieces needed to portray the time period and provide entertaining action. All of those bison and wolves running around didn't just work for peanuts.

Many surmised that the expanding budget of the movie, combined with its Western genre label, combined with it being a first time director, would equal a Hollywood disaster. Instead it won Best Picture at the 1991 Academy Awards and gained Kevin Costner honorary member status in the Sioux Nation. On top of that it is said he may have profited over $40 million on his personal investment in the film. Oh, yeah, and he won the Best Director Oscar.

The top prizes of Best Picture and Best Director weren't the only golden statues for *Dances With Wolves*. The film generated twelve nominations overall and won seven. The other five "Best" wins were for screenplay, cinematography, sound, editing, and original score. Nominations that did not nab "Best" grand prizes were for actor, supporting actor, supporting actress, art direction, and costume design.

The screenplay for *Dances With Wolves* started life as a screenplay, but then was reborn as a book, that then got turned into a screenplay. Michael Blake couldn't find a production home for his script in the mid-80s but liked the material enough to convert it into a novel. The novel became a hard sell as well but reached paperback publication in 1988. Kevin Costner then bought the rights to turn the book into a movie, a process that was probably helped along by the fact that Costner had acted in the movie *Stacy's Knights*, which at the time was the only other movie ever produced based off of a Michael Blake script. Side note of interest: there is a sequel to *Dances With Wolves* in novel format, written by Michael Blake, called *The Holy Road*. As of my typing this *The Holy Road* is rumored to be in development, possibly as a television mini-series. Michael Blake was working on getting the story turned into a movie, however, Costner was opposed to reprising his role in a sequel and Blake died in 2015.

Movies rarely nail down reality for display and *Dances With Wolves* is a film that gets lobbed back and forth in discussions of Native American cultural representation with regard to whether the movie is to be applauded or mocked for its portrayals. There are those who give it a thumbs up for the general attempt at being a positive reflection on a people that suffered through hard times and prejudices. However, when it comes to the specific tribes of Native Americans represented in the film, some are painted as heroic, while some are painted as completely villainous.

For Native Americans with a sense of humor and a good handle on the Lakota language, the characters speaking in said language within the film have been a source of chuckles. The Siouan Lakota language has gender-specific styles and the cast missed out on getting that training. Therefore, in the finished film, a lot of the male characters speak as if they are women.

As for a historical reference point that may have inspired the story of *Dances With Wolves*, there was once upon a time in real history a Lieutenant John Dunbar that worked as a missionary with the Pawnee. Also, Michael Blake did go on record to reveal his inspiration for the Stands With Fists character. Stands With Fists was influenced by the real life story of Cynthia Ann Parker, a white woman adopted into a Comanche tribe as a little girl. Well, some would say less "adopted" and more "kidnapped" as she was taken away after an attack on the settlement where she lived. She lived as a Comanche for approximately twenty-four years before Texas Rangers forcibly removed her from the tribe and placed her back into "white" society. Tragically, it is said that she never adjusted to the transition and even attempted to return to her Comanche family, which included three children, only to be drug back to what was deemed to be her proper place. She died of influenza in 1871. What a bummer. I should have ended this with that joke about ballroom dancing with wolves. Right? They should make a reality competition show where they send celebrities out on to the dance floor with a choreographed routine and at the same time release a wild animal form a cage to join them.

2. *Ghost* - directed by Jerry Zucker, screenplay by Bruce Joel Rubin. Domestic Box Office: $217,631,306

Patrick Swayze and Demi Moore star in *Ghost* as the lovely couple Sam Wheat and Molly Jensen. Romance gets hit with tragedy early on as Sam is murdered by a mugger and becomes a ghost. As he haunts around the love of his life, Sam realizes that she is in danger due to his murder not being a random mugging, but a part of a bigger conspiracy. In desperation he turns to a fraud turned psychic played by Whoopi Goldberg to try and communicate his worries to Molly.

Before *Ghost*, director Jerry Zucker was known for goofy comedies such as *Airplane! Top Secret!* and *Ruthless People*, all of which he directed with Jim Abrahams and his brother David Zucker. Who knew that such a dramatic romance with tragic, at times quite dark, supernatural elements would make for the perfect first solo directing gig? Best Director was not one of the five categories that the film was nominated for at the Academy Awards, however, Zucker captained over a ship that saw an Oscar go to Whoopi Goldberg for her supporting actor role and Bruce Joel Rubin for his screenplay. Best Picture, Editing, and Original Score were nominated categories where the film lost out. Whoopi Goldberg completed an awards trifecta by also winning a BAFTA and Golden Globe for her performance.

Spoiler alert! Actor Tony Goldwyn doesn't play a very nice guy with the character of Carl Bruner. No matter what Goldwyn has starred in, no matter what he may go on to do in his career, in my mind he will always be: that bad guy from *Ghost*!

Tony Goldwyn did not have to carry all of the creepiness of the film alone, aside from the spooky shadow creature effects within the movie, actor Vincent Schiavelli as the Subway Ghost also imprinted on my child mind after seeing the movie. I won't say he resides up there with Large Marge from her scary moment in *Pee-Wee's Big Adventure*, but his presence treads in that territory. It's not even his angry ghost on the subway performance that sticks, it's just his unique look combined with that angry ghost performance. Vincent Schiavelli is also one of the first images, after the Penguin and after Cat woman's suit, that comes to mind when I think of *Batman Returns*. In that movie he is the creepy Organ Grinder that follows Penguin's lead. Wait. Why do I think of Danny DeVito in his creepy makeup before I think of Michelle Pfeiffer in her Cat woman suit?

Twisted and sad facts interjection: Vincent Schiavelli died of lung cancer in 2005. Patrick Swayze died of pancreatic cancer in 2009. Cancer took both of them at the age of fifty-seven.

Ghost lands at number two for domestic box office earnings in North America. However, if you expand to look at the numbers for worldwide movie releases, the highest earning film at theaters in 1990 was: *Ghost*. As a hit overseas it's no surprise to see that the movie got an Asian reboot in 2010 with a Miho Nakazono and Shimako Sato screenplay being based off of Bruce Joel Rubin's original.

The song *Unchained Melody* will forever be associated with the movie *Ghost*; however, the song was originally created for another movie. *Unchained Melody* was the theme song for the 1955 prison movie *Unchained*. Alex North takes credit for the music and Hy Zaret for the lyrics. As used for the film *Unchained*, the 1955 version of the song was Oscar nominated for Best Original song. The version of the song used in and made popular by *Ghost* is the 1965 version recorded by The Righteous Brothers.

When I wrote about the movie *Dick Tracy* earlier I made mention of how important collectible movie cups were for us kids of the early 90s. McDonalds actually got into the VHS selling business for a while as well. For just $5.99 with the purchase of a Big Mac you could get the VHS of Ghost. Yep, we bought the movie *Ghost* at a fast food drive thru.

1. *Home Alone* - directed by Chris Columbus, screenplay by John Hughes. Domestic Box Office: $285,761,243

The year 1990 in movie box office numbers was an around the world success for the romance of *Ghost*, but in America the number one and two ranked movies swapped places with the top dollar amount being laid down to see Macaulay Culkin slapping his hands to either side of his face to exclaim: "Ahh!"

Home Alone is about a kid left home alone during the holidays, an oversight on his parents' part, a wish come true for him because he was tired of his obnoxious family. Once he has the house to himself, however, it's not all fun and games because two burglars have targeted it for robbery. The young boy works to outwit the burglars with booby-traps while his mother and father work to get back across the country to check in on him. Okay, never mind, it is all fun and games.

The movie *Home Alone* launched Macaulay Culkin off from child star to child superstar, reshaping his entire existence thereafter. John Hughes worked with Culkin on the movie *Uncle Buck* and chose him as the lead for *Home Alone* at conception. Director Chris Columbus listened to Hughes but went ahead and did a massive casting call for the part before deciding on Macaulay Culkin as was originally planned for him.

Macaulay, as with many child actors, has his share of horror stories and the bad press associated with growing up within the industry. However, as of this writing, I must point out that the guy hasn't washed out with the tide like many others. He did not keep the same working pace or stand in the Hollywood spotlight as he did during the *Home Alone* years, disappearing perhaps from "the scene" with regard to mainstream relevance, but he seems to be a more positive than not industry survival story. Currently he shares his quirky sense of humor with a popular comedy website and podcast called Bunny Ears and seeing where he is at in life through interviews I'm left to assume he will put more projects on his plate as and when he sees fit to enjoy them. Or, maybe I just jinxed him and you're reading this a decade from its original publishing date and Macaulay Culkin is in prison now known as Kid Cannibal Deluxe and that's not his rapper name, it's his label splashed across the headlines like the blood from his victims.

As someone that was a growing youngster in the era when Macaulay Culkin was an A-list child star, I find it interesting how casting manipulated our heartstrings with him. He made us laugh and have fun in *Home Alone*, but then they followed that up with the release of *My Girl*, whereas the supporting actor we connected with his feelings only to then have his character killed off by bees. He died! It was an unexpected gut punch upon first viewing, and thanks to the mass popularity of *Home Alone*, for many it felt like an early experience of someone you know dying. Then *Home Alone 2: Lost In New York* came out and all was right with the world again. But, then after that they hit us with *Good Son* and Macaulay Culkin is an evil little murderer! In looking back, it seems like the extreme role pivots had such a memorable impact that one might think Macaulay Culkin acted in far more blockbuster movies in that time period than he actually did.

Catherine O'Hara plays the role of the mother in *Home Alone*. It is a flip of the coin as to whether or not my brain pictures her in this movie or in *Bettlejuice* when I hear her name. However, when I hear her name my brain always boots up the factoid I heard about her having situs inversus. Situs Inversus is a rare condition where a person's organs are positioned opposite of where they would normally be in the body. According to the Internet Donny Osmond and Enrique Iglesias are two other celebrities with the condition.

As Kevin's, that's Culkin's character's name, mother tries to get back home to her son she encounters many delays and ends up hitting the road with Gus Polinski the "Polka King of the Midwest." The role is played by John Candy and is one of those minor parts where an actor who shines shows you that there is no such thing as a minor part in a movie. John Candy had the "magic" in him folks.

Actor Joe Pesci as one of the two burglars of the film has a different kind of magic. He's got the brash, tough guy act down for sure and in 1990 audiences may have been able to catch him in *Goodfellas* a couple of months before they then saw him in *Home Alone*. His partner in crime in the movie is played by Daniel Stern. The casting story told about *Home Alone* and the bandits is that Daniel Stern was one of the first choices for a role, but too costly. When Robert De Niro and Jon Lovitz declined to participate Joe Pesci came in and then the difficulty was finding someone that could roll with Pesci's acting energy. They then ended up going back to and hiring Daniel Stern.

"Keep the change you filthy animal." That quote is from the black and white gangster film *Angels with Filthy Souls* which Kevin watches within the film *Home Alone*. However, that film within a film isn't a real film at all, it's a parody take on the real 1938 crime title *Angels with Dirty Faces* and was shot specifically for *Home Alone*. It is a well done clip that became even more hilarious to me as an adult realizing it wasn't a real movie. Kevin uses the movie, cranks the television volume up, to fool a pizza delivery man and the burglars, tricking them into thinking that a machine firing maniac resides within the house.

Now, I will argue that violent movies do not turn people violent because, let's face it, we would all be murdering people left and right if that were true. However, I will admit that as a kid *Home Alone* influenced some behavior that could have gotten me injured, but then again that steep staircase alone could have done the job. At one of the homes I lived in my bedroom was in the attic and my brother and I would tie stuffed animals, as well as paint cans to the upper railing of the staircase via jump ropes, then swing them down to mimic some *Home Alone* booby trap action. We never tried to hit one another with the paint cans, but a giant Big Bird stuffed animal would from time to time catch one of us off-guard upon staircase ascension.

Kevin uses his BB gun to shoot the burglars in *Home Alone*. My brother and I also shot our BB guns indoors, leading to a broken mirror that we lied and told our mother involved Chinese Checkers marble throwing. And I do recall a single time that we decided to shoot one another outside with the BB guns, luckily not losing our eyes. However, we did not need *Home Alone* to influence that activity, we chose to do those things just because we had the guns and the free time to use them.

Home Alone resides atop the list of highest grossing movies in North America, but its brand of comedy did not get the big awards respect one might think should accompany commercial success. The only nominations received by the film from the Oscar giving Academy were for the music, Original Song and Original Score, with neither trophy won. The Golden Globes did nominate *Home Alone* in the Best Picture category and Macaulay Culkin for Best Performance in a Musical or Comedy, but no wins there either. I guess being the number one movie of the year will have to suffice in terms of legacy prestige.

1991

10. *The Naked Gun 2 1/2: The Smell Of Fear* - directed by David Zucker, screenplay David Zucker and Pat Proft. Domestic Box Office: $86,930,411

In 1990 Jerry Zucker diverted from his comedy roots and made the hit romance *Ghost*. His older brother David Zucker, however, made sure to keep spoof / parody comedy alive the following year with the sequel to 1988's *Naked Gun: From the Files of Police Squad!*

The Naked Gun 2 1/2: The Smell of Fear follows police Lt. Frank Drebin as he investigates the happenings around a Dr. Meinheimer and his work in the field of renewable energy. The big players in the energy sector ala oil, coal, and nuclear are none too pleased with Meinheimer's findings and a kidnapping involving swapping the scientist out with a look-a-like plot is afoot. Drebin's old flame Jane Spencer works for and is dating Dr. Meinheimer and the case takes Frank right back into her arms for some love triangle shenanigans. Naturally, David Zucker made sure to poke fun at his brother's movie *Ghost* by including a romantic parody scene involving wet clay and a pottery wheel.

The star of the *Naked Gun* movies, Leslie Nielsen, was also the lead in the television series where the basic premise of the character premiered. *Police Squad!* aired on ABC in 1982 and while many seemed to enjoy the wacky humor the series was canceled after a mere six episodes. The show developed a cult following as episodes were rebroadcast, giving the concept a boost in terms of marketability, which assisted the creators in being able to reboot the concept in the form of the first movie released in 1988.

Leslie Nielsen was originally known for his dramatic film roles, however, his career trajectory changed when he starred in another slapstick movie that involved the Zucker brothers: *Airplane!* . The generations of movie goers after that movie released probably remember Nielsen as strictly a comedic actor. Born in the early 80s, indeed I am to be counted amongst those who think only of zany chuckles when they think of the late actor. Leslie Nielsen died in 2010 and the humor continues at his grave with the phrase "Let'er rip" featured as the epitaph on his gravestone.

In all three of the *Naked Gun* movies Priscilla Presley stars as Frank Derbin's lover Jane Spencer. Born Priscilla Ann Wagner, Priscilla was formerly married to the King of Rock n Roll himself Elvis Presley. In *The Naked Gun 2 1/2*, at first on the outs with Frank, Jane is paired off with the Dr. Meinheimer character portrayed by Robert Goulet. Legend has it that when Elvis was alive he despised Goulet enough to have once shot out the screen of his television when the singer appeared on it. Elvis died in 1977 and did not have to witness his ex, they were already divorced when the television incident supposedly occurred, acting alongside Goulet.

Elvis was someone that managed to have successful singing and acting career and Robert Goulet, while a different type of talent, also juggled both of those careers. In 1962 Goulet won the Grammy for Best New Artist, but prior to that he started getting acting credits in 1954 with an appearance on *Howdy Doody* being his first credit listed on IMDB. Goulet actually appeared in an episode of the original *Police Squad!* television series prior to coming onboard the sequel film. Other popular movies you might have caught him in are as a dinner guest in *Beetlejuice* and then playing himself in the 1988 movie *Scrooged* starring Bill Murray.

The *Naked Gun* film series is also known for the reoccurring role of Nordberg portrayed by infamous sports star turned murder suspect O.J. Simpson. Simpson was found not guilty for the murders of Nicole Brown Simpson and Ronald Goldman, but the Razzie Awards made sure that he won the Worst Supporting Acting Award for *Naked Gun 33 1/3: The Final Insult*.

A blues singer in *Naked Gun 2 1/2* portrayed by actress Colleen Fitzpatrick may have not drawn the attention of pop culture trivia seekers at the time of the film's release, however, this actress went on to become well-known for a flash of time by her musical stage name: Vitamin C. The song *Smile* off of her 1999 debut album was a pop genre hit.

Another musical talent one might be able to spy in *The Naked Gun 2 1/2: The Smell of Fear* is "Weird

Al" Yankovic. He also made a cameo in the first film.

In its opening run at theaters *The Naked Gun 2 1/2: The Smell Of Fear* took over the top spot at the box office from the Kevin Costner *Robin Hood: Prince of Thieves*. There's a pretty good chance you're going to see more about Costner's film some notches farther up this top ten list.

9. *Father of the Bride* - directed by Charles Shyer, screenplay by Frances Goodrich, Albert Hackett, Nancy Meyers, and Charles Shyer. Domestic Box Office: $89,325,780

Father Of The Bride and its sequel are films that I saw as a youngster. I will point out though that the 1989 Steve Martin starring film *Parenthood* is the Martin movie we watched over and over again for some reason, not *Father of the Bride*. I have also caught my memory confusing the titles of the two when remembering certain scenes. There's no confusion with those and *Three Amigos* though! *Three Amigos* was probably the movie that made us kids pay attention to the other Steve Martin releases of the following years even when they were about more adult things.

The title of the movie explains the plot fairly well with Steve Martin being the father of the bride ala George Banks. Well, at least I feel like it's easy enough to guess what things are about. A man is freaking out some about giving his daughter away to the man she wants to marry. He doesn't want to lose his little girl, doesn't care for the new guy, and doesn't think they've known each other long enough to get married. Cue the comedy and heartwarming shenanigans.

The film is a remake of a 1950 film with the same name, based on a 1949 Edward Streeter novel. The 1950 *Father Of The Bride*, however, was Oscar nominated thrice over whereas the 90s version garnered box office success without the awards show celebrations. The original film starred Spencer Tracy, Joan Bennett, and Elizabeth Taylor as father, wife, and daughter. Acting opposite of Steve Martin was Diane Keaton and in her MTV Movie Award nominated feature film debut Kimberly Williams-Paisley played their daughter. Also, in the 1991 film, comedian Martin Short has a role as wedding planner and Kieran Culkin, brother to *Home Alone*'s Macaulay, is a member of the Banks family.

The original film, as did the 90s film, got a sequel. In the 60s there was also a television series adaptation of *Father of the Bride*. As of February 2018 Walt Disney Studios has a *Father of the Bride* remake listed as a project in the works.

Director Charles Shyer and Nancy Meyers who worked on the screenplay together were a married couple at the time. They also both worked as writers on the successful 1980 film *Private Benjamin*. Charles Shyer went on to direct the sequel to *Father of the Bride* in 1995 with help from Nancy on the script once again. He assisted on writing for her directorial effort *The Parent Trap* remake, before directing the Jude Law starring remake of *Alfie*. Nancy Meyers has her own directing career, along with writing, with films such as the aforementioned *The Parent Trap*, and then *What Women Want, Something's Gotta Give, The Holiday, It's Complicated*, and *The Intern*. Charles and Nancy divorced in 1999, but that's none of our business.

While on the subject of marriages, actress Kimberly Williams-Paisley has that hyphenated last name because she married popular country singer Brad Paisley in 2003. They have two children.

Father of the Bride 2 did not crack the top ten of box office sales when released in 1995. However, the movie was considered a financial success breaking into the top twenty earning films of the year; number seventeen. The plot for the sequel centers on Steve Martin having to deal with the mid-life crisis of not only his daughter's pregnancy making him a grandpa, but also his wife becomes pregnant.

8. *Sleeping with the Enemy* - directed by Joseph Ruben, screenplay by Ronald Bass. Domestic Box Office: $101,599,005

There is more than a twelve million dollar difference between the earnings of the number nine film on this list and the number eight film. I guess people thought *Father of the Bride* was cute, but they really wanted something with more dysfunction, to see someone: sleeping with the enemy.

Home Alone carried its 1990 success over into 1991 with an impressive eleven weeks as the top box office draw. *Sleeping with the Enemy* is the film that toppled *Home Alone* from that top spot. The situation was a win-win for 20th Century Fox as both movies were from their stable.

I was soon to turn nine years old when *Sleeping with the Enemy* released in February of 1991. You might not think such a relationship based psychological thriller would be on the watch list for a lad of that age, but the fact is the heat from Julia Roberts' star power carried over from 1990's *Pretty Woman* and my grandma, the buyer of movie tickets for me on the weekends, was sold. She sat through all of our action movie choices, often exclaiming "they don't play very nice," and we in turn watched her romances and romantic thrillers. Yes, if you must know, I've watched the 1989 drama *Steel Magnolias*, also featuring Julia Roberts, way too many times. *Steel Magnolias*, *Pretty Woman*, and *Sleeping with the Enemy* were a trio of Julia Robert films always on repeat when it came to VHS tapes playing on Granny's tv. Every now and then we made sure to slip in *Flatliners* starring Roberts as well.

Sleeping with the Enemy is about a woman played by Julia Roberts escaping an abusive marriage by faking her death. Her evil nightmare of a husband played by Patrick Bergin, however, tracks her down. The movie is based off of a 1987 Nancy Price novel.

Critics weren't really all that kind to *Sleeping with the Enemy* and if the same movie were released today it'd probably be a Lifetime channel movie, but, as I mentioned, the force was strong with Julia Roberts, and critics don't know everything.

I find it amusing that actor Robert Bergin played Robin Hood in a 1991 *Robin Hood* movie release. Amusing, of course, because a more epic Robin Hood movie that I've already hinted at being on this list was also released that year starring Kevin Costner. Movie studios often mirror each other, trying to compete with project subject matter. In the *Robin Hood* starring Robert Bergin actress Uma Thurman portrays Maid Marian. There is a chance I saw that *Robin Hood* movie, but it doesn't take up any space in my memory bank as far as I can remember.

The lead role of Laura Burney in *Sleeping with the Enemy* was not originally written for Julia Roberts. Instead, actress Jane Fonda was at the top of the production wish-list. When Fonda did not join the cast Kim Basinger was allotted the role, but then she backed out opening the path for Julia Roberts to then take it and become one of the youngest women ever to earn a seven figure payday for a single movie role.

It wasn't all sunshine for Julia Roberts after filming *Sleeping with the Enemy*, she made some new enemies herself. After production wrapped in Abbeville, South Carolina Roberts publicly referred to the city as "a living Hell" and "horribly racist." Needless to say Abbeville citizens were soured on supporting the actress and some even took out an ad in *Variety* to express their outrage.

Julia Roberts backed up her comments on Abbeville by explaining that she witnessed a black friend refused service in a restaurant while there. She clarified that she did not mean to feed Southern stereotypes, being a Georgia born woman herself, and did not mean to imply that all citizens of Abbeville were racist, but merely stated what was on her mind with the shock of having witnessed what she did.

Director Joseph Ruben would finish out the decade of the 90s directing the films *The Good Son*, *Money Train*, and *Return to Paradise*. Screenwriter Ronald Bass, also credited with 1988's *Rain Man*, would garner a lot of movie credits, two more of which in the 90s would see Julia Roberts on the cast: *My Best Friend's Wedding* and *Stepmom*. And for the sake of trying to make an amusing connection between director and writer on the subject of works titled after step-parent roles, before he directed *Sleeping with the Enemy*, Joseph Ruben directed the 1987 horror movie *The Stepfather*.

It is said, though not given credit, that *Ghost* screenwriter Bruce Joel Rubin did some rewrite work on the *Sleeping with the Enemy* script. Hey, there we go, some more quirkiness, Ruben and Rubin surnames.

7. *The Addams Family* - directed by Barry Sonnenfeld, screenplay by Caroline Thompson and Larry Wilson. Domestic Box Office: $113,502,426

It is impossible for me to read the title of this movie without the theme song popping into my head. *The Addams Family* movie and the music associated with it are especially memorable for me because they helped me win a prize at school. On Valentine's Day there was a contest to see who brought the most creative box for collecting valentines in. I decorated my box with a giant heart featuring a picture of the Addams Family from the movie. The key to winning, however, was the music, not the original *Addams Family* theme song, but the MC Hammer rap song that was released with the movie. Inside of my valentines box I hid a tape recorder and used it to repeatedly play the MC Hammer performed single *Addams Groove*. *Addams Groove* won a Razzie Award for Worst Original Song, but the person that made that call obviously had poor taste.

The Addams Family were created by cartoonist Charles Addams and appeared in his single-panel cartoons that appeared in publications such as *The New Yorker*. The macabre family debuted in 1938.

In the 60s the concept was adapted into a live-action television series which led to a television movie. The show aired for two seasons and the infamous theme song was created by Vic Mizzy. In the 70s there was an animated Addams Family show, but that lasted for only one season.

Then came the movie magic of the 90s! *The Addams Family* follows the family as they are reunited with Uncle Fester, a long lost brother to the head of the household Gomez Addams. Fester either has amnesia or is an imposter and his homecoming does not see him arrive alone. Rumor has it that there is a treasure to be found in the Addams Family home and the con artist that has adopted Fester intends to get to said treasure, shenanigans ensue.

If you have not seen the 1991 film *The Addams Family* I recommend you put this book down and go ahead and watch it and the 1993 sequel *Addams Family Values* as both of them are quite funny. The sequel is the one I always think of first, however, when I want to laugh pretty hard.

The cast that brought the Addams Family to life were perfectly chosen in my opinion. Anjelica Huston gained a Golden Globe nomination for playing Morticia Addams. Her lover on this side of the dark pit, Gomez Addams, was portrayed by the late Raul Julia. Their children Pugsley and Wednesday were Jimmy Workman and Christina Ricci, with Ricci truly being a standout presence. Christopher Lloyd donned a lot of makeup to play

Uncle Fester and Judith Malina was Granny. The ever helpful and intimidating servant Lurch saw Carel Struycken in the role and while the character known as Thing is only a disembodied hand that scurries around Christopher Hart took on those duties. Viewers get to see many more of the odd Addams clan during a family reunion, perhaps most notably the walking hairball that is Cousin It played by John Franklin.

The production of the movie sounds like it was an overall nightmare. Different studios owned different rights, Charles Addams widow also had to be convinced to sell some rights, eventually one studio sold the rights to another, only to find out that yet another studio actually held some rights, and then a rights holder for the television series come forward with a lawsuit explaining that the movie did not compensate him for his rights and should only have been based on the cartoons. The lawsuit was settled, and all the rights apparently chopped up and sorted out for the sequel to have been made.

Beyond the rights hokey-pokey, filming delays affected the film. The original cinematographer quit and then his replacement also left due to being hospitalized for a sinus infection. Director Barry Sonnenfeld, experienced in cinematography, took over that critical role himself to finish the film.

Other medical delays included Raul Julia having a blood vessel pop in his eye and Barry Sonnenfeld had to put things on hold when his wife fell ill.

The shoot was also said to have been torturous for Anjelica Huston as the corset she wore didn't exactly squeeze with comfort. Also the makeup work to alter her eyes and neck, along with some fake nails she had to wear added to her annoyances.

The Addams Family marked the feature film directorial debut for Barry Sonnenfeld. At one point Tim Burton was meant to helm the picture, which seems like a natural talent fit to the subject matter, but Sonnenfeld proved more than up to the task. Barry Sonnenfeld would go on to direct other blockbuster movies such as the first three *Men In Black* films. He also directed Will Smith in 1999's stinker *Wild Wild West*. Barry Sonnenfeld's latest credits are for ten episodes of the Netflix series *A Series of Unfortunate Events*. I prefer the Jim Carrey movie adaptation, did not care for the unfortunate show.

The Addams Family screenplay credits may have gone to Caroline Thompson and Larry Wilson, but it is said that there were many rewrites with Paul Rudnick being one person to provide such services. Paul Rudnick ended up getting sole screenplay credit on *Addams Family Values*.

In another example of strong 90s promotions, to this day I can still taste the breakfast cereal that came out to advertise the movie. The cereal came with a collectible flashlight and in my household we managed to get two of the four characters: the flashlights shaped like Thing and Cousin It.

A third Addams Family movie meant to reboot the franchise in 1998 was *Addams Family Reunion*, a direct to video effort not featuring the same cast members as the previously successful ventures. Many people do not realize that it exists, and I personally have never seen it. If you are a Tim Curry superfan perhaps you already know that he is Gomez in that flick. Daryl Hannah is Morticia.

I am writing this information about *The Addams Family* in 2018. The 90s films led to another cartoon series, comic books, and video games, as well as the third movie I already mentioned. However, in future news, a new animated feature is potentially to be released in 2019 featuring the voices of Oscar Isaac, Charlize Theron, Chloe Grace Moretz, Finn Wolfhard, Nick Kroll, Bette Milder, and Allison Janney. Ah, the future looks dark, so dark, just the way Addams Family fans should like it.

6. *Hook* - directed by Steven Spielberg, screenplay by James V. Hart and Malia Scotch Marmo. Domestic Box Office: $119,654,823

If you are a big fan of the movie *Hook*, I am about to disappoint you. When I was a kid I found the movie to be boring and as an adult I agree with my original assessment as a child: never going to be hooked on *Hook*.

Hook takes place in the Peter Pan mythology following an adult Peter played by Robin Williams.

When his old nemesis Captain Hook, portrayed by Dustin Hoffman, kidnaps his children, Peter must come to grips with who he is, remember his past, and travel to the magical world of Neverland to rescue them.   Julia Roberts is Tinkerbell, Bob Hoskins is Smee, and while there are loads more actors I should mention it's more fun to name the names of people who were thrown into the mix that make it seem like making a "Hollywood" movie was more important than making an overall enjoyable movie. Therefore, if you watch *Hook* you can expect to find Phil Collins, George Lucas, Carrie Fisher, Jimmy Buffett, and David Crosby popping in. Glenn Close got in there, though that's not saying her as an actress makes for a bad cameo, and also a young Gwyneth Paltrow makes one of her earliest film appearances.

I am biased against *Hook* due to personal preferences in the acting department.   Robin Williams as a lead can be very hit or miss for me, loved him in his later work on *World's Greatest Dad* and he was very solid in the thriller *Insomnia*, but in the early 90s *Mrs. Doubtfire* is all I needed from him and that was still a fairly heavy dose to stomach. Also, Dustin Hoffman is an actor that I really just don't like seeing in movies at all. Why is that? Why such disdain for Dustin Hoffman? I don't know. It's nothing personal, just is what it is. However, if you take Dustin Hoffman and add a dumb wig and some dumb eyebrows to him like in *Hook*, that exasperates the critical feelings.

When you think of movie directors, Stephen Spielberg is probably at the top of the mountain when it comes to Hollywood royalty. The year 1989 saw the release of the sappy drama *Always* and the franchise adventure *Indiana Jones and the Last Crusade*, and then 1990 was void of Spielberg directed projects coming to theaters.

In the 80s is when Stephen Spielberg originally set out to make the movie *Hook*. However, he lost his taste for the material and decided that where he was at in life did not match up with where he needed to be in order to bring filmmaker insight into the material. The production bounced around some and the ball eventually ended up right back in Spielberg's court and he took the gig again. When all is said and done, the movie gets stuck with the legacy of having its own director mention it as being one of his weakest works that he is not a fan of. More or less he proclaims he did not know what to do with the bulk of the movie and the entire middle section of the film is filler and spectacle for the sake of spectacle.

It did not help that the massive production apparently had a problem child in its Tinkerbell. Julia Roberts is said to have lost her mind with anxiety during the shoot and in turn stressed everyone else out and made the shoot a nightmare. The actress had risen to the top of Hollywood's A-list and was also dealing with personal issues in the romance department during this period. Julia Roberts movies were making big bucks at the box office, but she may have been paying with a bit of her sanity behind the scenes.

If you want to revisit, or lay eyes on it for the first time, I always say people should formulate their own opinions and not let blowhards such as myself sway their opinions, be sure to have a comfortable seat, *Hook* is way too long for how slow it moves.

5. *City Slickers* - directed by Ron Underwood, screenplay by Lowell Ganz and Babaloo Mandel. Domestic Box Office: $124,033,791

If you took nine-year-old me into a fantasy world with pirates and fairies, nine-year-old me wasn't impressed; trashing *Hook* again. Yet, take me to watch a movie about some older men going on a vacation cattle drive and nine-year-old me wanted to watch that movie again and again. Weird.

City Slickers has a plot in which Billy Crystal, Bruno Kirby, and Daniel Stern star as men reaching mid-life crisis status and deciding to get away from their woes in the city by going on a cattle drive adventure. As the going gets rough, the men learn life lessons and how to be tough from a grizzled cowboy played by Jack Palance.

The role of Curly in *City Slickers* earned Jack Palance an Oscar for Best Actor in a Supporting Role as well as a Golden Globe. When he won the Oscar Jack Palance decided to show off how fit he was for his age, doing some one-handed pushups on the stage. It was the third time that Palance had been nominated in that category over the span of his career. His first Supporting Actor nomination came in 1953 for *Sudden Fear* and the second was in 1954 for *Shane*.

In his book *Still Foolin' 'Em: Where I've Been, Where I'm Going, and Where the Hell Are My Keys* Billy Crystal relates a tale about the casting process for the role of Curly. Jack Palance did not come onboard as quick as hoped for and an offer was extended to actor Charles Bronson. According to Billy Crystal, Charles Bronson was angered by the offer, seriously cursing him out and insulted by the idea that he would take such a role. Charles Bronson may not agree, may have been proud to stick by his guns and direct his career, but the adoration Jack Palance received after starring in the role probably makes most people think Bronson was being a rude, egotistical idiot. Both Palance and Bronson are deceased, and not that it was a competition, but Palance lived longer. Jack Palance died in 2006 at the age of eighty-seven, while angry Charles Bronson perished in 2003 at the age of eighty-one.

Billy Crystal also has a story about Jack Palance's anger. Apparently on the first day of shooting the veteran actor got into an argument with director Ron Underwood. After the yelling match, Billy Crystal inquired of Palance what the argument was about and where the anger came from and got a reply along the lines of "It was my first day. I always get nervous on my first day."

Comedic actor Rick Moranis, of *Honey, I Shrunk the Kids* fame, was originally cast as the character Phil. However, he dropped out of the production to be with his wife who had been diagnosed with cancer. Daniel Stern replaced Moranis.

And while I'm on a doom and gloom kick involving this comedy film, might as well mention that lead actor Bruno Kirby, the character Ed, died in 2006 at the age of fifty-seven. Leukemia is what felled Mr. Kirby. If it helps make things less dreary here is a *City Slickers* fun fact about Bruno Kirby: he was allergic to the horses and had to keep taking allergy shots to remain on set. Wait, never mind, that's not a fun fact. It shows his dedication to the craft though!

Here's a positive thing! Jake Gyllenhaal made his feature film debut in *City Slickers* as Danny Robbins, son to Billy Crystal's character Mitch Robbins. Unless you don't like Jake Gyllenhaal and curse the fact that someone let him into Hollywood, then, I guess that's not so positive. I think Gyllenhaal does a pretty good job though, no hate coming from me.

As well-received as *City Slickers* was, director Ron Underwood will never get out of the shadow of his greatest movie which was released in 1990: *Tremors*. Argue if you want for *City Slickers,* try to convince me of the sacred value in *The Adventures of Pluto Nash* or *Mighty Joe Young*, but my mind is made up: *Tremors*.

Even though it is a comedy, the production of *City Slickers* got serious about capturing the settings and all of the action to take place at them by hiring Dean Semler to be the director of photography. Dean Semler took home an Oscar for his work on 1990s *Dances with Wolves*.

I suggest for more behind the scenes depth about *City Slickers* to actually pick up a copy of Billy Crystal's aforementioned book which covers the subject better than me. Personally, my mind has already wandered back to thinking about how awesome the Ron Underwood directed movie *Tremors* is. No, the 2005 movie *In The Mix* starring Usher is not better, *Tremors* is the best movie that Ron Underwood has and will ever direct!

City Slickers got a sequel in 1994 called *City Slicker II: The Legend of Curly's Gold*. The sequel did not reach the top ten list in that year. It peaked at number thirty-two in North American box office earnings.

4. *The Silence of the Lamb*s - directed by Jonathan Demme, screenplay by Ted Tally. Domestic Box Office: $130,742,922

Famous movie critics Siskel and Ebert did not agree on *The Silence of the Lambs*. Roger Ebert had his thumb up exclaiming the virtues of the film while Gene Siskel called it trashy. Opinions are a tricky thing, prone to changing, and when I was younger, while "trashy" is not something that would have

72

bothered me, I was specifically not a fan of Jodie Foster starring movies and *The Silence of the Lambs* did not reel in my cinematic appreciation. My thoughts on the film evolved over the years, it is a film best experienced by adults, and I must say I side with Ebert, the movie ticket buyers of 1991, and the Academy Awards on this one: *The Silence of the Lambs* is a solid film.

Based on the 1988 novel of the same name, *The Silence of the Lambs* takes you on a dark journey with a fresh F.B.I. recruit into the worlds of profiling and serial killer hunting. A murderer dubbed Buffalo Bill is on the loose and in the ultimate "it takes one to know one" approach to tracking down their prey the Feds begin a series of interviews with another killer, the imprisoned Hannibal Lector. It is up to agent Clarice Starling to decipher Lector's twisted wisdom to aid in the capture of the other fiend, but she's not confident with regard to whether or not the approach is paying off, unsure of whether she is really getting into Lector's head for information or that he has freely gotten into hers for his own devious purposes.

Dr. Hannibal Lector is the character that most will first associate with *The Silence of the Lambs*. He is not only a horror genre icon, but thanks to the performance of Anthony Hopkins the character transcends genre and resides in cinema history as a grand achievement in craft. Anthony Hopkins reprised the role in a sequel, *Hannibal*, and a prequel, *Red Dragon*, however, before the breakthrough of *The Silence of the Lambs* the character had already appeared in the 1986 movie *Manhunter*. Actor Brian Cox portrayed Lector in that Michael Mann directed film, which wasn't ill received, but somehow slipped into history without the fanfare that Hopkins was later able to capture with director Jonathan Demme. The story of *Manhunter* was remade as the aforementioned *Red Dragon* letting Hopkins fully take claim of the role for a moment. Then in 2007 the original book author nabbed a screenplay credit in the Lector involved franchise of his creation with the movie *Hannibal Rising*. Another prequel in the timeline to *The Silence of the Lambs* the story follows a young Hannibal Lector played by Gaspard Ulliel. Then 2013 saw the beginning of the *Hannibal* television series and yet another actor stepped into Lector's shoes, this time Mads Mikkelson. But, who is Hannibal Lector? Anthony Hopkins.

Gene Hackman actually invested in securing the book rights for *The Silence of the Lambs*, eyeing the Lector role for himself should they get the film off the ground. When he changed his mind it is said that Sean Connery was offered the part. Supposedly Connery found the script too icky and then, according to the autobiography of actor Derek Jacobi, *As Luck Would Have It*, the role came down to Jacobi, Hopkins, and Daniel Day-Lewis.

Michelle Pfeiffer is said to have been the first actress offered the role of Clarice Starling. She turned it down.

Jodie Foster stars as Clarice Starling and I have to ask my younger self, why such early animosity toward Jodie Foster keeping *The Silence of the Lambs* off of my radar of interests for so long? I don't have a comfortable answer, but the lack of appeal is not all on Foster. I grew up in the Midwest and I know my early knowledge of her involved her sexuality. I have never felt anti-gay sentiment or feelings in my life, however, the environments that I lived in pushed such an agenda when it came to what was or wasn't "cool."

As a growing boy Jodie Foster did not attract me in the ways we were being sold on sexualization and the movies. Therefore, my mind had to grow out of the dirt being heaped on it to form its own opinions better when it came to giving certain movies a chance to impress me without immediate dismissal or the need for the leading lady to be "attractive" to me. When you're young and trying to fit into the environment around you it can be easy to let the opinions of other pollute your mind and you nod your head along.

The Silence of the Lambs became a big movie and therefore opinions on it were more popular in conversation than say me ever having to explain why in 1991 I was still watching *Pee-Wee's Big Adventure* and *Follow That Bird* every chance I got. The kids were discussing the "adult" movies. At school you act like you're into adult things, like you have valid adult viewpoints, as you eagerly wait for the bell to ring so you can run home and play with some dolls.

When it was released, and continuously over the years, *The Silence of the Lambs* has actually gotten some ill press over the killer Buffalo Bill in the movie. The character is often pointed out as being an evil stereotype for promoting homophobia or transphobia. While I don't disagree that one can choose to attack the construction of the Buffalo Bill / Jame Gumb role, I don't subscribe to the theory of there being a purposeful agenda behind said character aimed at a specific sect of people. You can do that type of "picking apart" with most any movie or character if you choose to. Actor Ted Levine made the character memorable, ruling the screen in a creepy fashion whenever present, without personally connecting any transphobic wires in my mind as to "they are trying to tell us all trans or homosexual people are psychos." Dumb, fearful people in the real world around me might have tried to push such an agenda and maybe they could even use a movie as propaganda in an attempt to reinforce such, but that's not a blame the movie should shoulder, that's something that people in their self-important "everything revolves around my opinion" jibber-jabber do to movies all of the time, projecting meaning and purpose on to the art that the artist disputes.

There were many creative influences that went into the story of *The Silence of the Lambs*, both in book and movie format. Pick some serial killers and you might say that their twisted true crimes fed the dark muse at play. The F.B.I. and their procedures were also involved, literally with some consultation provided. John Douglas, a man known to be one of the pioneers of "profiling" techniques, provided insight to the filmmakers. John Douglas was the inspiration for the character Jack Crawford in the book, a character portrayed by actor Scott Glenn in the movie.

A behind the scenes tale often told about *The Silence of the Lambs* and the role preparation done by actor Scott Glenn sheds some light on the real horror that exists in the world. It is said that Scott Glenn picked the brain of John Douglas and Douglas suggested that one way to better understand the trials of his job was to listen to snuff tape recordings. Glenn is said to have emotionally bitten off more than he could chew, having a tearful breakdown after Douglas let him hear recordings of Lawrence Sigmund Bittaker and Roy Lewis Norris raping and torturing a young woman. This is a story to keep in mind if you think that all acting is just frivolous playtime, many expose themselves to some hard truth in order to bring you that fiction that flickers before you and your tub of popcorn.

The Silence of the Lambs was nominated for seven Oscars. All five of the main award categories were won by those involved with the production: Best Picture, Best Actor in a Leading Role for Anthony Hopkins, Best Actress in a Leading Role for Jodie Foster, Best Director for Jonathan Demme, and Best Screenplay Based on Material Previously Produced or Published for Ted Tally.

3. *Beauty and the Beast* - Directed by Gary Trousdale and Kirk Wise, screenplay by Linda Woolverton. Domestic Box Office: $145,863,363

The animated feature *Beauty and the Beast* centers around a young book-loving woman, Belle, that encounters a beast-man that holds her father prisoner. She swaps places with daddy and resides in the castle with the beast-man. On the Beast side of things, well, he's an arrogant Prince that was transformed, a curse that can only be lifted should a young woman fall in love with him for who he is and not what he looks like. He has pretty much given up hope, living in beastly form alone with his servants that have been transformed into household items such as candlesticks and teapots. It is a romantic musical journey with peril aplenty as a villainous suitor of the woman also comes to claim Belle for his own. Who will smooch who? Will the curse be lifted? Will Belle shave the Beast? Find out all that and more by watching Disney's *Beauty and the Beast*.

In 2017 Disney revisited *Beauty and the Beast* as a live-action movie starring Emma Watson. If you had to choose between one or the other, I would recommend the 1991 animated version. The new version brought nothing exciting or new to the table in my opinion and the CGI usage was quite drab and lifeless when objects were supposed to be coming to life and singing; the zest and spirit captured by the cartoon were lost.

Beauty and the Beast is a rare example of a cartoon that got nominated in the Best Picture category for the Academy Awards. It lost to *The Silence of the Lambs*, however, it won the money race at theaters. The film did receive six Oscar nominations and won two: Best Original Song and Best Original Score.

My childhood memories do involve having seen *Beauty and the Beast* at the movie theater. I specifically recall going to that showing because it was a special occasion in which my mother, not my grandmother, actually took me to the show. I think I got to take a friend. *Beauty and the Beast* may not be my favorite of the Disney movies from my childhood, but it ranks up there due to this memory.

When I started this entry of the book and listed the sole screenwriter as Linda Woolverton I did so with regard to the way the writing credits of the film are listed out on the Internet Movie Database. Her credit is the one earmarked "animation screenplay," however, there are ten more "story by" credits that were doled out. If you want to count the original tale and story authors as well then *Beauty and the Beast* had at least thirteen writers, but, of course, there were probably more contributors that did not qualify for credit.

The writing process for *Beauty and the Beast* was a departure in terms of approach by the studio. It was the first time that Disney actually used a screenwriter instead of working straight from art and storyboards.

While it did not win any awards outside of music at the Academy Awards, *Beauty and the Beast* did make history at the Golden Globes. *The Little Mermaid* was the first animated film to be nominated for Best Picture, Musical or Comedy, but *Beauty and the Beast* became the first animated film to actually win that category. The Best Score and Best Original Song Golden Globes also went home with *Beauty and the Beast*.

2. *Robin Hood: Prince of Thieves* - Directed by Kevin Reynolds, screenplay by Pen Densham and John Watson. Domestic Box Office: $165,493,908

Robin Hood is a character that has and will continue to be featured in entertainment products as long as humans and social class inequality exists. In the 90s we got a Kevin Costner lead exploration of the character, something that seemed more out to be "hip and cool for a new generation" rather than being a stuffy historical piece. The approach worked on me, I thought *Robin Hood: Prince of Thieves* was hip and returned to see the action again and again. Of course, I've probably never actually been "hip" in my life, my tastes from childhood are not to be trusted. Heck, can we trust anything people liked in the 90s to hold up and still be awesome decades later? Trick question! Yes! Plaid, neon spandex, and Pogs!

Robin Hood steals from the rich and gives to the poor, fighting back against the Sheriff of Nottingham while romancing Maid Marian, and along for the ride are his merry band of forest dwelling thieves and his sidekick Azeem. Kevin Costner plays the title role with Morgan Freeman helping him out as Azeem. Mary Elizabeth Mastrantonio is Marian with Alan Rickman as the Sheriff trying to steal her away, by force, from Robin Hood's love. Sean Connery fills in the bit part of King Richard. Christian Slater was still cool in the 90s, so, he was Will Scarlett in the film. Michael McShane plays Friar Tuck, Geraldine McEwan is the nasty witch Mortianna, Nick Brimble is Little John, and Michael Wincott is Guy of Gisborne. Slater and Wincott are known for their distinctive, gravely voices, the producers really should have tried to work Kiefer Sutherland and Lance Henriksen into the mix somewhere I do say.

It is said that Cary Elwes was offered the role of Robin Hood in *Robin Hood: Prince of Thieves* before Kevin Costner took it. If that is true then the amusement to be found in that tidbit is that Cary while turning down this role, went on to star as Robin Hood in the Mel Brooks comedy *Robin Hood: Men in Tights*. Men in tight tights!

Alan Rickman didn't seem keen on becoming the Sheriff of Nottingham, however, eventually signed on with the promise that he could take as many liberties with the character as he wished. The freedom allotted to Rickman explains the twisted comedy that is brought into the story via the over-the-top Sheriff. It is said that many of his lines were not from the script, but rather pieces that Alan and his own personal writing pals designed. Alan Rickman drew so much attention to what he was doing with the character, however, that it is said Kevin Costner got into the editing room to snip out some of Rickman's screen time so as not to be overshadowed in performance.

People like to make fun of Kevin Costner's performance, specifically the lack of a British accent. No one is accusing Costner of not preparing for the role with a dialect coach though. The choice of not using an accent is said to have been made by the director and personally I think that really helped the movie in terms of connecting to the young kids of 90s America. The goal of the movie was not to be historically accurate, it was: to be hip. Kevin Costner won a Worst Actor Razzie award for his performance.

The woman that falls in love with Robin Hood after seeing his bare butt during a waterfall bathing sequence, Marian, (butt stunt double, by the way) was originally a role for actress Robin Wright. Wright decided that the role was not right for her and focused on real love via a pregnancy which is what led to Mary Elizabeth Mastrantonio stepping in to swoon over a butt; the thieving butt of a thief stole her heart.

The stylization of *Robin Hood: Prince of Thieves* won over children, but my guess is that the hit song *(Everything I Do) I Do It For You* helped draw in a lot of the adult attention. This Bryan Adams performed song was Oscar nominated and I recall it being one of the rare cassette singles that my music despising mother purchased. Also, I do not deny the power of Kevin Costner's butt double in drawing the likes of my Grandma and Aunts into repeated viewing of the movie once *Robin Hood: Prince of Thieves* was out on video. Sometimes cinema is best when kept simple, give us some action sequences, some good tunes, and throw in some butt and you've got the recipe for a good ole "Popcorn flick."

1. *Terminator 2: Judgment Day* - Directed by James Cameron, screenplay by James Cameron and William Wisher. Domestic Box Office: $204,843,345

The Terminator was released in 1984, but somehow, even as my brother and I became action movie crazed, I never watched it until after having my mind blown away by the awesomeness of *Terminator 2: Judgment Day*.

The plot for *Terminator 2* involves a cyborg played by Arnold Schwarzenegger being sent back in time to protect a young John Connor, played by Edward Furlong, from an assassination attempt by the liquid metal T-1000 played by Robert Patrick. In the future there is a war of men vs robots and John Connor is a key human in said war, thus, with time travel being a thing, the robots want to snuff him out as a teen. It's hard to keep typing a plot synopsis without wanting to launch into poking fun at all of the plot holes and logic missteps in the overall concept, but forget this sentence, and forget the plot holes, they don't exist, they have been terminated. Where was I? Oh, yeah, the Terminator is a good guy, but in the first film he was a bad guy, therefore, John's mother Sarah Connor, who barely survived the attacks of the first film, is pretty suspicious about the new good guy act, and action, action, explosions, pow, pow, technical effects wizardry. Sarah Connor is portrayed by Linda Hamilton.

Piranha Part Two: The Spawning helped crack open the big studio door of Hollywood for James Cameron, but 1984's *The Terminator* kicked it open, and *Aliens* in 1986 took the door off of the hinges, which led to *The Abyss* in 1989, but then 1991's *Terminator 2* seems like the ultimate payoff of his directorial journey, the movie that showed that while he was coming and going through that open door hole he brought in everything he needed to take over the building within and remodel it as he saw fit. What am I saying? I'm saying *Terminator 2* is the movie that should go on James Cameron's headstone if we are going to bury him with a nostalgic thumbs up from my era of young cinematic experiences, ignore the cries for "Here Lies the Director of *Titanic*," and James Cameron's own personal push to be the *Avatar* guy.

Terminator 2 has a restricted rating, rated R, yet it was marketed for kids in the same way that many of the blockbuster successes of the time period were. As a kid I had the movie trading cards and marveled over the media blitz that drew attention to the state-of-the-art technology that went into the making of the film, specifically we were all hyped up to be amazed by the liquid metal effects of the T-1000 character. If you did not go see the movie you were going to be missing out on cinematic history! Most things don't live up to the hype in my experience, but as a kid and an action movie fan, *Terminator 2* did not disappoint. The concept was slick with the science fiction twists and the action featured gunfire and explosions, coupled with gritty destruction left and right, it was a movie that felt BIG. Crap, I just got myself excited all over again to watch it. Nah, better not, might not live up to the hype.

Terminator 2: Judgment Day is an Oscar winning film four times over. Best Sound, Best Sound Effects Editing, Best Visual Effects, and Best Makeup all went home with *T2* production crew.

Another way in which *T2* made itself an accessible, in terms of broad audience range, was the family dynamic at play in the story. You've got the strong single mother who is imprisoned in an asylum for knowing the truth about time travel and terminators. Then you've got her rebellious son that she has not seen in a long time and he wants a father figure that accepts him for who he is, someone not as square as the foster units ruling over him. The family is reunited with Arnie's Terminator to form the ultimate of dysfunctional

90s families, functioning dysfunction that was edgy and yet identifiable to any young teens, especially those dealing with divorced parents.

It's crazy that Edward Furlong's film acting debut is *Terminator 2*. How does a kid get such a blockbuster break? I don't know. It seems like it should be some elaborate and exciting story. Wikipedia mentions that a casting director discovered him at the Pasadena Boys and Girls Club. Why was the casting director there? When one considers all of the troubling stories that come out of Hollywood involving child actors, perhaps one wonders if there are lots of seedy troubles indeed in the Edward Furlong Hollywood story.

Aside from drug addiction admissions by the young actor, there is apparently a *T2* behind the scenes love scandal. The ages changes from telling to telling, some say he was thirteen and the woman twenty-six, others claim he was fifteen and she was twenty-eight, some say they didn't round third base together until after he was sixteen, but whatever ages, it is said that Furlong had a female stand-in on set that he then hired to be his tutor, but what she tutored in was love, sweet, erotic love. Eventually his guardian tried to get the older woman charged with statutory rape, but that failed. In 1999 the tutor sued Furlong for abusing her and for money owed when she provided him services as a career manager. The entire relationship, which is none of our business anyway, is even more confusing when you read that Edward

Furlong emancipated himself at the age of fifteen and was in charge of his adult affairs anyway.

While I've got your attention tabloid style, actress Linda Hamilton and director James Cameron were a hot and heavy item as well. She is said to have moved in with Cameron the same year as *T2* released and then gave birth to their daughter in 1993. The couple got married in 1997 and then divorced in 1999. Linda Hamilton gave James Cameron love, probably some adventure with her bipolar disorder, and also sacrificed her hearing for his *Terminator 2* movie. Linda Hamilton forgot to put in her ear plugs during a scene in which she fires a gun inside of an elevator, resulting in some permanent hearing damage. How many times might James Cameron have called out to his wife, only to be ignored because she could not hear him? Those little annoyances add up in a marriage, bless their hearts for trying. Actually, many purveyors of gossip will point out James Cameron having an affair with actress Suzy Amis as a contributing factor to the marriage's demise.

Actor Robert Patrick married his girlfriend during the filming of *Terminator 2*. They are still together in 2018 as I type this. Robert Patrick has always let it be known that *T2* changed his life for the better, taking him from a broke actor, to an actor who took the fight to Arnold Schwarzenegger in battles that will forever be remember by movie fans, which is darn good currency in landing acting gigs. Fun fact: Robert Patrick is the brother of Richard Patrick the lead singer of the band Filter.

Robert Patrick's part in the movie almost went to some other seemingly odd choices. It is said that James Cameron wanted singer Billy Idol in the role, however, an injury from a motorcycle accident kept Idol away from the job. Then Blackie Lawless, lead singer of the metal band WASP, has a tale of himself being cast as the T-1000. He says that at six foot four it was decided that he was too tall for the role.

Terminator 2: Judgment Day marks the start of James Cameron's name being associated with "the most expensive film of all time" marketing gimmick. *T2* was the most expensive until he topped it with *True Lies* which he then topped with *Titanic* which he then sank with *Avatar*. There usually isn't much truth in Hollywood numbers though, but even with high-end production costs James Cameron has proven to be a winning lottery ticket again and again in the eyes of those who pay to play.

1992

10. *A League of Their Own* - Directed by Penny Marshall, screenplay by Lowell Ganz and Babaloo Mandel. Domestic Box Office: $107,533,928

Out of the crop of films to be released in 1992 the Clint Eastwood Western *Unforgiven* went on to win the Academy Award for Best Picture. *A League of Their Own* made more money at the box office, however, landing at number ten in earnings with *Unforgiven* looking up at it with six million dollars less of a box office intake. But, there you have it, proof that two of America's greatest pastimes, baseball and shooting people while wearing a cowboy hat, can draw a crowd to theaters.

A League of Their Own is a fictionalized, comedic and dramatic account of the real-life women's professional baseball league that was formed when World War 2 hurt the sport of baseball by stealing away many of the men that generally put on a show playing it. Even if you have not seen the film you've probably heard the quote "There's no crying in baseball," possibly somehow it even got into your head with the sound of Tom Hank's voice exclaiming it.

The list of actors starring alongside Tom Hanks are way too many for me to want to list out, therefore, I present to you a brief list that leaves out many notable contributors: Geena Davis, Lori Petty, Rosie O'Donnell, Jon Lovitz, David Strathairn, and Madonna. The characters of Dottie and Kit, sisters portrayed by Geena Davis and Lori Petty, can be considered the main leads of the team story effort.

In a 2013 television interview director Penny Marshall told Bob Costas that she originally was interested in getting Demi Moore cast in a lead role. Demi Moore was pregnant at the time that they were ready to kick things off, however.

There were stunt people involved with the shoot, but much of the action on the field was actually performed by the actors who participated in some training beforehand. There are tales of all sorts of bumps, bruises, and broken noses, it was probably a wise decision not to toss a woman with child inside of her, Demi Moore, into the fray. Of course, a player giving birth during a baseball game scene could have been interesting!

Director Penny Marshall is the sister of director Garry Marshall and Garry is actually in the movie as Walter Harvey. He stepped in when another actor dropped out at the last minute. Aww, family favors in Hollywood are too cute.

Prior to shooting *A League of Their Own* Penny Marshall had already worked with actor Tom Hanks on the set of *Big*. Penny directed *Big* and it did big numbers in North America in 1988 as the fourth highest earning film of that year.

Other than as a director, Penny Marshall became a household name in acting. She was Laverne on the classic television show *Laverne and Shirley*. This show ran from 1976 to 1983, but as a kid I recall it still getting plenty of air time on the channels I surfed on my little black and white, eight inch screen television. Brother Garry Marshall directed two episodes of the show and appeared as a drummer in a couple of episodes.

In 1993 CBS made a television series based off of *A League of Their Own*. It did not last very long. As of 2018 there is another television series rumored to be in development by Amazon. *A League of Their Own* is also the name of a UK gameshow that is not about a women's baseball team specifically but does happen to be a quiz show that revolves around sports in general.

In the movie the women's baseball league is sponsored by a man that made his money in the business of candy bars. In real life Philip K. Wrigley was the sponsor and chewing gum was the name of his game; Wrigley's chewing gum. If you are a baseball fan you also know to associate Wrigley with the Chicago Cubs baseball team. It is not a coincidence that the baseball field that the Cubs play at is called Wrigley Field.

9. *Basic Instinct* - Directed by Paul Verhoeven, screenplay by Joe Eszterhas. Domestic Box Office: $117,727,224

Basic Instinct is touted as one of the most financially successful films of the 90s, featuring one of the most paused scenes in history when it released to home video, and responsible for a slew of erotic thrillers that came out for years afterward in hopes of catching some of the same heat. One could say that *Basic Instinct* itself was trying to capture some of the same heat generated by 1987's *Fatal Attraction* which also starred Michael Douglas as someone making the whoopie with an unstable lady.

The movie is about a detective investigating a murder and falling into a hot and heavy sex affair with the prime suspect. It stars Michael Douglas as Detective Nick Curran with Sharon Stone as the femme fatale Catherine Tramell.

Let's discuss the elephant in the room right away: Sharon Stone's vulva. Rumor has it that people were destroying their VHS tapes by rewinding and pausing so often during the infamous interrogation scene of *Basic Instinct*. In the scene Sharon Stone sits in a chair and while being questioned uncrosses and crosses her legs giving viewers a look beneath her skirt. She wasn't wearing any panties, thus, the female crotch shot heard around the world.

Sharon Stone would later claim that she was tricked into exposing herself in the scene. Originally she wore panties and director Paul Verhoeven told her that they were reflecting the lighting in a negative way and that she should remove them because her nethers would be hidden in shadow. It is said that she slapped Verhoeven after later seeing the film and herself so exposed. The director defends himself against her accusations and claims that Stone was always fully aware of what was going into that shot. Regardless, Sharon Stone should probably be given an award for acting all sexually charged in Verhoeven films, having to slobber all over Arnold Schwarzenegger on *Total Recall* and then Michael Douglas in *Basic Instinct* as if they were the most handsome of sex Gods, probably while taking home a far smaller paycheck.

The screenplay for *Basic Instinct* sold for $3,000,000 which at the time was a record-setting sale. Writer Joe Eszterhas, love him or hate him, has a rebel attitude that one might want to study if they plan to navigate the seedy waters of Hollywood. I've read his books *The Devil's Guide to Hollywood* and *Hollywood Animal* and recommend both. I'm not saying he is a positive role model, but rather he is quite blunt, and I know many writers feel like their voice gets muffled in the business of movie making even when they are the spark that started the fire in the first place, thus, the way Joe handles himself may just kick a little motivation into your spine.

In a not very gentlemanly move, screenwriter Eszterhas told the world about how he got to have a one night stand with Sharon Stone. The way he figured it, *Basic Instinct* was a big hit for her and she was saying thank you, while he felt he deserved the thank you. The behind the scenes sex lives of Sharon Stone and Joe Esterhas did not totally diverge after that night, they somewhat teamed up to find new partners when Stone starred in the movie *Sliver* that Esterhas wrote. A producer on that movie left his wife Naomi Baka for Stone and Joe Esterhas ended up with Naomi, eventually marrying her. Joe and Naomi have been married since 1994 and have four children together.

If you think *Basic Instinct* is smut, know that it is prestigious smut with regard to Hollywood award nominations, making it into two Oscar categories: Best Film Editing and Best Original Score. It didn't win for either of those categories, but the editor Frank J. Urioste and all of the time he spent watching Michael Douglas and Sharon Stone's sweaty bodies rubbing together had to have been proud of the effort. Previously Urioste had been nominated for Oscars in the editing category for *Robocop* and *Die Hard*, not winning on those either.

Gay rights activists did their best to disrupt the filming of *Basic Instinct* with protests. Sharon Stone's character likes to sleep with men and women and some of the gay community felt like her being portrayed as a killer was a negative statement about people who like to make love with people that identify as the same gender. The protests got so bad that the production began making fake call sheets with fake locations to throw protesters off the scent.

If you want to protest something bad about the movie it should probably be the big DNA plot hole. The crime would have been solved and the culprit arrested in a short matter of time if the story had not forgotten about DNA testing as a tool in the detective's arsenal.

8. *Wayne's World* - Directed by Penelope Spheeris, screenplay by Mike Myers, Bonnie Turner, and Terry Turner. Domestic Box Office: $121,697,323

Party time! Excellent!

The movie *Wayne's World* is based on characters from *Saturday Night Live* comedy sketches performed by Mike Myers as Wayne and Dana Carvey as Garth. The actual genesis of the Wayne character, however, is farther back in time with Mike Myers having performed a version of the character in 1987 on the CBC variety show *It's Only Rock & Roll*. The CBC is the Canadian Broadcasting Corporation, Mike Myers is Canadian. Dana Carvey was born in Montana. Carvey developed Garth based on his own brother that he dubbed a quiet genius and has said that the only direction Mike Myers gave him with regard to the character was "Garth loves Wayne."

The characters of Wayne and Garth host their own public access television show from out of the basement of Wayne's parents' house. It's not a show that is making them a fortune, but it does give them some local celebrity credentials and young people have made the show an underground success. In the movie they are discovered by a sleazy, handsome television executive played by Rob Lowe who wants to develop the show on a mainstream channel in order to sell products to the teens that tune in. Wayne and Garth struggle with how to keep their identities while pursuing their dreams and then on top of all of this there is the love story of Wayne and Cassandra, a part played by Tia Carrere. The sleazy television guy not only wants to steal the soul of Wayne's show, replacing it with a core of corporate greed, but also to steal away his girlfriend.

Why did we love this movie in the 90s? It lampooned the teenage culture of the time, the slackers putting it to the man if you will, yet at the same time championed them. Personally, however, I'm going to say I was drawn in by the music. Specifically the car ride lip synchronization scene in which Wayne and company introduced my young ears to the magnificence of the Queen song *Bohemian Rhapsody*.

I bought the Wayne's World soundtrack on cassette tape in order to own that epic single from Queen and found myself introduced to much more. To this day I can sing you the song *Dream Weaver*, as performed by Gary Wright thanks to the Wayne's World soundtrack. I was introduced to the bizarre-ness of Red Hot Chili Peppers via the song *Sikamikanico* and became interested in the works of Alice Cooper due to the fun track *Feed My Frankenstein*. My musical taste gradually went from old school country and Weird Al to straight up rock and roll and I am guessing this soundtrack helped that progression with the likes of Black

97

Sabbath, Soundgarden, Cinderella, and The Jimi Hendrix experience also being present.

Another element of the *Wayne's World* soundtrack that my young mind found interesting was the fact that one of the rock bands on the album was led by Tia Carrere. It was neat to be able to watch the attractive woman in the movie and then she was also belting out the energetic song *Ballroom Blitz* and crooning *Why You Wanna Break My Heart* into my ears via my Walkman headphones.

The pairing of the soundtrack and the movie just kept both spinning around for my entertainment consumption, and the main thing that fused those together was first and foremost *Bohemian Rhapsody*. The movie helped reignite interest in the song, sending the song from 1975 back up the music charts. The lead singer of Queen, Freddie Mercury, died just three months before the movie opened in theaters.

The filming of *Wayne's World* was not as fun spirited as the movie itself came across. Director Penelope Spheeris was trying to juggle issues on a production level that she was not used to and among the issues was the needy state of being that Mike Myers was in. She related in interviews about the tantrums Myers would throw on set over little things such as what butter products were available at craft services.

Post-production of the film turned into a nightmare as well with Myers and Spheeris arguing over the shaping of the footage. They are said to have reconciled after their differences caused a rift, but one will note that Penelope Spheeris did not come back to direct the sequel.

Mike Myers has been known to say that the entire *Wayne's World* shoot was a blur to him. His father was dying at the time and he has said he recalled finishing the movie shoot and then his dad dying, not much else.

Dana Carvey wasn't a happy camper during this time period either. He is said to have also gone on the outs with Mike Myers over character control, wanting to take more ownership of Garth while Myers did his best to influence everything with his control-freak agenda.

As difficult as he sounds like to work with, Mike Myers seems to know what he wants, and his vision did launch him into superstardom with the Austin Powers franchise before his career seemed to implode with 2008's *The Love Guru*; though 2003's *The Cat in the Hat* wasn't exactly a career benchmark either.

The sequel to *Wayne's World*, *Wayne's World 2*, is something I recall rushing out to see upon release, but it failed to capture the same magic sauce flavor as the original.

7. _The Bodyguard_ - Directed by Mick Jackson, screenplay by Lawrence Kasdan. Domestic Box Office: $121,945,720

In 1992 the second highest earning movie worldwide was _The Bodyguard._ In North America the interracial romantic thriller rose just over _Wayne's World_ to land in seventh spot on the highest earnings list.

Kevin Costner stars as a bodyguard, Frank, hired to protect a pop singer, Rachel, played by Whitney Houston. Rachel has a stalker sending her threats and while Frank is watching over her during this tenuous time in her life, the sparks fly, and love sings.

Screenwriter Lawrence Kasdan rose to fame with a lil 1980 film called _Star Wars: The Empire Strikes Back_ followed up by _Raiders of the Lost Ark._ Yes, other than George Lucas, he's the _Star Wars_ guy. His work on other projects such as _The Big Chill_ and _Silverado_, however, connected him to Kevin Costner, which is a relationship that eventually paid off in getting _The Bodyguard_ produced. Before he worked on _The Empire Strikes Back_, Lawrence Kasdan had written _The Bodyguard_ and in the 70s a variation of it was first proposed starring Diana Ross and Steve McQueen, followed by a Diana Ross and Ryan O'Neal version, neither of which took off.

The director of *The Bodyguard*, Mick Jackson, is a British born man with a diverse portfolio of movie projects. Before The Bodyguard he directed *L.A. Story* starring Steve Martin and then after *The Bodyguard* helmed the Dana Carvey private eye with amnesia flick *Clean Slate*. He would go on to be the director of the 1997 disaster piece *Volcano*, but from that silliness his path led him to the 2010 movie *Temple Grandin* which won him an Emmy and leading lady Claire Danes got lots of awards attention. *Temple Grandin* is a dramatic biopic about a pioneering woman in the livestock industry who also happened to be autistic.

The year 1992 truly is a rich example of how well the blending of films and music, specifically the marketing connection between films and their soundtracks, that has, in my opinion, been neglected as musical album sales bow to digital singles streaming, can be effective in giving a project immediate popularity along with ever-lasting life in entertainment legacy. There is a greater emotional memory formed for people with such music and moving picture synergy. *The Bodyguard* soundtrack became the highest selling soundtrack of all time with the Whitney Houston performed song *I Will Always Love You* helping it soar.

Whenever I am inspired to belt out some lines from *I Will Always Love You* it is always Whitney Houston's epic voice that I hear in my head. Many people may not even realize that she is not the first to perform the song. The song was originally written and recorded by Dolly Pardon in 1973. It reached number one on the charts in 1974, but then Dolly Pardon re-recorded the song for the 1982 film *The Best Little Whorehouse* in Texas, which she starred in with Burt Reynolds. The song went to number one again after the release of that movie. And then Whitney Houston sang it and it became the best-selling music single by a woman in history.

I was all set to write a few paragraphs on Whitney Houston's troubles, from a miscarriage during filming of *The Bodyguard* to her death in 2012, but let's shorten up the "troubled" angle and just sing some more I *Will Always Love You* instead.

Never mind, let's strike a tragic note. *The Bodyguard* is a film that has the unfortunate distinction of being a production on which someone died. Worker Bill Vitaagliano was crushed to death during the preparation of a scene. Some sources say he was killed by colliding scissor-lifts, others called them falling light cranes.

A proposed sequel to *The Bodyguard*, as revealed by Kevin Costner, was in the works and would have again gotten creative with the casting of the leading lady. Costner claims that Princess Diana was planning to star in it with the film loosely based around her real life. A draft of the script is said to have been delivered to Costner in 1997, a few months before Diana's death in a car crash.

Seriously though, that soundtrack! We owned a cassette copy of *The Bodyguard* soundtrack in my home and aside from *I Will Always Love You*, my young ears were drawn to the edgy pop track *Queen of the Night*. There is nothing weird about a ten year old boy growling out that he is the queen of the night; "Oh yeah, oh yeah, oh yeah!"

6. *Sister Act* - Directed by Emile Ardolino, screenplay by Paul Rudnick. Domestic Box Office: $139,605,150

After a lounge singer named Deloris witnesses a murder she goes into hiding as a nun at a convent. She soon takes over the all-lady choir and brings new spirit to their singing performances, which helps draw new people to the local church. Whoopi Goldberg headlines *Sister Act* as Deloris.

My mother was never one to say she was a fan of either movies or music, yet I keep remembering movies and music she enjoyed when I was young. She was a Whoopi Goldberg fan, specifically liked it best when Whoopi let out strings of obscenities in movies such as *Jumpin' Jack Flash* or *Burglar*. However, *Sister Act* worked for her too because she bought us a VHS copy to watch over and over again.

The Bette Milder starring movie *Outrageous Fortune* was another one my mother made sure that we owned on VHS, therefore, my mother might find it fun to know that Bette Milder was the original casting choice for the lead in *Sister Act*. As a singer Milder made total sense for the project, but she passed on it. Whoopi Goldberg wasn't a slouch about the singing though, she did her own singing in the movie, while some actors were dubbed with the singing voices of others.

One of the nuns in the movie, the timid Mary Robert that finds a very powerful voice, is played by actress Wendy Makkena. Now, this is where things get weird for me and *Sister Act*. Somehow the fake news got started that Wendy Makkena was the woman who voiced Ariel in *The Little Mermaid*. Who told me this? I grew up for some reason thinking that was true and I told everyone! Wendy Makkena was not involved with 1989's *The Little Mermaid* and on top of that it's not even her singing in *Sister Act*. Her singing voice was dubbed over, and Andrea Robinson is the singer heard. Wait, the weirder part is Andrea Robinson DOES have a *The Little Mermaid* connection, just not the 1989 Disney flick. In 2008 she has a singing credit for the direct to video *The Little Mermaid: Ariel's Beginning*.

The singing and mermaid conspiracies aren't the end of people not being who they are said to be when it comes to *Sister Act*. The screenwriter of the movie, while I noted it as Paul Rudnick, is credited to Joseph Howard. Joseph Howard does not exist. Other writers were brought in to make changes to the script, too many to name, but I'll name drop Princess Leia the script doctor Carrie Fisher, may the force be with her rest in peace, and Paul Rudnick decided that he did not want to take the blame for the script with so much of his material altered, thus the pseudonym.

Other people outside of the movie production thought a lot of different funny business was afoot and filed lawsuits against *Sister Act*. There was a two-hundred million dollar charge that the story was plagiarized from the book *A Nun in the Closet*. A script was said to have been written based on the book and pitched to the likes of Disney, Bette Milder, and Whoopi Goldberg. The judge sided with Disney in the court case.

In 2011, talk about taking your time, a nun named Delois, not Deloris, sued the powers that be involving the movie with the claim that it stole material from her 1987 autobiography *The Harlem Street Nun*. She didn't win either.

The director of *Sister Act*, Emile Ardolino, also directed the hit film *Dirty Dancing*. He died from complications involving AIDS the year after *Sister Act* was released. Emile Ardolino was an Academy Award winner for Best Documentary. The documentary was *He Makes Me Feel Like Dancin'* and followed ballet star Jacques d'Amboise as he taught ballet to kids in New York City.

5. *A Few Good Men* - Directed by Rob Reiner, screenplay by Aaron Sorkin. Domestic Box Office: $141,340,178

The sheer amount of movies that I was able to rent as a child via my grandmother on weekend visits is astounding. Stacks of VHS tapes would be rented, then she would take us to the movie theater as a primer, and if that movie on the big screen was exciting enough then we had the energy to stay up all night and the next day watching the rentals. It sounds unhealthy, sleep deprivation, all those Doritos and Mountain Dews, yet in my memory those days were the best, we were sharp, we were firing on all cylinders and soaking up creative inspiration at a rate that surely developed our minds to be movie trivia show masters if not professional martial artists trained in the ways of movie Seagal and Van Damme. Of course, as the world turns, you grow up and find out that those skills mostly just prepare you for running a free Internet blog or something, but time well spent I still say!

"You can't handle the truth!"

A Few Good Men is famous for the above quote and while I do not recall seeing the movie at the theater I do know that we would rent it frequently. At first glance it doesn't seem like the normal popcorn material for a kid my age, but our movie diet involved a vast buffet of choices. That mentioned quote alone is what I think helped sell *A Few Good Men* as something we wanted to see.

People were imitating Jack Nicholson's line left and right and we would rent the VHS and watch, getting that hit of movie watching high as he delivered it and we could repeat it ourselves, empowered as official members of the club that had seen the film and seen the line delivered. Again, not really much of a superpower to have I suppose, being able to recite movie lines, but sharing a common entertainment experience with others of the world is surely some sort of wonderful connection made, right?

The movie follows a military lawyer as he defends two soldiers accused of murdering another soldier. The twisted conspiracy behind the crime takes the lawyer up the chain of command until he is confronting a Colonel with grand ideals about his role in protecting the world as he sees it. Tom Cruise stars along with Demi Moore, Jack Nicholson, Kevin Bacon, Kiefer Sutherland, Kevin Pollak, James Marshall, and J.T. Walsh. You can also see Christopher Guest, Cuba Gooding Jr., and Noah Wyle in there.

Writer Aaron Sorkin has gone on to have quite the career with television shows such as *The West Wing* and *The Newsroom* under his belt, with movies such as *The Social Network* and *Moneyball*, as well as *Molly's Game*, which he directed, but *A Few Good Men* is listed as his first Hollywood credit, the one that let him take off and use his creative superpowers to influence entertainment for years to come.

A Few Good Men started out as a stage play written by Aaron Sorkin. He would write sections of the story on bar napkins while he worked in said bar. One inspiration for the play is said to have been Sorkin's sister who was in the Navy JAG Corps and her telling him about a hazing gone wrong case that she was working on. When the material took the leap from stage play to movie screen, renowned screenwriter William Goldman did a re-write, though took no official writing credit.

One of the notes from a movie executive that Aaron Sorkin did not care for during the process of bringing *A Few Good Men* to movie life is said to have asked: "If Tom Cruise and Demi Moore aren't going to sleep with each other, why is Demi Moore a woman?" The answer: "Women have purposes other than to sleep with Tom Cruise."

The interaction Sorkin had with the executive is a prime example of the everyday thinking that goes into movie formation. You the writer tell a story as it feels it should be told and then others pick at it in terms of trying to form something they think will make the most money, not what is the "truth." It is also a prime example of sexism, something that can swing both ways in Hollywood, but has historically been a weight pressed down most often on women in the industry. Demi Moore probably got paid way less than her male counterparts in the movie for the same amount of hard work and yet still someone had the gall to question why her character wasn't a sex toy for the leading male character.

Jack Nicholson is said to have been paid five million dollars for ten days of work on *A Few Good Men*. I think I am going to quit writing now and go work on my acting instead. I'm going to go look in a mirror and just yell "you can't handle the truth," over and over again.

The role of Lt. Sam Weinberg in the movie is portrayed by actor Kevin Pollak. Jason Alexander was originally cast in the role, but the production lost him when *Seinfeld* was renewed and Alexander from then on became mostly known as George Costanza. As for Kevin Pollak, he likes to share a story from the set of A *Few Good Men* in which his mother visited the set and spent her time hitting on and frustrating Jack Nicholson. He did a pretty good Nicholson impersonation when he told the story on Conan O'Brien's talk show.

When I think of director Rob Reiner I always see him as a jolly fellow and think of him as the director of *The Princess Bride* and *When Harry Met Sally*. It's easy to forget that he also brought us the severe drama of A *Few Good Men* and right before that the horror of *Misery* based off of the Stephen King story.

4. *Lethal Weapon 3* - Directed by Richard Donner, screenplay by Jeffrey Boam and Robert Mark Kamen. Domestic Box Office: $144,731,527

All of the *Lethal Weapon* movies were rotating heavy through my childhood movie rental adventures and the third installment was the first one that I got to see on the big screen. Therefore, when I think of the series the first set piece that comes to my mind is the opening of the third installment when Riggs is trying to stop the armored car robbery. Actually, that action set piece isn't even the opening set piece, the defusing of a bomb gone wrong is the opening set piece for *Lethal Weapon 3*, and the armored car shenanigans occur after they've been demoted for said bomb incident. The armored car scene, however, left a greater impression on me as a kid and even influenced my own playtime with my action figures. I would have them hanging off of the sides of speeding vehicles and such to mimic the gutsy actions of Riggs, not have them contemplating which wires to cut on a bomb. I guess as a kid you could say I wasn't into developing too much tension with my toys, lots of gunfire and explosions, lots of spit drenching the front of my shirts.

Lethal Weapon 3 is the continued action adventures of loose cannon cop Martin Riggs, played by Mel Gibson, and family man "getting too old for this shit" cop Roger Murtaugh, played by Danny Glover. They are trying to stop an arms dealer or something, but if you're tuning in for plot over action I think you might have chosen the wrong movie series. Joe Pesci returns as the annoying Leo Getz and Rene Russo is introduced into the mix as Lorna Cole, a tough as nails new romantic interest for Riggs.

One of the fun parts of *Lethal Weapon 3*'s production was that the filmmakers got to really conduct a lot of the destruction seen on the screen. The opening building explosion really took out the building, which was a pegged for demolition former City Hall in Orlando, Florida. They made sure that when the place toppled it would go in a forward motion so as not to fall backward on to where the new City Hall stood. The actual mayor of Orlando poses in the movie as a policeman and sarcastically applauds Riggs and Murtaugh for causing the explosion.

Also, spoiler alert, the final action scenario of the movie where a housing development is set ablaze was in reality: an actual housing development that they set ablaze. The location was in Lancaster, California. The construction at the housing site was unfinished due to the company undertaking it having financial problems. The movie production was given free rein to destroy the houses so long as they cleaned up afterward.

After the end credits of the movie there is an extra explosion as a joke playing off of the opening of the film. This time the production team of the film blew up a hotel in Florida that was scheduled for demolition.

Screenwriter Jeffrey Boam has the odd distinction of having two "written by" credits on the same movie, as he was hired to rewrite his own script after someone else had been hired to rewrite it. Yes, that makes sense, just keep reading it over and over again. It is also said that Princess Leia was another ghostwriter that worked on the script for *Lethal Weapon 3*. Carrie Fisher really got around Hollywood with the written word!

In the original draft of *Lethal Weapon 3* Rene Russo's character was a man. No, they did not have a gay Riggs subplot, but rather it was another man just as crazy as Riggs, I guess meant to spark off some competition of daring deeds or something. In that version of the script Riggs is having an affair with his partner Murtaugh's eldest daughter! After the sex change was made, Russo's character became of romantic interest to Riggs and the daughter affair subplot was mostly erased. In the movie Murtaugh still suspects his daughter might be having a relationship with Riggs, but his suspicions are unfounded.

As a kid the *Lethal Weapon* movies were good fun. As an adult the viewing experience has been somewhat tainted because the movies feature so many genre aspects that have become cliché and the subject of parody, it's hard to see them without thinking on those too familiar things. They still have an energy about them though and are must see films for any action genre buff.

3. *Batman Returns* - Directed by Tim Burton, screenplay by Daniel Waters. Domestic Box Office: $162,831,698

They did it again! Batman returned and so did the massive marketing push with all the bells and whistles to draw in the attention of the same children that made the first Tim Burton *Batman* a success in 1989. The sequel was an event that we had to bear witness to. I remember liking it well enough, my inner child critic not so harsh. Today, while I appreciate the kinkiness of Cat woman's suit, I find *Batman Returns* campy and unwatchable. I do not say that as a comic book fan or caring about realism or any specific thing. The characters as presented, and the world as presented is fine by me, I just get bored when I try to watch it. As adult and macabre as it is, it's still for kids and nostalgia just doesn't reconnect me to caring about *Batman Returns* for some reason.

The 1989 *Batman* to me is coated in a certain style of grime, it has grit with its violence. *Batman Returns*, even with the Penguin being all sorts of creepy looking and Cat woman looking like a dominatrix it still feels more childish to me than its predecessor. Sponsors did not view the film in that way and there were many complaints from the likes of McDonalds who felt the sequel was "darker." It did not stop McDonalds from making collectible *Batman Returns* cups though. We had to have them! I can remember the excitement of sitting in a vehicle in a McDonalds drive-thru, peering out of the window, and seeing those

Batman Returns cups being advertised. I cannot think of the movie without being transported back into that easy-sell mind and that drive-thru lane. Oh, so many McNuggets did I eat.

It is actually the toys and offshoot products associated with the Batman franchise that eventually pushed Tim Burton out. He did not get the directing gig for the third film because corporations wanted brighter colors and more kid friendly action to sell. The franchise imploded with those demands and got really dumb really quick before Christopher Nolan came along and re-booted things for adults.

Michael Keaton returned for this sequel to become Batman. He did so with a large pay bump that got talked about enough that one might think it priced him out of appearing in the third film. However, he was offered the third film, *Batman Forever*. Keaton said, while doing the press for the 2014 film *Birdman*, that he turned down the chance to reprise the role because the script was terrible, and he couldn't understand the direction they were wishing to take the franchise in. As a kid I recall that we were told that *Batman Returns* would be the final Batman movie for Michael Keaton because he decided that violence in movies was bad and he would no longer do violent movies. Who told us that? Where did that rumor come from? Michael Keaton has since appeared in movies with violence in them and even provided some voice over work for one of the most violent video game series in *Call Of Duty*.

Annette Bening was originally cast as Cat woman. Michelle Pfeiffer was watching the casting news closely due to a childhood fascination with the character. She says that it devastated her when she did not initially get the part. Fate ended up smiling on both women, however, with Annette - Bening dropping out of the production due to pregnancy and Michelle Pfeiffer getting to replace her. Perhaps they both got their dream roles at that point in life, a mother and a cat woman, though only one of them lucked out and got to avoid the torture device that the Cat woman suit proved to be. As uncomfortable as the Cat woman suit was to not only wear, but to get into, Michelle Pfeiffer still played the role with seductive flair, a real pro that Michelle Pfeiffer.

Due to his unique proportions one might think Danny Devito was born to play Oswald Cobblepot also known as The Penguin. He didn't find the process of getting into character any more comfortable than Michelle Pfeiffer did. The makeup process for Penguin took 3-4 hours each day. The oozing black liquid that is constantly leaking from Cobblepot's mouth? Danny DeVito likes to take credit for whipping up that effect himself, "a concoction that I came up with after working with the makeup and the special effects people." Um, yeah, sounds like maybe the special effects and makeup department came up with it. It is said to have been a "mild" mouthwash with food coloring in it. Maybe DeVito DID invent the black ooze, dabbling in the effects department, but this seems like a nice time to point out that once actors start doing interviews in bulk you'll see them start to take credit for pretty much everything in a movie, suddenly they wrote it, got to direct their own scenes, redesigned the sets, inspired all of the music, and fed crackers to starving gaffers at the craft services table.

Christopher Walken plays the role of the villainous Max Shreck in *Batman Returns*. This character is one of the worst ones in the film and I really could have done without him. It's not Walken's fault or the character's fault in general, it's really just that there is too much silliness crammed into one convoluted plot and if I were going to cut characters his would be one of the first on the chopping block. Cat woman is created by him when he pushes his secretary Selina Kyle out of a window. Then he has a hand in giving Penguin power in the city all in order to get his own plans for a power plant approved, just an evil, scheming business man with wacky hair. In an early draft the character was supposed to be Harvey Dent also known as Two-Face.

Pee-Wee Herman was a big deal, I would even watch non-Pee-Wee features if I knew Paul Reubens was in it just so that I could see him and point him out: "There's Pee-Wee!" In 1991 he was arrested for indecent exposure, caught jerkin' the gherkin in an adult theater. We heard all about it as kids, yet, instead of labeling him as a bad pervert, we still embraced him as a good pervert. I would watch the 1992 release of *Buffy the Vampire Slayer* fully amused that Paul Reubens was one of the vampires. At that time, however, I blinked and somehow missed it that he was also in *Batman Returns*. Paul Reubens briefly portrays Penguin's father in the opening of the film. A wasted cameo really, it would have been better if he got to be a vampire in it also.

2. ***Home Alone 2: Lost in New York*** - Directed by Chris Columbus, screenplay by John Hughes. Domestic Box Office: $173,585,516

Three of the top four movies of 1992 were sequels. *Home Alone 2* is the sequel to *Home Alone*. This time Kevin McCallister isn't at home though, he is lost in New York, New York City to be exact. See, it seems obvious that the film is a sequel to *Home Alone*, but I just wanted to clarify it because his home isn't in New York. Chicago is not in New York. Yep.

Instead of being forgotten at home, in the state of Illinois, Kevin instead boards the wrong flight when the family is taking a trip to Miami. He ends up in New York City all by himself and must once again adapt as the exact same two burglars from the first film are also there and yadda, yadda: booby traps. He is also having to keep up a ruse at his hotel, tricking the nosy concierge into thinking he is actually there with his father, not a kid home, err, a kid alone.

Home Alone 2: Lost in New York is another movie that I was excited about and rushed to see as a kid, but as an adult, don't really care about it so much. I'm not being overly critical or jaded, there are plenty of movies from my childhood that I love to revisit, for example the 1986 children's classic *Critters* never gets old.

There isn't too much to discuss when it comes to *Home Alone 2* as a film. If you saw the first *Home Alone*, this is pretty much the same movie with slight differences due to the "kid loose in the big city" aspect. They really repeat a lot of the antics from the original, paying homage to dialog, and Kevin even gets another older "scary" person to befriend in a heartfelt way that then comes to his rescue; in the original there was the snow shovel guy and in the sequel you get the pigeon lady. The pigeon lady is played by Oscar winner Brenda Fricker, the Best Supporting Actress at the 1990 ceremony for the 1989 film *My Left Foot: The Story of Christy Brown*. I'm not sure what her agent was doing to her. "You won the ultimate acting prize, now let's get you covered in bird dung and then we've got you all lined up to appear in *So I Married an Axe Murderer* as well!"

Donald Trump makes an appearance in the movie, says a line to the kid. Yes, THE Donald Trump, same orange fartbag that became the President of the United States of America. A dual autographed photo of Trump and Macaulay Culkin would be an interesting item. Sorry, I have to think about things that would be cool to sell on eBay as I write this, you know, because books don't really make me any money.

118

Home Alone 2 got a novelization to go along with the movie release. Written by Todd Strasser, the audiobook version is read by actor Tim Curry who played the concierge in the movie. Todd Strasser also wrote the novel for the first *Home Alone*. I remember having both books, vividly remember the covers with pictures of Macaulay Culkin on them. I'm sure that I read them. I don't remember reading them. The original *Goosebumps* series by R.L. Stine began in 1992. I remember reading those.

The World Trade Center was featured in the movie as Kevin goes around the city. After the 9/11 attacks some television broadcasts of the movie edited out the towers. It's a move that doesn't make sense to me, the buildings get destroyed in a terrorist attack, so, we can't let people see that they existed in old movies? Maybe I am being insensitive, maybe society is trying to be too sensitive, I don't know.

1. *Aladdin* - Directed by Ron Clements and John Musker, screenplay by Ron Clements, John Musker, Ted Elliot, and Terry Rossio. Domestic Box Office: $217,350,219

Four writers are listed as "screenplay by" for the credits of the 1992 Disney animated film *Aladdin*. However, over eighteen different people took some story credits and if they were willing to give eighteen people acknowledgment that probably means there was another hundred that

119

contributed for no credit. Howard Ashman doesn't get a writing credit, yet it is known that he wrote a treatment and lobbied for *Aladdin to get produced by Disney. Howard Ashman was perhaps best known as a musical lyricist having worked on The Little Mermaid and Beauty and the Beast for Disney. He died in 1991 but did get a composer credit for his work on the film.*

At the Oscar awards the following year the music department took home two Oscar statues without Howard Ashman. Ashman's frequent collaborator Alan Menken shared the Best Original Song Award with Tim Rice for the song *A Whole New World*. Then Alan Menken got the prize for Best Original Score. The same prizes went to the same fellows at the Golden Globes.

Out of all of the music from *Aladdin*, only one of the songs gets stuck in my head and that is the opening song *Arabian Nights*. I do not know the lyrics of the song, aside from the title portion and that when one sings it they should belt it out as loud and in as weird a key as possible. The lyrics of *Arabian Nights* changed from theatrical to home video release. A line about "they cut off your ear if they don't like your face" was replaced with a line describing the immense land and intense heat of the world setting.

Aladdin is the tale of a street urchin, Aladdin, that finds a lamp containing a wish granting genie. He uses his wishes to make himself seem like a rich prince in order to try and woo Princess Jasmine.

The evil Jafar and his parrot Iago have their own plans to overthrow the kingdom with Jafar marrying Jasmine instead. Oh, and Aladdin has a pet monkey named Abu.

Robin Williams provided the voice of the Genie and really that loud character pretty much ruled over the entire movie, second perhaps only to the music. It is claimed that the screenplay for *Aladdin* was not nominated for the Academy Awards due in part to so much of Robin William's work on the film was ad-libbed by him.

There was a deal in place with Williams in which he took a pay cut for the work, but in exchange Disney promised not to use his name or image to promote the film and the genie character would be used sparingly. A rift formed between the actor and Disney once they started pumping out promotional materials and toys involving the popular genie character. Subsequently, Robin Williams did not return to voice the character in the direct to video sequel *The Return of Jafar*. Both parties came to terms and made up by the year 1996 it would seem because Robin Williams once again voiced the role for the direct to video *Aladdin and the King of Thieves*.

The voice of Aladdin was provided by Scott Weinger who has quite the Disney filled resume. The singing voice for the character, however, was Brad Kane. Meanwhile, the princess the men are trying to obtain, was voiced by Linda Larkin while

Filipina singer Lea Salonga provided the singing talent.

Jonathan Freeman voiced the villain Jafar, a role that originally was supposed to be voiced by Patrick Stewart. Scheduling conflicts kept Stewart out of the production. Jafar's bird sidekick came to life via the annoying to many voice skills of comedian Gilbert Gottfried. Gilbert would go on to become known by many as the voice of the Aflac duck in television commercials for said insurance supplement company. He would also be known as the guy who lost the Aflac duck job due to offensive Twitter jokes.

Directing duo Ron Clements and John Musker prior to *Aladdin* worked together on *The Great Mouse Detective* and *The Little Mermaid*. Following *Aladdin* they continued in animated features with *Hercules, Treasure Planet, The Princess and the Frog,* and *Moana.*

1993

10. *Cliffhanger* - Directed by Renny Harlin, screenplay by Michael France and Sylvester Stallone. Domestic Box Office: $84,049,211

The definition for "cliffhanger" is: an ending to an episode of a serial drama that leaves audiences in suspense or a story or event with strong elements of suspense. The 1993 action film *Cliffhanger* could be described by some as the latter definition choice, however, let's not pretend that the creators of the film did not just intend the title to mean: a man who hangs off of cliffs. It is a title that makes rudimentary sense to me, yet with a hint of silliness. Therefore, when I go through old movie reviews that people wrote about *Cliffhanger*, or complaints people specifically involved in rock climbing had about realism and technical inaccuracies, it seems to me that they should have discarded those complaints before they even watched the movie. The title, the movie poster, the trailers, who really thought they were getting an educational film about rock climbing?

One of the specific complaints often cited, with regard to rock climbing not getting a realistic portrayal, is the usage of a bolt gun in the movie for firing bolts directly into the rock face of the mountain. The impact of a bolt coming from such a device and into rock would not create a solid anchor point for a climber, rather the bolt would split, break, or shatter the chunk of rock it penetrates. And then, of course, the athletic feats pulled off by Sylvester Stallone, come on, no one is buying that. Well, except the people who buy tickets to see movies in theaters, otherwise I wouldn't be writing about this movie.

The plot of *Cliffhanger* centers on expert climber Gabe Walker as portrayed by Sylvester Stallone. The movie opens with him being involved in a tragic climbing incident in which a woman he is intending to save dies. Gabe is going to give up rock climbing but is convinced to go out on the mountain to help rescue some stranded climbers. It turns out that the call for a rescue is a ruse by some bad guys who have crashed onto the mountain after stealing cases of money. They want Gabe and his pals to use their mountain climbing expertise to help them recover the cases of cash that were redistributed across the mountain during the crash. The baddies in this movie are led by Eric Qualen portrayed by actor John Lithgow. All of this story and the cast are led by the director of *Die Hard 2* Renny Harlin.

The most iconic set piece of *Cliffhanger* is probably the opening sequence in which the rescue goes wrong. Two characters hang from a wire, one trying to hold on to the other, but the glove slips off, and down the woman plummets to her death killing Gabe's desire to climb rocks or be responsible for saving people. The problem with the scene, for me and I am sure many others, is that it became so iconic in 90s pop culture history that parodies of it warped being able to take it seriously when viewing it within the context of its original action movie source. The prime example of this is when in 1995 Jim Carrey mocked the scene for the *Ace Ventura: Pet Detective* sequel *Ace Ventura: When Nature Calls*.

The stunts in *Cliffhanger* did not come cheap. Stuntman Simon Crane set a record for stuntman paychecks by getting a cool million dollars to perform a midair stunt which involved him going from one plane to another.

Even with the epic scope of the environmental setting and with the stunt sequences, the plot and overall vibe of *Cliffhanger* makes me think that it would be more suited for a direct to video release in more modern times. However, in 1993 *Cliffhanger* had blockbuster theatrical appeal and was even nominated for three Oscars: Best Sound, Best Sound Effects Editing, and Best Visual Effects.

9. *Schindler's List* - Directed by Steven Spielberg, screenplay by Steven Zaillian. Domestic Box Office: $96,065,768

The Academy Award for Best Picture from the 1994 ceremony honoring the films of 1993 went to *Schindler's List*. The movie is based on a Steven Zaillian screenplay based off of the novel *Schindler's Ark* by Thomas Keneally. *Schindler's List* is the story of Oskar Schindler, a real historical figure, who used his businesses in Germany to save the lives of Jews by hiring them to work there during World War II and the Holocaust.

In many of the production notes for films directed by Steven Spielberg a common theme seems to be that he has a hard time committing to a project initially. There are often tales of him debating whether or not he is in the right frame of mind or the right person for the job, followed by lists of directors that he tries to pawn the gig off on. I point this out, but I won't try to go full bore therapist and analyze it, but the same back and forth debate within himself seems to have been the case on *Schindler's List* as well.

It is said that Spielberg tried to recruit Roman Polanski to direct *Schindler's List*, but Polanski passed. Roman Polanski himself is a holocaust survivor and his mother died in Auschwitz. He may not have been ready to explore the subject matter, but Polanski would eventually get around to his own Holocaust film with *The Pianist* in 2002. *The Pianist* won Polanski Oscars for Best Director and Best Adapted Screenplay, while lead actor Adrien Brody nabbed the Best Actor statue.

Another director Sydney Pollack declined Spielberg's invitation to direct *Schindler's List*, but then Spielberg found a taker for the gig in Mr. Martin Scorsese. Of course, Steven Spielberg changed his mind and decided that he was the right man for the job after all, and it is said that Martin Scorsese got the rights to direct *Cape Fear* as a parting gift from the production.

Ultimately Spielberg settled on a vision for the film that he wished to move forward with, however, some of the artistic choices were not the types that thrill production studios, for example, shooting the film in black and white. In order to get full backing for how he saw *Schindler's List* Spielberg is said to have cut a deal to also direct *Jurassic Park*, a blockbuster style film with broader audience and merchandiser appeal. He shot *Jurassic Park* first due to the mental/ emotional drain he sensed would be coming pursuant tackling holocaust material, which would render him perhaps creatively impotent for the dinosaur romp if he were expected to jump right into it.

Director Spielberg did not fill his pockets with the payment he received for directing *Schindler's List*. He used the money to found the USC Shoah Foundation Institute for Visual History and Education. The purpose of the foundation centers around documentation of the holocaust, specifically they conducted video interviews of survivors and witness testimonials.

When you think of actors to lead a Holocaust drama and are searching the Hollywood pool of names, floating to the top is obviously *Darkman*! No? Liam Neeson stars as Schindler in the movie, which may have surprised some as he was not the type of Hollywood royalty one might have expected to be wooed for such duties. Oh, if you didn't get the *Darkman* reference, Neeson starred in that 1990 Sam Raimi picture, a cheesy superhero-ish tale with an acting performance by Neeson that I think could have easily killed off any future movie career for him beyond B flicks.

The likes of Mel Gibson, odd considering how his drunken anti-Jewish rants would twist public perception of him years later, and Kevin Costner auditioned for the lead part of Schindler. Warren Beatty is said to have gone far in the audition process before Spielberg decided he wanted to work with someone less known. Of course, if Spielberg was of that mindset it makes one wonder about the statement sometimes shared that Harrison Ford of Indiana Jones fame was offered the part and declined.

All of the going back and forth over the different elements of *Schindler's List* paid off in the end if one considers Academy Awards the best currency. Aside from being forever labeled a Best Picture, Schindler's List won six more Oscars, including Best Director, though none for the acting.

8. *The Pelican Brief* - Directed by Alan J. Pakula, screenplay by Alan J. Pakula. Domestic Box Office: $100,768,056

The Queen of the American Box Office Julia Roberts plays a law student named Darby Shaw in *The Pelican Brief*. She writes a legal brief detailing her theory on why two Supreme Court justices were murdered. Her paper hits the nail on the head and soon her own life is in danger. A reporter named Gary Grantham, played by Denzel Washington, is also drawn into the conspiracy. Some of the other acting talents featured in *The Pelican Brief* are Sam Shepard, John Heard, Stanley Tucci, Tony Goldwyn, and John Lithgow. Yep, a whole lot of dudes circling around Julia Roberts.

It surprised me to discover *The Pelican Brief* on the top ten earners list in North America for 1993. Why? Because I find the movie to be pretty boring.

The Pelican Brief is based on a John Grisham novel. Turning John Grisham novels into movies was big business in 1993; another adaptation will be featured on this list. If you read the book first, the movie is almost always worse, but the same thing can happen to me sometimes in reverse; seeing the movie first ruins a book. In the case of *The Pelican Brief* I have not read the book, but just by judging some of the differences, I'd wager the book is a more interesting read.

It is said, something I have not confirmed by my own reading, that the lead characters of Darby and Gary have a romantic relationship in the book. Julia Roberts went into the production of the film ready to realize the sparks on screen with her co-star Denzel Washington. However, the romance was nixed for the film and Washington gets blamed. It is relayed that at the time Denzel Washington was being careful about onscreen romances, specifically interracial ones, because he felt a lot of his fan base consisted of African-American women and he wanted them to realize his appreciation for them by not kissing white women in films. Hollywood, some theorize and form Washington's opinion for him when they talk about why he might not have wanted to lock lips with Julia Roberts, has a problem with diversity, mainly pushing white women forward as romantic interests and what is to be considered beautiful. Denzel Washington, by this theory, was doing what he could to work against that.

The working chemistry, therefore is not to be blamed, when it comes to the lack of romance between Darby and Gary in the film. One should not confuse *The Pelican Brief* with the 1994 Julia Roberts and Nick Nolte movie *I Love Trouble*. Julia Roberts and Nick Nolte were said not to get along at all on the set of that film with Roberts describing Nolte as "disgusting" and Nolte in turn describing Roberts as "not a nice person." Both movies feature leading characters that are reporters and I know some people in their 1990s haze of memory tend to forget which movie is which when it comes to behind the scenes trivia.

Alan J. Pakula, the director of *The Pelican Brief*, also directed the 1976 film *All The President's Men*, *Sophie's Choice* in 1982, and in the year prior to *The Pelican Brief* his movie *Consenting Adults* was released. *The Pelican Brief* was Pakula's next to last directing job on a major feature. It was not until 1997 that he helmed another project, *The Devil's Own* starring Brad Pitt and Harrison Ford, which was his last before dying in 1998 at the age of 70. His death was a bizarre car accident in which the car traveling in front of his ran over a metal pipe. The pipe was then launched through the windshield of Pakula's vehicle striking the director in the head. This pipe into head action caused

Pakula to swerve his vehicle off of the road and into a fence.

7. *In the Line of Fire* - Directed by Wolfgang Petersen, screenplay by Jeff Maguire. Domestic Box Office: $102,314,823

In the Line of Fire stars Clint Eastwood as an aging secret service agent, Frank, that is getting phone calls from a "whacko" that taunts him over his past failure to keep JFK from being assassinated. The stalker is played by John Malkovich and goes ahead and lets Frank know that he will be killing the current president. The challenge is set, Frank and company must track down the caller and stop the assassination from taking place. Rene Russo, Dylan McDermott, John Mahoney, Fred Dalton Thompson, Gregory Alan Williams, and Gary Cole round out the cast.

The film lacks an opening credit sequence, but the soundtrack gets right to work with an interesting piece of music. I felt like the song started out almost whimsical, but the pace quickly reached thriller movie tempo, yet before you can get to having either too much fun or get too tense, a somber horn weaves through. It is the type of horn that is often around in police procedural productions or even in movies involving work on a military base, or, as in this case, plots involving secret service agents, something that keeps you checked in that there is going to be serious business afoot. The music has a lot of character.

Ennio Morricone was the composer for *In the Line of Fire*. Early on in his career he was known as the composer of choice for director Sergio Leone, whom he was classmates with. Among his musical Oscar nominations are the films *Days of Heaven*, *The Mission*, *The Untouchables*, *Bugsy*, *Malena*, and then after a long career with zero wins the Academy gave him an honorary award in 2007. Fast forward to 2016 and Ennio Morricone honored his own skills by finally outright winning the Oscar for Best Original Score for the Quentin Tarantino film *The Hateful Eight*.

Clint Eastwood plays some piano in the movie.

In the acting department the opening scene sets up Clint Eastwood fans with good ole Eastwood attitude. He gets to have a point blank "Dirty Harry" moment, blasting some bad guys away, which doesn't seem to get him too emotional, though his partner is shaken up a bit. The tone is set up in such a way that you know the film will get dark and violent, but then you get plenty of wit in the banter of the dialog as things progress from said opening action. The lighthearted chuckles not only help balance, but also give an edge to the horrible violence yet to come, working organically, never confusing you about the seriousness that opening horn music told you about.

Perhaps the most comical bit in *In the Line of Fire* is the romance between Eastwood's character and Rene Russo's character. Well, not the concept of the romance itself, though maybe after so many movies it seems a bit cliché if anything is wrong with it. However, the romance leads to a comical, attempted love scene where they go to make love and the camera stays at floor level, letting you see all of the gear and weaponry they must drop as they unclothe. Thanks in part to the romantic music playing over the scene, the moment does not go too far into say the territory of a *Naked Gun* movie.

Another scene, if I am to sound jaded by Hollywood formulas and overly critical, that comes across almost too goofy involves a rally speech event. Frank is watching the excited audience for potential assassins when a balloon pops. He mistakes it for gunfire and sounds the false alarm getting himself in professional trouble as the secret service agents rushing the stage to protect the president embarrass the powers that be. Now, the scene in general works fine and dandy for me, the false alarm bit, that's fine, it helps show the shaky ground that Frank is on, gives the Eastwood bravado some doubt to tangle with. The problem for me, however, is that it shows John Malkovich's villain character in the audience and he is literally the person popping the balloons. The false alarm did not need to literally come from the villain popping balloons, balloons are known to pop, it would have been less silly to me if they just popped and Frank jumped into action based on the mere tension and stress of duty without us then also seeing that Malkovich literally did the popping.

Also, one more complaint, there is a pivotal death scene where the bullet wounds and just overall "the moment" of the kill aren't portrayed all that well. Too "staged," more akin to a death in a play to me than a big Hollywood film, even though the scene itself just prior to said death was one of the most harrowing moments of the story yet.

I can't and won't truly dissect the script or story telling with ill intentions, who wrote what or directed what, who called the shots here or there is all behind the scenes knowledge I am not privy too. Perhaps moments I did not like one hundred percent also made the original writer squirm in his seat as well. When all was said and done with the production, screenwriter Jeff Maguire got a Best Writing Oscar nomination and the film does still hold up in an entertaining and solid enough fashion; the balance I spoke of in the film's tone, it is maintained well enough, never tilting things too far away from the dark center, even though time and what has become cliché over it tries to give the movie a shove in terms of how younger generations may view the work.

Jeff Maguire followed up *In the Line of Fire* with a credit for *Timeline* in 2003 and then in 2006 he has a credit for *Gridiron Gang*. After that: nothing. Maybe he will sell another script after I have written this, but his short list of credits is a good example of how tough it can be to get movies made and be a prolific screenwriter.

Existing in the dark center of the movie is the character played by John Malkovich. His Best Supporting Actor Oscar nomination is a testament to the strength of the character and his performance, obviously. Tommy Lee Jones nabbed the golden man statue, however, for his role in *The Fugitive*.

Would I recommend *In the Line of Fire*? Sure, it's not too bad, fans of any of the actors should add the film to their collection. It runs a little long for me in terms of I got tired of John Malkovich calling Clint Eastwood to discuss things time and again.

Wolfgang Petersen, the German born director of *In the Line of Fire* also directed *The Neverending Story*. You should probably check that one out too. *The Neverending Story* of 1984 followed by *In the Line of Fire* from 1993 would make quite the odd double feature viewing experience.

6. *Indecent Proposal* - Directed by Adrian Lyne, screenplay by Amy Holden Jones. Domestic Box Office: $106,614,059

My grandma is a fan of staying up late to watch smutty movies. I will always remember teasing her one evening when I arrived at her house late to find her fully engrossed in one of the sequels to *Wild Things* on a pay cable channel. She paid for the tickets and rentals of a lot of the movies that I would see in the 90s and she was for sure the target audience for *Indecent Proposal*. Thus, even though it doesn't sound like subject matter that would interest a kid, I was well aware of the movie when it released. The movie gave grandma a hint of smutty intrigue via its premise but delivered name actors exploring dramatic relationships and romance. She did not take us to the theater to watch it. However, I would catch a viewing of it on VHS rental later on.

The indecent proposal in *Indecent Proposal* comes from a billionaire played by Robert Redford. He offers a couple, played by Demi Moore and Woody Harrelson, one million dollars if he can have one night with the wife. The couple accept the offer and what doing such a thing does to a relationship then unfolds in a dramatic fashion.

This is a movie that probably hit some nails on their heads for the target audience of the time, resulting in it being a solid box office hit. However, the hype around the intriguing premise ended up having more going for it than the movie itself. It did not wow me or make me want to fall in love with anything other than money. The premise is so strong that as I type this there is news that a script for a remake has already been commissioned.

What other erotically charged films had screenwriter Amy Holden Jones written prior to *Indecent Proposal*? In 1992 her script about a luscious St. Bernard was released as the movie *Beethoven*. The writer of the script is also known for 1988's *Mystic Pizza* which would become a bargain bin hit in retail stores after Julia Roberts rocketed to fame.

Amy Holden Jones based the *Indecent Proposal* screenplay off of a novel by Jack Englehard. However, it is said that the basic premise is mostly what survived from book to movie translation with the novel being more about cultural friction between Jewish folks and Arab folks.

The director of this film is no stranger to controversial material dealing with sex. Adrian Lyne is also the director of the films *Flashdance*, the foodie porn *9 1/2 Weeks*, *Fatal Attraction*, *Jacob's Ladder*, the 1997 version of *Lolita*, and then the 2002 murder and adultery tale of *Unfaithful*.

Indecent Proposal was nominated for seven Razzie awards; the anti-Oscar awards for the worst movies of the year. Worst Picture, Worst Screenplay, and Worst Supporting Actor were all categories that it won in. I'm not going to "go up to bat" for the movie, but maybe due to hype and box office popularity critics were a little too harsh on the film in 1993. If you're going to a movie with the title of *Indecent Proposal* and there is indeed an indecent proposal within the movie, I think you're getting what you expected to pay for and there is nothing wrong with guilty pleasure movies that bring joy to grandmas around the world.

5. *Sleepless in Seattle* - Directed by Nora Ephron, screenplay by Nora Ephron, David S. Ward, and Jeff Arch. Domestic Box Office: $126,680,884

Whether or not you are personally a fan of the movie *Sleepless in Seattle*, the fact is that when it comes to romance movies this is one that has etched itself a place in history, a premiere spot in the romantic movie Hall of Fame, a film that no matter how dated it may get will remain relevant with a supportive fanbase for decades more.

Sleepless in Seattle paired up Tom Hanks and Meg Ryan as romantic interests, something 90s audiences adored, a movie coupling of likable perfection. The movie is about a widower with a young son that calls in to a radio show and gets his dad to go on air speaking about love he had and lost. Many people upon hearing the story find that their heartstrings have been pulled and among them is a reporter named Maggie. The story becomes one about whether or not these two people will get together and live happily ever after in love.

Before *Sleepless in Seattle* director and writer Nora Ephron did some relationship investigating with Meg Ryan in the 1989 movie *When Harry Met Sally*. She did not direct *When Harry Met Sally* but was the screenwriter. In that feature Meg Ryan was paired up with Billy Crystal. However, after *Sleepless in Seattle*, Ephron, along with the rest of the world, realized there was a lot of magic in pairing Tom Hanks up with Ryan, and she would get the duo together again in the 1998 romance *You've Got Mail*. I find that fans of *Sleepless in Seattle* also end up being fans of *You've Got Mail* as well, but there is no denying that *Sleepless in Seattle* is the one about "finding the one" that really dug in deep in terms of pop culture, romance movies, and at the risk of sounding non-PC: *Sleepless in Seattle* is one of the ultimate "chick flicks."

Before you get too gooey with the feels, let me try to creep you out some. The role of Sam, played by Tom Hanks, has a sister in *Sleepless in Seattle* that is played by actress Rita Wilson. In real life Rita Wilson is married to Tom Hanks. Okay, I guess I wanted that to seem creepier than it really does. It's two actors doing a job, not doing taboo sex role-playing. Why did I even type this? Why am I not deleting it? Perverts.

A lot of people tend to ask: what ever happened to the kid from *Sleepless in Seattle*? The actor Ross Malinger, Jonah in the movie, seems to have plugged away at acting, mostly television gigs, until 2006. It is said that around that time he retired from the business and went into car sales. If you look up the car business that he went to work at the second Google search result I get at this time is people complaining about being ripped off by fraudsters. I believe what they are deal in, if still in business, is replica or reproduction cars.

Well, now we know what the real person portraying Jonah grew up to be. I wonder what the fictional character would have went on to become? It's probably best to just forget the actors and focus on the fiction if you want to keep enjoying movies.

The final film that Nora Ephron wrote and directed was 2009's *Julie and Julia*, which is not too shabby a watch featuring Amy Adams and Meryl Streep. In 2012 Ephron died at the age of seventy-one from pneumonia as a complication of the acute myeloid leukemia she had been diagnosed with.

If you like *Sleepless in Seattle* then there is a chance you've gone back farther into Hollywood's romantic history to check out the 1957 film *An Affair to Remember*. The characters in *Sleepless in Seattle* reference the movie and some of the plot points end up mirroring the older movie, such as the all-important meeting up at the Empire State Building. *An Affair to Remember* stars Cary Grant and Deborah Kerr as a couple that fall in love and then plan to reunite at the Empire State Building in six months to see if they have all of their life affairs in order so that they can be together in a relationship.

Authors note: my spellcheck program keeps auto-correcting the name Amy into the word May. It did it with my mention of Amy Adams and when I wrote the name Amy Holden Jones for the *Indecent Proposal* entry. Of course, this has nothing to do with *Sleepless in Seattle*, but here you go, a backstage window into the woes of writing this book. Amy, Amy, Amy, and, yep, every one of them corrected by the computer program to May.

4. *The Firm* - Directed by Sydney Pollack, screenplay by David Rabe, Robert Towne, and David Rayfiel. Domestic Box Office: $158,348367

What is a bigger box office draw than a movie based on a John Grisham book and starring Julia Roberts? A movie based on a John Grisham book starring Tom Cruise! After 1993 movie producers should have been throwing all of their money at trying to get Julia Roberts and Tom Cruise together in a movie based off of a John Grisham book.

The Firm follows a young lawyer, Mitch, played by Tom Cruise, and his great new job at a law firm. Mitch discovers that the firm is deep into laundering money and helping out the Mafia and soon FBI agents come to him and Mitch's life is in danger as he must play a game of double-agent lawyer to bring down the corrupt and murderous folks that employ him. Gene Hackman, Jeanne Tripplehorn, Holly Hunter, Ed Harris, Hal Holbrook, David Strathairn, Gary Busey, Paul Sorvino, Steven Hill, and the Quaker Oats man with type 2 adult-onset diabetes: Wilford Brimley.

The movie and the book for *The Firm* differ, as tends to be the case with adaptations, but John Grisham is said to have complained and stopped at least one change the filmmakers had planned. The role that went to Gene Hackman was indeed a male role in the book, however, Meryl Streep was being eyed for said role before Grisham apparently put his foot down.

Gene Hackman ended up making the cast and there is said to have been some kerfuffle over credits and name billing on promotional materials. Tom Cruise had a deal in place already that stated only his name could appear first and above the title on promotional materials. Gene Hackman wanted similar billing and when he was denied he made sure that his name was taken off of any and all promotional materials. Therefore, some movie fans were surprised when they went to the movie and saw him in it.

Gene Hackman is a novelist himself. In 1999 he penned, with the help of Daniel Lenihan, *Wake of the Perdido Star*. As writing partners Hackman and Lenihan also wrote the books *Justice for None* and *Escape from Andersonville*. Gene Hackman would go solo in writing his 2011 Western *Payback at Morning Peak* and then again in 2013 with the police thriller *Pursuit*.

Gene Hackman might be a John Grisham fan in general. He has starred in three movie adaptations of Grisham material: *The Firm*, *The Chamber*, and *Runaway Jury*.

Out of all of the cast on *The Firm* only one actor received attention from the Academy Awards and that was Holly Hunter, nominated for the Best Supporting Actress Oscar. At the same awards show Hunter was also nominated for the Best Actress in a Leading Role category for her part in the 1993 release *The Piano*. She did not win for her limited amount of time in *The Firm* but did indeed take home the grand prize of Best Actress for *The Piano*. Also in 1993 Holly Hunter appeared, and was nominated for a Golden Globe for it, in the wonderfully titled television movie *The Positively True Adventures of the Alleged Texas Cheerleader-Murdering Mom*. It could only have been a better title if they had fit the word "chainsaw" in there somewhere.

At the 1994 Oscar Awards ceremony, which awarded films released in 1993, Holly Hunter wasn't the only actress nominated in dual categories. Emma Thompson also landed in both Best Actress Lead and Supporting with her lead in *The Remains of the Day* and support in *In the Name of the Father*. Emma went home empty-handed, but she did win Best Actress the previous year for *Howard's End*. No other actresses were nominated within both of those acting categories within the same year during the 90s.

The Firm was the last theatrical release that actor Steven Hill acted in. Hill and Tom Cruise have a *Mission Impossible* connection with Steven Hill having played the role of Daniel Briggs in the television series during the late 60s.

The soundtrack for *The Firm* is somewhat unique in that the bulk of it is Dave Grusin playing the piano. His solo work on *The Firm* did earn him an Oscar nomination, but not a win. Dave Grusin did win an Oscar prior to this legal thriller, however, taking home Best Original Score for the 1988 film, directed by Robert Redform, *The Milagro Beanfield War*.

A television series that also worked as a sequel to the film was created. In *The Firm* produced by NBC you get to find out what is going on with Mitch and the Mafia ten years after the events of the original film. The show was canceled after a single season.

3. *The Fugitive* - Directed by Andrew Davis, screenplay by Jeb Stuart and David Twohy. Domestic Box Office: $183,875,760

Harrison Ford plays Dr. Richard Kimble in the 1993 released film *The Fugitive*. The good doctor has been framed for the murder of his wife and while he is on the run from the law, specifically a U.S. Marshall played by Tommy Lee Jones, he seeks out the one-armed man actually responsible for the murder. There is a conspiracy afoot!

When *The Fugitive* came out the hype train for it went full steam with the stunt sequences of the film being touted as impressive feats one must buy a ticket in order to see. As a kid one of my favorite things to see in action movies was someone either jumping or falling from a great height, add a waterfall and all the better. Therefore, the scene in which Dr. Kimble jumps off of a dam and into the water really entertained eleven year old me. The movie did not disappoint on the big screen and also became a regular thriller of a rental for me once it was on VHS.

Tommy Lee Jones won an Oscar for Best Supporting Actor for his portrayal of U.S. Marshal Samuel Gerard. The role isn't really much different than most of his no-nonsense characters in movies. When Tommy Lee Jones stays in that dry lane he is indeed quite entertaining as a presence. When he exudes personality in a more out-going manner you get Two-Face in *Batman Forever*. Don't be Two-Face in *Batman Forever*. Actually, he is a bit over-the-top, but in somewhat perfection as the warden in *Natural Born Killers* too, so, there is a fine line he can balance there for performance diversity if he dares to continue exploring.

Tommy Lee Jones did continue exploring Samuel Gerard with *The Fugitive* spinoff movie *U.S. Marshals*. *U.S. Marshals* did its best to pack in the stunts and action having Jones chase down a new fugitive, this time an accused murderer played by Wesley Snipes.

The Fugitive is based off of a television series of the same name that aired in the 60s. It ran for four seasons and garnered an Emmy win in 1966 for Outstanding Dramatic Series. The first three seasons of *The Fugitive* tv show are in black and white, but the final season was filmed in color. CBS brought *The Fugitive* back as a television series in 2001 with Tim Daly as the lead. The show got axed after a single season.

When it came to writing the movie based off of the television show, the process became convoluted with ideas and over the years one can be sure there were many ideas pushed forth for the script. Where *The Fugitive* really got crowded in staff in a notable way, however, was in the editing department. Six different people were given an "edited by" credit and when the editing of the movie got nominated for an Oscar that meant all six were eligible to take to the stage. The win did not come to pass, but the amount of people given credit for editing a single film was a record at the time. The editors were: Don Brochu, David Finfer, Dean Goodhill, Dov Hoenig, Richard Nord, and Dennis Virkler.

The two writers that ended up with the sole screenplay credits were David Twohy and Jeb Stuart. David Twohy previously had written *Critters 2* and *Warlock* and after *The Fugitive* moved on to *Waterworld*, *G.I. Jane*, and *Pitch Black*. He also is a director, something he appears to have dabbled with before 1993, but really got going stronger in 1996 with the Charlie Sheen science fiction film *The Arrival*. Along with writing the first three of the Vin Diesel starring *Pitch Black* films, David Twohy also directed those; *Pitch Black*, *Chronicles of Riddick*, and *Riddick*.

Jeb Stuart on the other hand was already known for *Die Hard* and *Another 48 Hrs.* and post *The Fugitive* wrote on *Just Cause*, *Fire Down Below*, and *Switchback*. He directed *Switchback* in 1997, which isn't too bad a thriller flick starring Dennis Quaid and Danny Glover, and in 2010 he wrote and directed a movie I had never heard of until now called *Blood Done Sign My Name*.

147

Prior to *The Fugitive*, director Andrew Davis may have assumed his career might revolve around the star power of Steven Seagal having directed Above *the Law* in 1988 and *Under Siege* in 1992, the latter of which also had him working with Tommy Lee Jones. It seems that he was able to avoid fading with Seagal, yet, while directing films that are notable enough that most people have heard of them, they weren't huge hits like *The Fugitive*. Andrew Davis directed *Chain Reaction* starring a pre-*Matrix* Keanu Reeves, *A Perfect Murder* with Michael Douglas and Gwyneth Paltrow, the forgettable Arnold Schwarzenegger movie *Collateral Damage*, the PG rated *Holes*, and then *The Guardian* where Kevin Costner tells Ashton Kutcher how to be a rescue swimmer. *The Guardian* is the only movie I have ever seen while on an airplane. Out of those later movies, my guess would be that *Holes* has the largest fanbase due to it being based off of a popular youth novel, though not one that I personally grew up with, so I missed the window of grander appreciation for that material I suppose. I did grow up with Steven Seagal movies though. It's sad that Seagal kind of went from being an action movie star to being just a pretentious, mumbling guy that I guess works as a representative for Russia. Seagal's career went direct to video with unwatchable, in my opinion, movies where his fighting action is him just kind of waving his hands around, people fall, and I bet he really is standing around farting a lot and mumbling philosophy about how his don't stink or something while stunt actors do the heavy lifting.

I do find it fun to imagine how *The Fugitive* would have turned out if instead of Harrison Ford director Andrew Davis had gotten the studio to go with Steven Seagal.

2. *Mrs. Doubtfire* - Directed by Chris Columbus, screenplay by Randi Mayem Singer and Leslie Dixon. Domestic Box Office: $219,195,243

Robin Williams was a manic master of jibber-jabber and the 90s were the perfect decade for his brand to have a strong run at pop culture relevance. It was a decade of neon and jibber-jabber!

When Robin Williams killed himself in 2014 it may not have been a total surprise to those that knew him best, but many fans around the world were surely shocked due to the effervescent personality he bounced around with when being filmed. His suicide is a dark exclamation mark on his legacy, yet, going out in a dramatic fashion is also befitting of such a man. It can seem like the world is all about laughing and tragedy and Robin Williams was a world unto himself that he was able to share bits and pieces of with us, making our own worlds all the more experienced and better.

Of course, I thought Robin Williams was dang annoying in movies more than not. *Mrs. Doubtfire* was an exception for me as a kid, however. Many, many times I watched *Mrs. Doubtfire* and while I may have lost my actual enthusiasm for it, or quit laughing at it in short-order, it still remained in some way a soothing formula of a feature to keep getting put into the VCR from time to time.

If you really think about the scenario of *Mrs. Doubtfire*, it is totally bonkers just like the actor playing the lead. Yet, the movie is able to keep a warm heart alive within the material. *Mrs. Doubtfire* is about a divorced man who wants to spend more time with his children and does so by dressing up as an elderly lady and getting hired by his ex-wife to be a housekeeper and nanny for the children. Aside from Robin Williams the movie stars Sally Field, Pierce Brosnan, Robert Prosky, Harvey Fierstein, Mara Wilson, Lisa Jakub, and Matthew Lawrence.

Mrs. Doubtfire is based on a 1987 British novel by Anne Fine. In 2003 a television movie was made based off of the same book and titled *Madame Doubtfire*. Michael Leeb played the title character.

A sequel to the 1993 film was in the works with Robin Williams interested enough in reprising the role that he took meetings with the screenwriter. His death put an end to sequel talks. However, in 2015 Alan Menken announced a musical adaptation was in the works. The musical as of this writing has a status update by Menken as: stalled.

It took four hours each day to transform Robin Williams into an elderly woman. The process became a popular talking point about the film during promotions and at the Academy Awards the following year *Mrs. Doubtfire* won Best Makeup.

The prize was given to Greg Cannom, Ve Neill, and Yolanda Toussieng.

What happened to the kids from *Mrs. Doubtfire*?

Mara Wilson played the youngest daughter Natalie. *Mrs. Doubtfire* was her big screen debut and helped launch her into a decent career. I think many movie fans from the 90s probably recall her best as Matilda in the movie *Matilda* based off of the Roald Dahl book. She still does some acting and has also turned her attention to writing. An article that she wrote for the website Cracked in 2013 became a popular read, entitled: *7 Reasons Child Stars Go Crazy (An Insider's Perspective.)* Mara voices the character Jill Pill on the industry lampooning Netflix cartoon *BoJack Horseman*.

Actress Lisa Jakub, the eldest daughter Lydia, got expelled from her Canadian school for being absent during the filming of *Mrs. Doubtfire*. Robin Williams wrote a letter to the school in an attempt to woo them into forgiveness, but it is said they framed the letter to be treasured without budging on their decided punishment of the girl. Lisa continued acting and when I see her picture I always recognize her from her part in the 1996 blockbuster *Independence Day*. She retired from acting in 2001, at the age of twenty-two, with her final acting credit being listed in 2000. She also turned to writing with her book *You Look Like That Girl* being published in 2015 and the book *Not Just Me* in 2017. If you are into yoga you might have some common interests with Lisa Jakub for she is a fan of the practice and is specifically trained to teach Kripalu yoga.

Matthew Lawrence played Chris, the son of Mrs. Doubtfire. There you go Hollywood, there is your sequel: *Son of Mrs. Doubtfire*. Matthew Lawrence is still acting and maybe one day he will land a role that gets him more acclaim than his acting brother Joey Lawrence. Joey Lawrence became a teen heartthrob after starring in the show *Blossom* and then went on to the sitcom *Melissa and Joey*. Matthew Lawrence's sitcom career isn't chopped liver though! He played the character Jack Hunter in the popular *Boy Meets World* show and then reprised the role for the spinoff *Girl Meets World* years later.

1. *Jurassic Park* - Directed by Steven Spielberg, screenplay by Michael Crichton and David Koepp. Domestic Box Office: $357,067,947

The film *Jurassic Park* directed by Stephen Spielberg, based off of a script by Michael Crichton and David Koepp, based off of a novel by Michael Crichton, quite possibly may have been THE event movie of my lifetime. I mean that in a personal way, I'm just not sure any other movie will be able to be released with such perfect timing and with such content as to get me as excited as I was for *Jurassic Park*. *The Land Before Time* is a cartoon that I grew up watching with fervent dedication and when the promotional blitz for *Jurassic Park* began I salivated at the chance to see realistic dinos in action.

After finally seeing *Jurassic Park* at the theater I recall being content and vocalizing such, keeping the hype of what I had experienced going. I also remember my brother stating that he thought it was too slow and boring. The truth is I sort of agreed with my brother, though would never admit it. However, the dinosaurs, the roaring T-Rex, movie magic had cast a spell over me and I would go on to watch *Jurassic Park* many times over the course of my youth and lifetime in general. Perhaps, the slower parts of *Jurassic Part* helped prime me for being a more mature movie-goer when it came to plots I was willing to tackle? The pacing does not bother me anymore and the roar of the T-Rex always takes me back, always gives me that same energetic buzz that was placed within me during my youth. *Jurassic Park is a landmark film for me, that no matter how "off" any of its elements, science and logic specifically, may be through adult eyes is still a joyful experience. I am not saying Jurassic Park is my favorite movie of all-time, but in terms of movies experienced it makes some sort of list of mine outside of this book I am sure.*

Jurassic Park is about science blending with amusement and then the consequences of playing God. Scientist are able to create dinosaurs through new DNA extraction techniques and then the owner of the bioengineering company uses said dinosaurs as attractions in a new theme park idea.

He brings in some scientific experts to evaluate the park before it is opened to the public and then, thanks to sabotage by someone trying to steal trade secrets, the dinosaurs escape their enclosures, and everyone is in danger of becoming a meal.

Steven Spielberg directed *Jurassic Park* as part of a two picture deal that allowed him more artistic freedom when it came to presenting his other big picture release of the year *Schindler's List*. The year was very successful for the director as *Jurassic Park* ruled atop the box office and *Schindler's List* won him the big Academy Awards. *Jurassic Park* also won some Oscar awards: Best Sound, Best Sound Effects Editing, and Best Visual Effects.

The book *Jurassic Park*, written by Michael Crichton became of interest to filmmakers before it actually reached publication in 1990. Michael Crichton seems best known for his work in the realm of novels, however, he was the director of some notable films himself. The original 1973 film *Westworld* was written and directed by Crichton, a property that would later be turned into a television series by HBO. His next directing gig came in 1978 when he wrote and directed a film adaptation of his novel *The Great Train Robbery*. Other films adapted from Michael Crichton novels, aside from *Jurassic Park* sequels, include: *The Andromeda Strain* (which also became a tv mini-series,) *Rising Sun*, *Congo*, *Disclosure*, *Sphere*, *Timeline*, and *The 13th Warrior*, a film on which he also did some reshoots as a director. He also wrote for the popular show *ER* and on the script for the disaster and action film *Twister*.

When it came time to adapt *Jurassic Park* into the screenplay a second writer was brought in, most likely due to the dense amount of content in the book compared to what could be featured in a movie, and then on top of that Michael Crichton's closeness to his own material, having a new set of eyes take a pass was probably quite beneficial in terms of streamlining the flow of the story. The second screenwriter, David Koepp, had written the scripts for 1991's *Toy Soldiers* and the 1992 movie *Death Becomes Her*. Following *Jurassic Park*, Koepp would get to work on the sequels, as well as many other notable films including *Carlito's Way*, *Mission Impossible*, *Panic Room,* and *Spider-Man*. David Koepp has ventured into the role of director on films such as *Stir of Echoes*, *Secret Window*, *Ghost Town*, *Premium Rush*, and the don't waste your time trying to watch it even if you are in love with Johnny Depp: *Mortdecai*.

The memorable music for *Jurassic Park* was worked on by composer John Williams of *Indiana Jones* and *Star Wars* movie fame. As epic as the theme song for *Jurassic Park* is, whenever I think of it the very first thing, in fact the song that got stuck in my head the very moment I started writing about *Jurassic Park* is, Weird Al's song *Jurassic Park*. The song is found on Weird Al's 1993 album *Alapalooza* and uses the plot of the dinosaur movie while also being a parody of the Richard Harris song *MacArthur Park*.

The leading man in *Jurassic Park* is said to have been a role turned down by both Harrison Ford and William Hurt before going to Sam Neil. However, when it comes to the male actors in *Jurassic Park*, I find it humorous to know that the role taken by Jeff Goldblum is one that actor Jim Carey auditioned for. Jim Carey in *Jurassic Park* movies is just a fun alternate universe, "what if," scenario to me.

Laura Dern is said to have been Spielberg's first choice, aren't they all, for the role of Ellie. Yet, some power in charge is said to have offered the role to Robin Wright firstly. Wright turned it down.

Christina Ricci is another notable name that went through the audition process, trying out for the young teen Lex. Actress Ariana Richards ending up taking the role and likes to say that Spielberg chose her because the screaming on her audition tape woke his wife up and made her think their kids were actually in peril.

Actor Wayne Knight is at the center of devious human activity in *Jurassic Park*. He is probably known best as Newman from the television show *Seinfeld,* but it was his performance in *Basic Instinct* that director Spielberg says got his attention and made him seek out Knight for *Jurassic Park*.

To avoid relating an endless stream of behind the scenes casting stories, I shall now sum up some of the other acting contributions for *Jurassic Park* by listing names: Richard Attenborough, Samuel L.

Jackson, Bob Peck, Martin Ferrero, Joseph Mazzello, BD Wong, and many more.

The real stars of the movie are the dinosaurs though, right? Brought to life by cutting edge animatronics and CGI combined with sound effects, with many a roar being a mixture of real animal sounds, the dinosaurs were awesome. We went to the movie to see the T-Rex, but the Velociraptor was really put on the radar of "cool, scary things" by the film. It should be noted that although the title of the film is *Jurassic Park*, the majority of the dinosaur species featured did not actually exist in the Jurassic Period. *Cretaceous Park* doesn't really have the same dramatic impact when you say it though.

1994

10. *Pulp Fiction* - Directed by Quentin Tarantino, screenplay by Quentin Tarantino. Domestic Box Office: $107,928,762

The first movie that I ever became officially involved with in a working capacity in Hollywood was *Silent Night, Zombie Night*. I produced, observed, learned, and got lined up on a curb along with the other zombies by the Los Angeles police; they thought we were a gang having a war in the street. *Silent Night, Zombie Night* got screened at the New Beverly theater, meaning that it was the first movie I was involved in that I also got to see at a theater. Quentin Tarantino bought that movie theater not long after our screening of the zombie movie. But, this book entry isn't about *Silent Night, Zombie Night*, I just thought that little trivia bit worked well as an opening before talking about my foot fetish. Wait, I mean Quentin Tarantino's foot fetish, err, movie *Pulp Fiction*.

As was the case for many, *Pulp Fiction* became an introduction to the work of Quentin Tarantino as a director, due to mass hype, which in-turn then had me looking back to *Reservoir Dogs*, and also realizing that the movie *True Romance*, which I was a big fan of, was also based off of a script by him. Over the years my thoughts on Tarantino have bounced around, with me enjoying some of his work greatly, and in more jaded moments being critical of his long-winded dialog or "paying homage" to other movies by using their scenes as his own. He made a name for himself and it is a unique name and career that he has had, kudos to him, let us love and hate him for it.

Pulp Fiction is a film with a twisted gathering of stories involving gangsters, drugs, and violence, the plot of which I will not type out, if you are a student or fan of film, *Pulp Fiction* should probably be on one of those "before you die" watch lists. For me personally, as a writer that graduated into writing for the moving pictures, *Pulp Fiction* was an early inspiration in my life for approaching a story from an outside the traditional box angle in the delivery of it. If you ask me for an example of successful, non-linear story-telling, *Pulp Fiction* is the example to be found in my inner film encyclopedia.

If one were to want to delve into the subject of postmodernism and films, *Pulp Fiction* is one chock-full of content that fuels intellectual debates in that regard. Are we that crowd? Probably not. I don't think I write for that crowd. I doubt too many people interested in meditating on the state of society as influenced by postmodern media offerings of all varieties have happened to come across this book and decided to give it a read. Then again, who knows, maybe you prime intellectuals were slumming it and checking out titles such as my book *Beerasaurus Sex* and linked on over to *America Goes to the Movies the 1990s* and decided to see if I talked some more about boobies. I totally did. Did I do this right? My self-referencing sarcasm and what-not? Did I just go postmodern?

While Quentin Tarantino has the sole screenplay credit for the writing of *Pulp Fiction*, there were many influences and creative contributions by others. Specifically Roger Avary, who does have a "stories" credit on IMDB and is listed as getting to share the Best Screenplay Oscar that Pulp Fiction won but doesn't hold an actual "written by" credit on the film. Some of the scenes were scenes from the original *True Romance* script that did not make it into that Tony Scott directed movie. Roger Avary's contributions to *True Romance* did not get him a real screenplay writing credit on IMDB either. Roger Avary also directs. The 1993 film *Killing Zoe* was written and directed by Avary and then a film that I really enjoyed *The Rules Of Attraction*, based off of a Bret Easton Ellis novel, was also written and directed by Roger Avary.

I recall one of the biggest stories surrounding the release of *Pulp Fiction* was the casting choice of John Travolta as Vincent Vega. It was a seedy, new type of role for the actor and how my generation saw him, previously Travolta was the *Look Who's Talking* guy or the guy from *Grease*. *Pulp Fiction* is said to have helped reinvigorate Travolta's career and ever since then that is a theme that article writers try to attach to the casting choices of Tarantino films, playing a game of, what starting to be forgotten actor might he dust off next?

I never saw *Pulp Fiction* at the movie theater, it was a VHS rental many times. Considering the different statements people consider the film to make in terms of the craft and industry and the critical division over its content in terms of worth, "one man's garbage is another man's treasure," I am somewhat surprised to see that *Pulp Fiction* ranked in the top ten earning films in America for 1994. *Interview with a Vampire* was the eleventh highest earner, which was something I recall being a huge success in the households I traveled through, and even *The Client*, another Tom Cruise featuring production, a safe bet legal thriller only made it to slot number thirteen. The art of risk, "daring to be creative" was alive and well in Hollywood in the 90s, *Pulp Fiction* being a prime example.

If one wants to look at history through the lens of trashy reality and modern reexamination of situations, for some, anything that was made by Miramax is now tainted. *Pulp Fiction* was the first feature fully funded by Miramax, a company that really helped push Indie films into the mainstream arena during the 90s. The issue now is the fact that Harvey Weinstein was one of the powers behind that company. Weinstein became the focus of the #Metoo movement in which the rumors of his sexual harassment and demands of women were brought to light as horrible truth, behavior that people came together to denounce not just on behalf of the women working in an industry, but for all that are seeking out their Hollywood dreams and don't want to be forced into doing things that will haunt them later that shouldn't have anything to do with whether or not their skills can land them a job.

Uma Thurman, who starred in *Pulp Fiction*, would also go on to star in Quentin Tarantino's two *Kill Bill* movies. When Harvey Weinstein's horrid behavior became news headlines, the relationship between Tarantino and Weinstein naturally came into question, as they were men that had worked together on many projects. Uma Thurman was injured in a car accident, a stunt gone wrong, during the filming of *Kill Bill* and it was an incident that she felt was avoidable and the possibility that Tarantino had forced her into the situation also brought into question some of his other practices in filmmaking, specifically the treatment of women on set and in his stories. Tarantino has denied that he wishes to perpetrate violence against women or to hold them back in any way.

Violence, sex, racial representations, language usage, all of these things and even the kink of his foot fetish have kept Quentin Tarantino on the hot seat when it comes to controversy and the public spotlight. Whether or not his kinks go beyond sucking toes and into actually wishing to do violent things to women is not my place to judge or know, I am not inside of his head, I do not have a relationship with him nor have I worked with him, and from my seat as a fan of films it's not my prerogative to try and use the art to decipher the man, but to take the art for what it is and may mean to me personally, whether that is inspiring, entertaining, or boring and off-putting. *Pulp Fiction* was selected for preservation in the United States Film Registry by the Library of Congress for being "culturally, historically, or aesthetically significant," and that seems like an accurate decision.

9. *The Mask* - Directed by Chuck Russell, screenplay by Mike Werb. Domestic Box Office: $119,938,730

The year 1994 belonged to Jim Carrey. It is the year that saw *Ace Ventura: Pet Detective, The Mask,* and *Dumb and Dumber* all release and change Carrey's status as an actor into being: a star. *Ace Ventura: Pet Detective* is a movie that I liked because that was the cool thing to do at the time, but deep down I was on the fence about whether or not I actually liked it at all. When *The Mask* came out, my friends embraced it and I did not, never got into it. However, *Dumb and Dumber* was hilarious.

Jim Carrey is not the only name that was thrust into stardom in part due to *The Mask.* Cameron Diaz made her acting debut in *The Mask* going from being a model to being a leading co-star in one of the biggest movies of 1994, while turning the ripe old age of twenty-one during the filming process. She has spoken in interviews about memories of Jim Carrey and the crew helping her celebrate her birthday but speaking from the angle of having seen the things people go through to "make it" in the acting game, what a story and experience to have your first acting gig be such a success. I bet that there are some coming of age stories behind the scenes that would make for a good movie. The

Cameron Diaz filled role, Tina, is said to have almost gone to Anna Nicole Smith, which makes it sound like the producers may not have been taking their chance at box office triumph too seriously.

The Mask was originally a comic book character created by Mike Richardson in the early 80s. Dark Horse comics put out tales of people wearing a mask that took away their morals and inhibitions. The concept led to much darker exploration of character and circumstance than *The Mask* movie treads into. The comic material went through many different creative iterations as Hollywood attempted to turn it into a money machine with it almost becoming a horror movie instead of the over-the-top comedy that it is. Of course, depending on who you talk to, maybe *The Mask* did still turn out to be quite frightening.

The first clue that the studios were trying to make a horror franchise out of *The Mask* might be that they hired director Chuck Russell to direct. His previous films were *A Nightmare on Elm Street 3: Dream Warriors* and *The Blob*. Perhaps Russell did not want to get pinned in a genre corner, however, and led the production into new creative territory. After *The Mask*, Russell would not go back to the horror genre either, directing the action movie *Eraser* starring Arnold Schwarzenegger. Out of all of Chuck Russell's films though, I would have to pick the 1988 *The Blob* remake as the one I find most entertaining.

The Mask was nominated for Best Special Effects at the following year's Oscar ceremony, but lost. Jim Carrey was nominated for a Golden Globe and lost, but on the bright side he also lost in the category of Worst New Star at the Razzie Awards. Who won Worst New Star? An actress almost cast in *The Mask*: Anna Nicole Smith. She got her Razzie for appearing in *Naked Gun 33 1/3: The Final Insult.*

8. *Speed* - Directed by Jan de Bont, screenplay by Graham Yost. Domestic Box Office: $121,248,145

The premise of *Speed* is one of those high-concept gimmick sounding ones that a high-brow audience might snicker at. However, keeping things simple can pay off especially in the action genre when you want nothing more than to shove popcorn into your mouth and get high on adrenaline.

Initially *Speed* was brushed off by some in script form as "*Die Hard* on a bus," featuring a plot about a bad guy that has installed a bomb on a bus and after the bus reaches 50 mph it can't go back under that speed or it will explode. Insert a hero cop and a plucky woman passenger and hit the gas pedal. *Die Hard* director John McTiernan passed on directing the Graham Yost script, however, he is said to have some hand in the gig going to Jan de Bont. Jan de Bont was better known as a cinematographer at the time, having indeed worked in such a capacity on *Die Hard*.

To distance the project away from being "*Die Hard* on a bus" the script went through some major rewrites, with Joss Whedon taking a pass on it that altered the tone and the characters. The only accredited screenwriter for the project Graham Yost has supposedly stated: Whedon is responsible for 98.9% of the dialog in the finished film.

As a kid digesting all of the action movies that he could, *Speed* immediately drew interest from me. They packaged the movie quite well in terms of adding to the root genre appeal. Keanu Reeves was a "cool" actor to me, *Point Break* having been an epic experience to see on the big screen for young eyes. Pairing Reeves with Sandra Bullock was also a good move because she was already made familiar to me via *Demolition Man*, which was another favorite of mine from that time period. Of course, I also knew Sandra Bullock from viewing *Love Potion No. 9* because the boys were not the only ones renting movies during weekend visits to Grandma Laurie's house. Side note: we have always called it Grandma Laurie's house, even when Grandpa Laurie lived there too. Odd?

I would not be surprised if *Speed* gets revisited by Hollywood in the future via reboot. They did make a sequel, *Speed 2: Cruise Control*. Keanu Reeves declined to return, and Sandra Bullock ended up on a cruise ship with Jason Patric trying to thwart a cruise ship highjacker played by Willem Dafoe. The sequel was not as good, but those of us that enjoyed *Speed* were actually just as excited to check it out anyway. Now, I suppose by its title alone *Speed 2: Cruise Control* should be hung on a wall in the bad sequel Hall of Fame.

Speed director Jan de Bont did return to direct *Speed 2: Cruise Control*. Sandwiched in-between *Speed* movies he shot *Twister* and then later he directed 1999's *The Haunting* and *Lara Croft Tomb Raider: The Cradle of Life* in 2003.

You know what freaked the movie studio out during the production of *Speed*? Not the dangerous stunts during which people could have been injured or worse for the sake of an entertainment product, but Keanu Reeves' hair. He shaved his hair very short for the role, some say after the director requested that he get an "adult" haircut, a move which had not been approved by the producing powers and now their displeasure and threats to postpone shooting for his hair to grow back, whether true or not, are a part of the *Speed* movie legacy. Seriously though, it takes a lot of people to make a big studio movie, and a lot of people put a lot of thought into things such as hair, and then get fixated and potentially turn a haircut into a stress induced medical condition for others.

Keanu Reeves performed a lot of his own stunts during the shooting of *Speed* and Sandra Bullock went and learned how to drive a bus beforehand. A lot of the action could have been avoided if Reeves' character, Jack Traven, when attempting to get the bus to stop before reaching 50 mph had just chosen to shoot out the bus tires.

7. *Clear and Present Danger* - Directed by Phillip Noyce, screenplay by Donald E. Stewart, Steven Zaillian, and John Milius. Domestic Box Office: $122,187,717

Based on the Tom Clancy novel of the same name, *Clear and Present Danger* sees Harrison Ford reprising the role of Jack Ryan; a character he previously brought to life in *Patriot Games*. *Clear and Present Danger* is about covert actions being taken against a drug cartel and when Jack Ryan becomes acting director of the CIA he discovers said covert actions being conducted without his approval. He rushes in to rescue some captured operatives and gets lots of material to yabber about when he turns snitch on the President and his cronies that are doing the shenanigans.

Both of the Tom Clancy movie adaptations starring Harrison Ford made it into our cycle of action movie rentals, the legendary weekend binges I have surely mentioned a thousand times already; yeah, I spent the 90s watching movies. However, they were not favorites really and I did not see either one at the theater. When it came down to choosing between *Patriot Games* and *Clear and Present Danger*, I personally always went with *Patriot Games*. I'm pretty sure I preferred it because I dug the female villain played by Polly Walker.

The main art for *Clear and Present Danger* features Harrison Ford with a flag draped around his shoulders. It's silly to me. He looks so serious with that flag that I can't take it seriously.

A lot of time, effort, and talent went into the making of *Clear and Present Danger* the movie. It made a lot of money at the box office. I can list out what awards it got nominated for, like the Oscars for Best Sound and Best Sound Effects, and I just did. People poured their blood, sweat, and tears into the production I am sure. But, I'm kind of bored trying to write about it and am going to just end this entry quite short. I'm totally in charge here! I probably should have spent all this time making a clickbait website instead and just making list articles.

It's funny to imagine if Harrison Ford and Jim Carrey had swapped roles in 1994, with Carrey running the CIA and Ford making funny faces while running around in *The Mask*. It's one in the morning as I write this, things are funnier to ponder in the early morning hours I guess. What time are you reading this at? Don't bother telling me, I'm not paying attention. Now I'm thinking about Harrison Ford and his *Clear and Present Danger* co-star Willem Dafoe and what it might have been like if they had been the actors in *Dumb and Dumber* instead of Jim Carrey and Jeff Daniels.

6. *Dumb and Dumber* - Directed by The Farrelly Brothers, screenplay by The Farrelly Brothers and Bennett Yellin. Domestic Box Office: $127,175,374

Ace Ventura: Pet Detective was one of the rare theater experiences where my parents actually took us to see it. And by parents I mean my mom and I think my new-ish step-father as this would have been around the time period where my parents' divorce was still a fresh and traumatic event. Going to the movies probably seemed like a positive thing to help distract us kids from all of the on-going life changes occurring. Sadly, it wouldn't be too long before getting to go to Grandma Laurie's on the weekends was a rarer event. When my parents divorced we the kids lived with mom full time and she moved us about two hours away from were granny resided

My parents thought that *Ace Ventura: Pet Detective* was one of the worst movies that they had ever seen. My older brother, like most kids I knew, loved it and all of its wackiness. Impressionable as I was to the opinion of adults, I was stuck in the middle in terms of opinion. I wanted to like it and I wanted to hate it, I wanted to choose the right opinion to have for everything to be okay and my life to work out. I leaned toward keeping my parents thinking I was an intelligent kid by not fully embracing the antics of Jim Carrey or praising the movie too heavily.

The Mask did not draw me in either. However, when I saw *Dumb and Dumber* I loved it. My mother dared to watch it and even she gave it some chuckles of approval. The whole whirlwind of critical decision making on the intake of Jim Carrey went full steam pro-Carrey after that.

Seriously, *Dumb and Dumber* is a hilarious movie and even as it ages the quirkiness of the work makes it a treat. Of course, *Dumb and Dumber* wasn't released until the end of 1994, so, for most of the year I had to sit through a lot of *Ace Ventura* and *The Mask* quotes spouting out of people without feeling like I wanted to be a part of that scene.

All three Jim Carrey starring films released in 1994 went straight to number one at the box office on opening weekend. The feat was a first for an actor. Perhaps the directors of *Dumb and Dumber* surfed the tail-end of the Jim Carrey wave of '94, but as I explained in my film preferences above, *Dumb and Dumber* stood on its own as the superior film to me and the Farrelly brothers, not just Jim Carrey were responsible for that. The movie launched their careers and prepped audiences for their fun brand of comedy. *Kingpin, There's Something About Mary, Me, Myself, and Irene*, and *Hall Pass* are some of the Farrelly Brothers movies that I enjoy. The brother's first names are Bobby and Peter.

Bobby and Peter did not direct the 2003 prequel *Dumb and Dumberer: When Harry Met Lloyd* nor did Jim Carrey and co-star Jeff Daniel's return to play their younger selves. However, the original gang of actors and directors got back together in 2014 for *Dumb and Dumber To*! Lighting was not captured in a bottle twice. I don't think I cared for the sequel, but to be honest, I can't remember what even happened in it. Oh, and I avoided the prequel altogether, have never seen it. Oh, oh, there was also a cartoon series made, but I missed out on ever seeing that.

Jeff Daniels as the actor to team up with Jim Carrey is said to have not been a popular choice. The directors have told a story in which they claim Jim Carrey wanted to act with Jeff Daniels and thus they offered Daniels a lowball sum of money hoping he would turn it down. Instead, supposedly against his agent's wishes, Daniels accepted the small sum and joined the cast. On his side of things Jeff Daniels has said that no scenes with himself and Carrey together were shot for the first two weeks of production because the producers were still not keen on him and wanted to have some time to think about possibly replacing him. However, they must have liked what they were seeing from him and decided that he could carry his end of the comedy.

Jim Carrey won for Best Comedic Performance as well as Best Kiss, along with his movie kissing partner Lauren Holly, at the 1995 MTV Movie Awards for *Dumb and Dumber*. He was also nominated for Best On-Screen Duo with Jeff Daniels, but somehow they failed to get that moon-man statue. The MTV Movie Awards were something I was getting to see for the first time, because we got cable television in our home after my parents divorced. Cable television opened up a whole new portal into the going-ons of pop culture to me and over the next few years one of the main reasons to tune in to the MTV Movie Awards was to see what silly thing Jim Carrey might do during the event.

5. *The Flintstones* - Directed by Brian Levant, screenplay by Tom S. Parker, Jim Jennewein, and Steven E. de Souza.   Domestic Box Office: $130,531,208

The original *The Flintstones* cartoon is a program that I recall watching with no more or less regard than *The Jetsons*, which I think aired back to back on whatever station I was watching. I would watch them and think they were okay, but never sought them out. I had a little eight inch black and white television in my room for a long time and generally watched whatever came on the UHF channel 25, which was a local religious channel that aired lots of poached Disney and other family programming.

I was a kid with an affinity for anything involving dinosaurs but did not become a legit fan of *The Flintstones*. However, when we bought two miniature dachshund dogs, animals that brought a lot of joy to me in my youth, they were bestowed the names of Pebbles and Dino. I mentioned my parents' divorce in the *Dumb and Dumber* section previously, well, I lost my lil weenie dogs due to that divorce. I guess my mom didn't want the animals when we moved. Poop. Now I'm just depressed. Flintstones, meet the Flinstones, they're, wahhhhhh!

Nope. I did not like *The Flintstones* movie, never got interested in it, did not go to the theater to see it, did see it on VHS at some point later on though. If they had made the movie as a cartoon I think I would have had more interest in it. For some reason a live-action Flintstones adventure just did not appeal to me as much as it apparently appealed to all of the people that helped it succeed at the box office.

The plot for the movie was nothing too interesting. Cliff Vandercave, played by Kyle MacLachlan, conspires with Miss Stone, played by Halle Berry, to swindle the company Slade International out of a lot of money, to pull it off they'll need someone else to take the blame. The plot then involves Fred Flintstone, played by John Goodman, getting a promotion even though he is not the brightest bulb at the company, for the express purpose of tricking him into being the patsy. If you are not familiar with *The Flintstones* at all, the setting for all of this is the "stone age" where there are dinosaurs, rock houses, and cars are powered by sticking your feet out of the bottom and running.

John Goodman was a solid casting choice for Fred Flintstone. His wife Wilma was portrayed by Elizabeth Perkins. The best friends and neighbors of the Flintstones were Barney Rubble portrayed by Rick Moranis and Betty Rubble portrayed by Rosie O'Donnell. All of those actors are okay choices for the look of the roles, but, for the most part, none of them were the type of talent that drew me in personally as a kid in terms of "must see" due to being transfixed by their star power. In fact, as a teen in the burgeoning mid-90s, I think the movie needed even more sex appeal to be of interest. I know, I know, that doesn't make sense, it was meant to be a kids movie, and Halle Berry did her seductive best.

The Flintstones was the last theatrically released movie appearance of Elizabeth Taylor. She was Pearl Slaghoople. I guess that's one way to bookend a legendary career.

The rights to *The Flintstones* cartoon were secured to become a film at some point in the 80s. Then the writing process for the script began and while the feature lists a trio of names, actor Rick Moranis, who sat in on some writer's meetings, has been quoted as saying there were at least eighteen different writers. Other sources make a claim of at least thirty-five writers.

At an early stage on the project Richard Donner was hired as the director. However, a script was never settled on, Steven E. de Souza of *Die Hard* and *The Running Man* fame took the first crack at it, and eventually Donner and company lost interest and Stephen Spielberg's company Amblin Entertainment bought up the rights to make the film. Brian Levant landed the directing gig from Spielberg because he was a genuine fan of the original *The Flintstones* cartoon series, said to have even been a collector of Flintstones related items.

Brian Levant directed *Problem Child 2* and *Beethoven* prior to *The Flintstones*. Both of those movies were ones that I watched repeatedly as a kid, though I will say the first *Problem Child* was rented more often than the second. This director seems to have stayed in the family film lane more than not when it comes to directing gigs. *Jingle All The Way* was his directing gig following *The Flintstones*. In 2000 he returned to direct a prequel to *The Flintstones* ala *The Flintstones in Viva Rock Vegas*. He had to work with an all new cast and the second film did not receive the same love as the first one did from the masses.

It is said that director John Landis did some reshoots on *The Flintstones*.

After not being a fan of the original live-action adaptation of *The Flintstones*, do I think it is a property that should get revisited in such a manner in the future? Actually, yes. Feel free to hire me to write and direct it, thanks.

4. *The Santa Clause* - Directed by John Pasquin, screenplay by Leo Benvenuti and Steve Rudnick. Domestic Box Office: $144,833,357

Released in November of 1994, I recall *The Santa Clause* being a hit amongst my peers. I also recall watching the movie at the theater during a weekend trip to Grandma's house. The weekend trips by this point were less than every other weekend, however. The picture for *The Santa Clause* was blurry to me because for some reason I had either forgotten or broken my glasses directly prior to entering the theater.

Tim Allen and the show *Home Improvement* were fan favorites in America, which helped *The Santa Clause* in ticket sales I am sure, though a Christmas movie featuring Santa Clause probably had a good chance regardless. The plot involves a man that accidentally bumps off Santa and then must become Santa himself. Fun stuff more than not, way better than *The Flintstones*. And, no, I was not a fan of *Home Improvement*.

Tim Allen was not the only major *Home Improvement* connection with *The Santa Clause*. Director John Pasquin was also the director of said television series. Heck, I'm surprised they did not cast one of the kids from *Home Improvement* to play the son in *The Santa Clause*. Throw in the Tool Time Girl and Wilson peeping over a fence and maximum synergy could have been realized.

Jim Carrey became the first actor to have three movies open number one at the box office in 1994. Tim Allen on the other hand got to experience having a number one movie at the box office, a number one television show on television, and his book *Don't Stand Too Close to a Naked Man* was number one on the New York Times Best Seller List all within the same week in November.

Even though *The Santa Clause* brought in the audiences in 1994, a sequel did not get made until 2002. Tim Allen became Buzz Lightyear in the *Toy Story* franchise between the holiday features. A third film, also starring Tim Allen, came to be in 2006: *The Santa Clause 3: The Escape Clause*. I have seen all of the films, but only the happenings of the first one really sticks in my memory after all of these years, can't tell you a thing about the sequels aside from Martin Short plays Jack Frost in the third film.

3. *True Lies* - Directed by James Cameron, screenplay by Claude Zidi, Simon Michael, Didier Kaminka, and James Cameron. By Domestic Box Office: $146,282,411

The movie *True Lies* stars Arnold Schwarzenegger as a terrorists fighting spy who has some trouble at home due to his wife, played by Jamie Lee Curtis, being bored and seeking some excitement outside of their marriage. She does not realize that her husband is really a spy and soon she gets pulled into his world of action as he tries to save the world and their marriage.

Other actors that play pivotal roles in *True Lies* include Eliza Dushku as the daughter, Tom Arnold as the sidekick, Bill Paxton as the man trying to woo Curtis with lies of being a spy, Tia Carrere, Art Malick, and Charlton Heston.

True Lies is a movie that became a different experience at different times in my life. It released when I was a young teen that appreciated it for the action sequences. There was a lot of talk about the Jamie Lee Curtis striptease scene, but at that age, even though I was interested in scoping out ladies on film, the sex appeal fell flat for me. I've never had " a thing" for Jamie Lee Curtis.

When I got older the more adult aspects of the plot, loaded with humor, paired with the action in new ways, taking the film to a new level of fun and funny. However, as I have gotten even older still, I have to admit that my appreciation for the film has waned some with the spoof style humor not having aged all that well thanks to over-saturation of like-minded products in the pop culture market. If you have not seen the movie, it's worth a watch, but it's not a classic that I feel the need to return to personally. I'd pop in *Commando* or *Predator* before I'd pop in *True Lies* again. Of course, "pop in" doesn't really make much sense in the digital world of movies anymore, does it? As someone who always declared he preferred physical copies of movies I admit that currently I am all digital with a Roku television. Insert a book length rant here about technology moving too fast and movie studios trying to sell the same movies over and over again on whatever the new format is, with special attention in the rant given to the amount of movies lost in transition, never making their debut on the newest technology.

After the box office success of *True Lies* a sequel was circling in the minds of everyone involved. Some people are said to have envisioned a franchise to rival the James Bond franchise and perhaps render it irrelevant. However, director James Cameron spent a long time making his next blockbuster film *Titanic*. Then the real terrorist attacks of 9/11 occurred and the subject matter of a spy facing off against terrorists became something Cameron could not envision himself approaching again with humor. More rumors have popped up over the years, but furthering the *Avatar* series of films seems like something Cameron is more interested in. There have been *True Lies* television series rumors floating around for a while now as well.

Actress Eliza Dushku played the young daughter to Schwarzenegger and Curtis in *True Lies*. She would go on to both movie and television fame with roles in *Buffy the Vampire Slayer*, *Angel*, *Dollhouse*, and *Wrong Turn*. As an adult she would also publicly address an abuser that took advantage of her during the filming of *True Lies*. According to Eliza Dushku the stunt coordinator for the film, Joel Kramer, sexually abused her when she was twelve. Dushku was injured during filming, breaking some ribs during a stunt, and further insinuates that Kramer may have let her get hurt on purpose due to her telling another adult about his behavior and said adult confronting Kramer.

Joel Kramer denies the abuse and claims he doesn't even remember Dushku breaking her ribs.

Eliza Dushku's publicly released statement detailing the events from her viewpoint seems important to me as something to be documented and shared in full. It is as follows:

"When I was 12 years old, while filming True Lies, I was sexually molested by Joel Kramer, one of Hollywood's leading stunt coordinators.

Ever since, I have struggled with how and when to disclose this, if ever. At the time, I shared what happened to me with my parents, two adult friends and one of my older brothers. No one seemed ready to confront this taboo subject then, nor was I.

I am grateful to the women and men who have gone before me in recent months. The ever-growing list of sexual abuse and harassment victims who have spoken out with their truths have finally given me the ability to speak out. It has been indescribably exhausting, bottling this up inside me for all of these years.

I remember, so clearly 25 years later, how Joel Kramer made me feel special, how he methodically built my and my parents' trust, for months grooming me; exactly how he lured me to his Miami hotel room with a promise to my parent that he would take me for a swim at the stunt crew's hotel pool and for my first sushi meal thereafter. I remember vividly how he methodically drew the shades and turned down the lights; how he cranked up the air-conditioning to what felt like freezing levels, where exactly he placed me on one of the two hotel room beds, what movie he put on the television (Coneheads); how he disappeared in the bathroom and emerged, naked, bearing nothing but a small hand towel held flimsy at his mid-section. I remember what I was wearing (my favorite white denim shorts, thankfully, secured enough for me to keep on). I remember how he laid me down on the bed, wrapped me with his gigantic writhing body, and rubbed all over me. He spoke these words: "You're not going to sleep on me now sweetie, stop pretending you're sleeping," as he rubbed harder and faster against my catatonic body. When he was finished, he suggested, "I think we should be careful." [about telling anyone] he meant. I was 12, he was 36.

I remember how afterwards, the taxi driver stared at me in the rear-view mirror when Joel Kramer put me on his lap in the backseat and clutched me and grew aroused again; and how my eyes never left the driver's eyes during that long ride over a Miami bridge, back to my hotel and parent. I remember how Joel Kramer grew cold with me in the ensuing weeks, how everything felt different on the set.

And I remember how soon-after, when my tough adult female friend (in whom I had confided my terrible secret on the condition of a trade that she let me drive her car around the Hollywood Hills) came out to the set to visit and face him, later that very same day, by no small coincidence, I was injured from a stunt-gone-wrong on the Harrier jet. With broken ribs, I spent the evening in the hospital. To be clear, over the course of those months rehearsing and filming True Lies, it was Joel Kramer who was responsible for my safety on a film that at the time broke new ground for action films. On a daily basis he rigged wires and harnesses on my 12-year-old body. My life was literally in his hands: he hung me in the open air, from a tower crane, atop an office tower, 25+ stories high. Whereas he was supposed to be my protector, he was my abuser.

Why speak out now? I was 12, he was 36. It is incomprehensible. Why didn't an adult on the set find his predatory advances strange or that over-the-top special attention he gave me. Fairly early on he nicknamed me Jailbait and brazenly called me by this name in a sick flirty way in front of others (at the time, I remember asking one of my older brothers what it meant). Sure, I've come to understand the terrible power dynamics that play into whistle-blowing by subordinates against persons in power, how difficult it can be for someone to speak up. But I was a child. Over the years I've really struggled as I've wondered how my life might have been different if someone, any grown-up who witnessed his sick ways, had spoken up before he lured me to that hotel room.

Years ago, I had heard second hand that Joel Kramer was found out and forced to leave the business. I learned recently that in fact he still works at the top of the industry. And a few weeks ago, I found an internet photo of Joel Kramer hugging a young girl. That image has haunted me near nonstop since. I can no longer hide what happened.

Hollywood has been very good to me in many ways. Nevertheless, Hollywood also failed to protect me, a child actress. I like to think of myself as a tough Boston chick, in many ways I suppose not unlike Faith, Missy, or Echo. Through the years, brave fans have regularly shared with me how some of my characters have given them the conviction to stand up to their abusers. Now it is you who give me strength and conviction. I hope that speaking out will help other victims and protect against future abuse.

With every person that speaks out, every banner that drops down onto my iPhone screen disclosing similar stories/truths, my resolve strengthens. Sharing these words, finally calling my abuser out publicly by name, brings the start of a new calm."

2. *The Lion King* - Directed by Roger Allers and Rob Minkoff, screenplay by Irene Mecchi, Jonathan Roberts, and Linda Woolverton. Domestic Box Office: $312,855,561

For someone that claims to despise musicals, I sure do know the lyrics to a lot of songs from Disney animated musicals. *The Lion King* came out around the time that I was in the sixth grade and was really one of the last Disney cartoons that I embraced as a part of my childhood. I look at all of the Disney cartoons that have been released thus far and for me it just sort of ends at *The Lion King*. Yes, I am known to belt out a line or two of *Colors of the Wind* from *Pocahontas*, the next animated feature that was released in line after *The Lion King*, but I can't tell you anything about what happens in that movie.

The Lion King follows a lion cub, Simba, born to King Mufasa. The lions rule over the rest of the animal kingdom and Simba's uncle Scar wants that power. Scar sets up Mufasa to be killed and lays the blame on Simba, which causes the heartbroken youngster to run away from his home. Simba grows up away from his family and responsibility, but eventually it is time for him to return and face his past and devious uncle. All of the death and guilt trips are accompanied by jolly music and humor.

There are people given directing credit and screenplay credit for *The Lion King*, but the ultimate list of names that worked in those departments is so lengthy that one has to wonder how much credit is still due. Additionally, *The Lion King* is touted as being one of the first "original" stories produced by Disney, but if one pulls back the curtain they might find a Japanese cartoon, based off of a 1950s comic, *Kimba the White Lion* and wonder if the creators of *The Lion King* may have just watched that and then copied it. See, I was going to write about the spawning of the idea and the creative process for the film, but the truth is Hollywood is a lot of smoke and mirrors, lies and credits, and lots of bullshit to pass around. Have a plate of bullshit! Mmm. Hakuna Matata!

The music for *The Lion King* had two Oscar awards bestowed upon it. The John Elton and Tim Rice crafted song *Can You Feel The Love Tonight* won for Best Original Song, while Hans Zimmer won Best Original Score. The songs were addictive and aside from the Oscar winning one, the following selections are also still stuck in my head: *Circle of Life*, *I Just Can't Wait to Be King*, *Hakuna Matata*, *I've Got a Lovely Bunch of Coconuts*, and *Nobody Knows The Trouble I've Seen*.

The soundtrack also featured the song *The Lion Sleeps Tonight*, however, that was one that I was very familiar with and had looping around in my head before the movie came into existence. The family of the fellow that composed that original song filed a lawsuit for not getting some coin from Disney for usage of it. In 2006 that suit was settled with the company that had licensed the song to Disney.

The Santa Clause at number four on the yearly earnings list was also a Disney backed production. It was not the only one with a *Home Improvement* connection. The popularity of that television show did not only do wonders for Tim Allen's career, but also thrust the young actors playing his sons into the spotlight. The eldest two boys Zachery Ty Bryan and Jonathan Taylor Thomas were promoted by teen magazines as "hot" and who to have a "crush" on. When teens got done choosing sides of Hollywood flesh, adorning their walls with posters and clippings, I'd wager Jonathan Taylor Thomas ended up with the bigger fanbase in that time period. He also landed the voice gig of child Simba in *The Lion King*. Matthew Broderick voiced adult

Simba, the bulk of the work, but as kids we were all made very aware that Jonathan Taylor Thomas was in the movie.

James Earl Jones voiced Simba's father Mufasa. I bet it would be weird having James Earl Jones as your father. I can just imagine his booming voice telling you to clean your room.

Other key voice talents featured in the movie are: Jeremy Irons, Moira Kelly, Nathan Lane, Ernie Sabella, Whoopi Goldberg, Cheech Marin, Robert Guillaume, Rowan Atkinson, Madge Sinclair, and Jim Cummings.

The Lion King inspired a Broadway musical of the same name. I have never seen the stage musical, though I have seen the colorful costumes in commercials over the years, as well as sections of the program performed on awards shows. It enjoyed a long period of being THE show everyone had to see. *The Lion King* stage musical won six Tony Awards and became one of the most successful shows in Broadway history.

1. *Forrest Gump* - Directed by Robert Zemeckis, screenplay by Eric Roth. Domestic Box Office: $329,694,499

Whereas *The Lion King* is the last animated Disney feature I can recall being fond of, *Forrest Gump* is the last movie that I really have a memory of getting to watch at the theater on a weekend at

Granny's. Perhaps that means nothing to you, but with regard to the shape of my life and how movies have played a part in it, it marks, if nothing else, the end of one path and the start of another. Perhaps I saw other movies after *Forrest Gump*, but *Forrest Gump* is the last fragment of memory in which I can still see myself leaving the theater with grandma and my brother. I can still hear my opinion that due to all of the narrative talking in the film, sitting through the movie was sort of like reading a book, but I thought it was okay.

Now, that was my last childhood memory of going to the movies as a part of a weekend at grandma's house. However, in 2005 as an adult I did randomly visit my grandma and ended up going with her and my aunts on their "girl's weekend" to watch *Walk the Line*. *Walk the Line*, a Johnny Cash biopic, is the last movie I can recall seeing at that theater we frequented in my youth before it shut down entirely.

Feel free to pause here to reflect on your own theater memories. If you're anything like me, when I was a teen and into my young adulthood the movie theater was a place of comfort, a place that sort of felt like a "home" in an otherwise nomadic life. Over the years the experience has changed at movie theaters and I've lost that feeling of home when I go. Yes, reflect on the memories, make sure you do so in such a way as to induce a sadness within yourself. Let us mope together. And if you have bought the actual print on paper version of this book let us draw sad doodles on the borders of this page as a healing exercise. Awww. As someone once said, "Life is like a box of chocolates."

Forrest Gump follows a slightly "slow" fellow through life adventures, many of which were real to life historical moments, and with keen interest paid to his love of a woman named Jenny. The movie is based on but differs a great deal from the 1986 novel of the same name authored by Winston Groom. I have never read the original novel; however, I did read the sequel novel *Gump and Co.*. The sequel novel is more of the same type of adventures, not really all that intriguing and I can fully understand why a sequel movie has never been made. I think I once heard that Tom Hanks declined to reprise the role due to the strain it took to keep talking in Forrest Gump's "simple" manner. It can also be a strain an audiences having to hear it for lengths of time. It is fairly impossible to watch *Forrest Gump* and then walk away from it without imitating his voice.

Also, when it came time to discuss a sequel, the uphill battle to profit was probably on the mind of the studios. *Forrest Gump* earned well in North America and worldwide, but it is said that the tally of costs overall did not net the film a profit by the end of 1994. Home video probably ended up helping put some scratch in some wallets, but still in the game of chasing dollars you want to be as fast as you can be in order to impress investors.

The effort that Tom Hanks put into the lead role of the movie won him the Oscar for Best Actor. It was the second year in a row that he won said trophy with his role in *Philadelphia* being a winner the previous year. *Forrest Gump* won six Oscars in total with Best Picture, Best Director, Best Screenplay Based on Previously Published Material, Best Film Editing, and Best Visual Effects rounding out the winner's circle.

Michael Connor Humphreys is the name of the actor that played the child version of the Forrest Gump character during such memorable sequences as "Run, Forrest! Run!" He did not continue to pursue acting as a career, however. When he was old enough Humphreys joined the military, serving in Iraq. As of 2018 it looks like his IMDB credits are starting to get some life again with a part in a television project I am not familiar with called *Knight's End*.

In *Forrest Gump* there is a shrimp obsessed character named Bubba that Gump befriends in Vietnam. This character is portrayed by actor Mykelti Williamson. Bubba and Forrest daydream about becoming partners in a shrimping business after the war. Inspired by the movie, a real Bubba Gump Shrimp Company went into business as a restaurant in 1996; eventually becoming a chain. Actor Chris Pratt, who was not in *Forrest Gump*, but is well known for *Guardians of the Galaxy* and *Jurassic World*, used to work at a Bubba Gump Shrimp Company and as the story goes waited on an actress there that put him in his first movie.

The director for *Forrest Gump*, if you're not one to follow directors as closely as famous actors, Robert Zemeckis, was the director for *Back to the Future* and its two sequels. He also directed *Death Becomes Her*, *Who Framed Roger Rabbit*, *Contact*, *Cast Away*, and then went on a digitally captured performances spree with *The Polar Express*, *Beowulf*, and *A Christmas Carol*.

Sally Field and Robin Wright were the main leading ladies of the film *Forrest Gump*. Sally Field played the title character's mother and Robin Wright filled the shoes of his romantic interest Jenny. Robin Wright garnered a Golden Globe nomination, but neither lady went up for the coveted Oscar statue. Aside from Tom Hanks, the only other actor nominated for an Oscar was Gary Senise in his supporting role as Lieutenant Dan.

1995

10. *Die Hard with a Vengeance* - Directed by John McTiernan, screenplay by Jonathan Hensleigh. Domestic Box Office: $100,012,499

Die Hard with a Vengeance is the third film of the *Die Hard* action series. Bruce Willis returned as John McClane and along with the Samuel L. Jackson played character Zeus is sent around the city by a terrorist in a deadly game of Simon Says. The game and threats involved are all a distraction, however, from the Federal Reserve gold heist that is truly afoot.

At this time the Internet Movie Database website, IMDB, does not list an actual screenplay credit for the movie. I chose to list Jonathan Hensleigh because the bulk of the script was based off of his action script called *Simon Says*. The script was not originally meant to be a *Die Hard* script, but rather it was converted and altered to become a part of said action universe. Fox studios turned it into a *Die Hard* movie after Warner Brothers failed to turn it in to a *Lethal Weapon* movie after the production of it as *Simon Says* with Brandon Lee in a role did not happen.

Jonathan Hensleigh is a writer with connections to some big action movies such as *Con Air*, *Armageddon*, and the Nicolas Cage starring remake of *Gone in Sixty Seconds*. However, the amount of work he did on those stories, while said to be quite influential, seems to have ended up landing him script doctor appreciation more than full-fledged writing credits. In 2004, however, he got a writing credit and directed the rebirth of *The Punisher* movie series in which actor Thomas Jane played Frank Castle out to get revenge against John Travolta's Howard Saint. Hensleigh also directed a 2007 horror movie with the title *Welcome to the Jungle* and then the 2011 crime biopic *Kill the Irishman*.

Many other scripts were considered for conversion into what would become *Die Hard with a Vengeance*. One such script was called *Troubleshooter*. This script would have had the action taking place on a cruise ship, but the concept got voted down with the plot reminding too many people of the Steven Seagal movie *Under Siege*, which was already being called *Die Hard* on a ship. The script *Troubleshooter* still got used by Hollywood, however, supposedly being worked around to create *Speed 2: Cruise Control*.

While the first two *Die Hard* movies were based off of novels, the third film is the first to be based off of a script from the starting line. A novelization of *Die Hard with a Vengeance* was penned afterward, however, by author Deborah Chiel. Deborah Chiel has also written book adaptations for films such as *The Accused*, *Great Expectations*, *Lean on Me*, *Sabrina*, *A Walk in the Clouds*, and *Mona Lisa Smile*.

Director John McTiernan also directed the first *Die Hard*, as well as *Predator*, *The Hunt for Red October*, *Medicine Man*, *Last Action Hero*, *The 13th Warrior*, *The Thomas Crown Affair*, and *Rollerball*. Some of those credits are more notable than others, but quite notable indeed. However, as of my writing this, his last directing credit was in 2003 for the John Travolta led movie *Basic*. McTiernan's career vanished after he went to prison for perjury during a case involving his usage of private investigator Anthony Pellicano to illegally wiretap telephone calls. It seems John McTiernan would listen in on the calls of a *Rollerball* producer with whom he was having some disagreements. After 328 days in jail and some house arrest on a one year sentence, McTiernan found himself bankrupt, and though not without famous supporters, apparently ostracized from the filmmaking industry.

I have seen the first three *Die Hard* movies a bazillion times. The first one is still the one that holds up the best. *Die Hard with a Vengeance* was my preferred watch over *Die Hard 2*, but as time has passed neither one of them stands out as being something I really plan on ever watching again. I'm getting old and those movies have too.

9. *Se7en* - Directed by David Fincher, screenplay by Andrew Kevin Walker. Domestic Box Office: $100,125,643

The movie *Seven*? Oh, you mean Sesevenen! *Se7en*. The title of the movie may be stylized for promotional materials, but as I continue to type I am going to go with *Seven* as the spelling. I feel dumb enough as it is on a day to day basis, typing the title with the number seven in place of a letter would only compound my feelings of intellectual inadequacy with each stroke of the key deviating from my barely there grasp of spelling and the English language. I know words dang it! Maybe not all of the right ones, but I know you don't put numbers in words! Do you?

Numeronym: a number based word. Most commonly, a numeronym is a word where a number is used to form an abbreviation. Example: K9 can stand for "canine." In some instances numbers take over entirely for words while providing the same meaning. Example: 411 means "information" or if you say 101 properly in a sentence you might be referring to the "basic introduction to a subject." And then we have the Internet and things such as leet or leetspeak where words can be spelled out with numbers or mean different things, but, still, *Se7en* doesn't make sense to me, and there, that was it, the last time I am going to spell it any other way than *Seven*.

Se7en stars Morgan Freeman and Brad Pitt as lawmen searching for a serial killer that dispatches his victims in grotesque ways inspired by the seven deadly sins of: pride, greed, lust, sloth, gluttony, envy, and wrath. Spoiler alert: the killer is played by Kevin Spacey. If you have not seen the movie, my telling you the actor who plays the killer does not really ruin anything aside from the talent reveal. At the time of production Spacey was getting some attention for the success of *The Usual Suspects*, therefore, the makers of *Seven* wished to keep his addition to the cast secret, a surprise to be seen when the killer is first seen. Spacey's name was kept out of the promotional materials and the opening credits. These days many people don't want to be associated with actor Kevin Spacey because many have accused him of sexual misconduct.

Prior to *Seven*, director David Fincher's foray into big features was *Alien 3* and that movie was an experience that he has said made him wonder if his career in movies might have been ended before it could even really begin. He became interested in *Seven* as a project to help him out of the *Alien 3* backlash he felt, something edgy that he could really let loose with in a creative sense without disappointing a franchise fanbase such as what came with *Alien 3*. As a kid, I was not aware of *Alien 3* being a disappointment. I liked it.

The ending of *Seven*, half a spoiler alert, is infamous in terms of "shock value." The conclusion of the film is said to have been one of the big draws for David Fincher when he signed on to the project. However, keeping the ending as it was written in the original script became a fight between the director, the actors, and the studio. The studio never intended for a copy of the script featuring the ending as it was to be given to Fincher. The powers that be preferred a more action involved conclusion with safer, commercial appeal. The ending of *Seven* would go down in history as one of the most memorable despite Hollywood's attempt to sanitize it.

Aside from helping fight to keep the ending of *Seven* intact, actor Brad Pitt also handed over his physical well-being to the production. His character in the film receives an arm injury which reflected an actual injury suffered by Pitt. Brad Pitt fell against a car windshield during the shooting of a rainy chase sequence and he severed a very real tendon in his arm.

Seven became one of my favorite movies when it came out. As a dark, serial killer piece with a twisted ending, it was perfect for a kid that studied way too many books about serial killers and other horrors. It felt intelligent, yet delivered on pulpy entertainment values, a solid package for a dirty, moody teenage mind in development.

8. *Casper* - Directed by Brad Silberling, screenplay by Sherri Stone and Deanna Oliver. Domestic Box Office: $100,328,194

Maybe life wasn't all peaches and sunshine in 1995, maybe the ghost and goth aspect are what drew me in, but I wasn't completely removed from allowing myself to enjoy "kids" movies still, and *Casper* was indeed a flick that I thought was fun upon release. I recently watched *Casper* again, on the wrong side of thirty-five years old: thirty-six, and while it's not a movie I am compelled to gush over, I found the corny sense of humor and slapstick antics, both at times darker than one might expect, to be amusing.

The plot for *Casper* centers around a paranormal therapist, having been faking his skills until now, and his daughter moving into a creepy mansion to communicate with the spirits. Specifically, a scheming duo wish for the ghosts to be sent packing so that they can get into the mansion and find the treasure that is supposedly hidden there. The cast includes Bill Pullman and Christina Ricci facing off against Cathy Moriarty and Eric Idle with the help of some CGI ghosts, the main one being Casper voiced by Malachi Pearson. When Casper isn't CGI in the movie the actor that you see is Devon Sawa.

I'm not sure where the plot for *Casper* the movie came from, it's a fairly generic, "pull it out of a hat" Hollywood plot, in fact, *The Addams Family* movie, also starring Christina Ricci, also featured a weird house with some people up to no good searching for riches. However, the ghost character himself was born as a children's book idea. Casper the Friendly Ghost was created by Seymour Reit and Joe Oriolo in the 1930s. Instead of the children's book being where Casper's adventures really took flight, the concept was sold to Paramount and became an animated cartoon. In 1949 Casper became a character with his own comic series published by Harvey comics.

Casper marks the first major feature gig for director Brad Silberling. Prior to landing the job, hired by Steven Spielberg, Silberling was directing television shows. His feature following Casper was the 1998 romance *City of Angels* starring Nicolas Cage and

Meg Ryan. Hmm, from a teen ghost falling in love with a teen girl to an adult angel falling in love with an adult woman, I sense Brad Silberling had early career interest in subject matter involving the afterlife.

7. *Jumanji* - Directed by Joe Johnston, screenplay by Jonathan Hensleigh, Greg Taylor, and Jim Strain. Domestic Box Office: $100,475,249

I grew up with *Jumanji* as a children's picture book. It was among many other titles that I would check out from the school library in Kindergarten. However, I only checked it out, or any other books really, if all of the copies of *Scary Stories to Tell in the Dark* were already claimed.

The book *Jumanji* was a creation of author Chris Van Allsburg. Another book by the same author, *The Polar Express*, is one that I perused, but *Jumanji* is the only one that I really cared for.

Now, one might think that having enjoyed the book experience that I would be interested in a movie based on the material, however, that was not the case at all. I had zero interest in the *Jumanji* movie. I eventually watched the movie on home video, but my initial disinterest in the movie had steered me correct with regard to whether or not I would like the flick. I cannot say that I hated the movie by any means, but after watching it, I did not care for or about it.

Jumanji tells the tale of some kids, played by Kirsten Dunst and Bradley Pierce, that find a magical board game with a jungle adventure theme. When they play the game the characters and dangerous events described by the game come to life and really put them in peril. Robin Williams was cast as the star of the film, a man released from within the board game, a previous child player that had been sucked into the game world. Yeah, I don't recall that guy being in the book.

Book creator Chris Van Allsburg did not end up as one of the three with final screenplay credit, but he did write some drafts and has a "screen story" credit. One of the accredited screenwriters already appeared on this list of films from 1995: Mr. Jonathan Hensleigh writer of *Die Hard with a Vengeance*.

Joe Johnston, the director of Jumanji, previously had directed *Honey, I Shrunk the Kids*, which I was a big fan of as a child. He also directed *The Rocketeer*, which for some reason never appealed to me. He has also directed *October Sky, Jurassic Park III, Hidalgo*, and entered the superhero game with *Captain America: The First Avenger*.

A sequel to *Jumanji* called *Jumanji: Welcome to the Jungle* was released in 2017 starring Dwayne "The Rock" Johnson. However, in 2005 a movie called *Zathura: A Space Adventure* was made, also based on a Chris Van Allsburg book with a *Jumanji*-like plot involving a game with more of a science fiction slant bringing real danger to the players. It is to be understood that *Zathura* is not merely a rip-off of the *Jumanji* idea, sure the author dipped back into the same creative well, but rather takes place in the same world in which *Jumanji* as a board game exists. Uh oh, could there be more games with more themes? And this thought has nothing to do with much of anything related to *Jumanji*, but: wouldn't it be wonderfully horrible if someone made a movie out of that buzzing game *Operation*?!

Most likely there will be *Jumanji* sequels made after I have published this book. There have already been video games and an animated series based off of the property. The animated series ran on television from 1996 to 1999.

6. *GoldenEye* - Directed by Martin Campbell, screenplay by Jeffrey Caine and Bruce Feirstein. Domestic Box Office: $106,429,941

GoldenEye brought back the British spy character James Bond for his seventeenth film and introduced a new actor filling the shoes: Pierce Brosnon. The producers must have seen Brosnon in *Mrs. Doubtfire* and thought: elite spy! Actually, it is said that Brosnan was considered for the James Bond role in the 80s but could not commit to the movie due to scheduling conflicts on another project.

When a person says the title of *GoldenEye* I do not call to mind the movie immediately. The first product that pops into my mind associated with said title is the first person shooter video game that became very popular on the Nintendo 64 system.

I am not a fan of the James Bond movie franchise overall, just do not find the movies all that interesting. It seems odd that in my childhood packed with action stars that James Bond never became required viewing.

The character of James Bond, as well as the stories for previous Bond films, were based off of novels by Ian Fleming. However, *GoldenEye* broke the trend in terms of story with the tale being an original thunk up by someone else. The person that did that thunking, err, thinking, was Michael France. France received story credit, but not screenplay credit. Michael France also wrote on *Cliffhanger*, 2003's *Hulk*, did some story work for *The Punisher* released in 2004, and then wrote 2005's *Fantastic Four*. His credit list ends up being a little short, however, as Michael France died from illness at the age of fifty-one.

The 1995 film *GoldenEye* saw James Bond trying to stop a rogue agent from using a deadly satellite weapon for devious purposes. Cue the stunt men! And the "Bond Girls."

Aside from the action set pieces and the overall swagger of the lead spy for the film series, I suppose fans like to tune in to see the "Bond Girls." Bond Girls are the actresses cast in the movie, generally being seduced into bed by James Bond. If you think the concept is misogynist and sexist I would not disagree with you. The label of "Bond Girl" sounds like a demeaning sort of property tag as if they belong to Bond and he can do with them as he pleases before tossing them aside for a new one.

In *GoldenEye* Judi Dench is the actress playing the sexpot rolling in the sheets with James Bond. I'm kidding. Judi Dench played Bond's elder handler known as M. This did mark the first time that this character was portrayed by a female. So, I guess there's a stab at female empowerment? Bond Girl duties mainly went to Poland born actress Izabella Scorupco. Famke Janssen is also in the movie with villainous femme fatale duties. Janssen's character is Xenia Onatopp and, um, okay, that name is better suited for a porno or parody movie. She likes to crush men between her thighs.

Prior to Pierce Brosnon taking over Bond duties, actor Timothy Dalton was James Bond. A new movie starring him had been planned, however, legal issues and fighting back and forth over rights and money involving the franchise held up production until Dalton's contract expired. In subsequent interviews Dalton has stated that he did get an offer to play James Bond in *GoldenEye* once the legal issues were all settled. However, he declined to reprise the role because the studio wanted a commitment for several movies instead of just the one.

Actor Pierce Brosnon would go on to play the role of James Bond for a total of four films. Director

Martin Campbell moved on to other things such as *The Mask of Zorro* and the sequel *The Legend of Zorro* before he himself returned to the Bond franchise with *Casino Royale*. *Casino Royale* would mark the second time that Martin Campbell directed a film in which a new actor debuted as James Bond. Daniel Craig took over James Bond duties from Pierce Brosnon for *Casino Royale*. The Daniel Craig starring Bond films saw the series getting a bit grittier than previous installments.

5. *Ace Ventura: When Nature Calls* - Directed by Steve Oedekerk, screenplay by Steve Oedekerk. Domestic Box Office: $108,385,533

In 1994 the movie *Ace Ventura: Pet Detective* was a surprise hit at the box office that helped add a lot of zeros to the future paychecks of actor Jim Carrey. The first film was the sixteenth highest grossing movie in North America in that year and I am sure studio executives were eager to strike while the iron was hot with regard to rushing out a sequel. Smart move, as the sequel got into the top ten for earnings on the year for 1995 and actually won over some of us that were on the fence about the brand with the first film. I recall liking *Ace Ventura: When Nature Calls* better than the first film. Is it actually better, however? Or perhaps a year of becoming familiar with and being bombarded with all things Jim Carrey softened up my critical side, making it more ticklish and readier to laugh? The scene where he crawls out of the fake rhino butt had me in stitches!

Jim Carrey himself had a good deal of power over the production of the movie and gave many people the impression that he was not happy with the film at all. It has been said that he worried a great deal about the portrayal of the tribesmen in the film being too offensive and he did not like that his character was written to be afraid of bats. The plot of the movie has him hunting down a stolen bat.

While some actors came away from the production stating that the work was awkward due to Jim Carrey not seeming like he wanted to be there, there are yet other tales about Jim Carrey trying to make the best of things. One move he helped facilitate was the hiring of his friend Steve Oedekerk as the director. Tom DeCerchio was the director, the director of *Celtic Pride*, and he either quit or was let go after shooting commenced. Steve Oedekerk was not known as a director at the time, but Jim Carrey felt comfortable with him already, knowing that they shared a sense of humor. Tom DeCerchio's feature film directing career seems to have stalled somewhat after 1996. Coincidence?

It sounds like Jim Carrey might have been trying to get used to the new Hollywood powers he had to wield at this point and time in his career.

The scene where he crawls out of the fake rhino butt, ha, ha, oh, my, that's funny stuff.

4. *Pocahontas* - Directed by Mike Gabriel and Eric Goldberg, screenplay by Carl Binder, Susannah Grant, Philip LaZebnik. Domestic Box Office: $141,579,773

As I have mentioned earlier, I pretty much quit caring about Disney cartoons after *The Lion King*. I have watched many since and specifically thought the movie *Up* had some touching moments, but as for repeat watching and being a fan, that kid in me just isn't there anymore and the adult in me has never been all that in awe of what Pixar ended up bringing to the Disney table in later years. I had zero interest in *Pocahontas* but did eventually see the movie due to having younger siblings that popped it into the VCR.

Even if I have not seen *Pocahontas* very many times it has still scarred me for life. The song *Colors of the Wind*, or at least a portion of the lyrics, belts out of me frequently enough that I should probably sue someone for implanting it in my brain.

What else is there to say about the movie? Um, there was probably a cute animal in it. The lead character lady Pocahontas is cute I suppose.

There has been debate over the years as to the historical accuracy and the handling of Native American characters in the film. Obviously it is not historically accurate, well, okay, I get it, people are indeed probably dumb enough to take their history lessons from Disney fiction. I bet some people were fooled. The true story of Pocahontas in the history books was much grimmer. Oh, what a dark and sordid history America has in the colors of its wind.

Pocahontas never had a romance with John Smith I don't think. If I recall some sources say she was ten years old when he arrived. Then at some point she was abducted by English colonists, taken away to become a Christian, married a different John, and changed her name to Rebecca.

If you want to accept *Pocahontas* as a simple cartoon and forget history, or if you want to take up the social cause of getting the facts straight, I pretty much agree with your stance either way. You do you.

Now I feel kind of bad that I am skipping over the historical debate and not writing an entire novel now on the subject of the evils people have done to each other over the eons. Sigh.

The evil music of *Pocahontas* won two Oscars: Best Original Song and Best Original Musical or Comedy Score. Alan Menken and Stephen Schwartz took those honors.

Alaska born actress Irene Bedard provided the voice for Pocahontas and reprised the role in the direct to video sequel *Pocahontas 2: Journey to a New World*. I didn't see that one. In the 2005 Terrence Malick film *The New World* Irene Bedard played the role of Pocahontas' Mother. I did see that one.

Mel Gibson voiced John Smith in *Pocahontas*. Christian Bale, Linda Hunt, and other folks such as Billy Connolly also provided their voices and acting to the feature.

3. *Apollo 13* - Directed by Ron Howard, screenplay by William Broyles Jr. and Al Reinert. Domestic Box Office: $172,071,312

When you think of the directing "masters" of Hollywood, most people probably consider Stephen Spielberg as the king. However, in the conversation, and up there on that imaginary mountain, there would be a seat for Ron Howard as well. I am not saying that all of his movies are great, neither are Spielberg's, but that he has earned and deserves to be an icon in the industry at the job position of director. His brother Clint Howard is also awesome, but his legacy is an entirely different thing. Ron Howard directed the 1995 released film *Apollo 13*, while Clint Howard, who did appear in *Apollo 13*, could be seen in quite a few films, one example being *Ice Cream Man* where he used his thespian powers to portray a man released from an insane asylum that wants to turn children into ice cream cones.

Apollo 13 depicts a space mission in 1970 when some astronauts had to abort their trip to the moon due to some technical issues. The astronaut's lives hang in the balance as they try to solve the problems with their ship and return home. Based on a true historical event, the production went to great lengths to try and keep strong doses of scientific accuracy and reality, but at the end of the day it's a Hollywood feature and you can't let the viewer's butt fall asleep in their seat, gotta manufacture some extra tension whenever possible. People have discussed at great length the inaccuracies of the film when compared to real life, specifically I can find many sources that try to correct the dialog in terms of what was said in the film and then what the true to life quote really was. Yeah, that's a waste of time to get hung up on.

Audiences seem to find Tom Hanks likable and trustworthy, they like his face in their movies, therefore, he was probably the perfect casting choice to lead *Apollo 13*. Along for the ride with Tom Hanks were Kevin Bacon, Ed Harris, Bill Paxton, Gary Sinise, and Clint Howard played the wife opposite of Hank's character. Okay, I got carried away with all of the male star power in the film and recast the role of Marilyn Lovell there, Kathleen Quinlan actually played the part. Tom Hanks, by the way, was Jim Lovell. Supposedly the real Jim Lovell wished for Kevin Costner to play him.

Apollo 13 is a solid film. The drama and peril are all juggled well and when thinking of "safe" entertainment, in that you know what to expect and it provides it, a "safe bet" sort of film for studios looking for box office dollars, *Apollo 13* to me is a supreme example.

The film was nominated for a total of nine Academy Awards, but only won two: Best Sound and Best Film Editing.

2. *Batman Forever* - Directed by Joel Schumacher, screenplay by Lee Batchler, Janet Scott Batchler, and Akiva Goldsman. Domestic Box Office: $184,031,112

Superhero movies were going through a rough patch, not the cream of the box office crop generally during my youth. Tim Burton brought some prestige back to the genre with the successes *Batman* and *Batman Returns*. However, the third film in that franchise, *Batman Forever*, just about killed off superhero movies altogether in my opinion. Terrible movie. Second highest earning movie of 1995. It was a hit.

The plot of *Batman Forever* has Batman facing off against Two-Face and the Riddler, a love interest/psychologist pursues Batman, and Robin shows up to be a sidekick, and who really cares about a plot: Batman's suit had nipples on it! People seemed to hate the fact that nipples were put on to Batman's suit, but talk about nipples endlessly is what they did, giving the Batman suit nipples some of that "bad press is better than no press" publicity steam.

Instead of a dark and grimy Gotham City this time around, things were brighter and glittery. I would not have been surprised if the movie had turned into a musical with Batman doing jazz-hands.

Burton infused the "camp" factor of the old Batman television series into his work, yet did so with gritty, goth flair. As a kid I liked the Tim Burton movie *Batman*. After I saw *Batman Forever* I was like: "You broke it!"

The Tim Burton movies featuring Batman are said to have gotten too dark for the taste of the studios. *Batman Returns* specifically did not generate as much money as they had hoped because the grim characters weren't "toy friendly" enough. Yes, a major contributing factor to Tim Burton stepping away from making a third Batman movie is because not enough toys were sold off of his movies. Therefore, out of the gates, the studio wanted *Batman Forever* to be one giant toy commercial.

One of the things they did right in terms of producing a blockbuster experience is packing the movie full of movie stars. Let's talk about those.

Michael Keaton did not return as Batman. The reason why he did not return depends on who you ask. Out of the studio came the excuse for recasting of: Keaton wanted too much money. Michael Keaton, however, says that he turned down the money and walked away because the script was terrible. An offer is said to have been made to actor Ethan Hawke, but in the end Val Kilmer took the role. Director Joel Schumacher credits his having enjoyed Val Kilmer's performance in the Western *Tombstone* for the casting decision.

Val Kilmer and director Joel Schumacher did not get along during the filming of *Batman Forever*.

Schumacher has said that Kilmer was rude to most people and after he called the actor out on it Kilmer quit talking to him for a two week period of filming. If the director and lead actor are not speaking, it's kind of hard for the creative magic to happen in terms of vision and performance aligning.

In Val Kilmer's defense it sounds like wearing the Batman suit was pure torture every single day with the nipples not adding extra comfort. He has described the process of putting on the suit as being a lengthy team effort. Then, once in the suit, turning one's head or hearing anyone clearly was impossible. At a Chicago Comic Expo he compared wearing the suit to experiencing what it is like to become old: "No one really listens to you anymore. You can't really talk or hear. You're always falling over, and someone has to help you go to the bathroom and get dressed.

The role of the Riddler was originally developed for Robin Williams. The deal fell through and for a while created a rift between the actor and Warner Brothers because Robin Williams wanted the role and thought that getting to play it was a sure thing. Jim Carrey, another comic known for jabbering out gibberish at a high rate of speed, in the midst of being a huge box office draw ended up getting the part.

The Riddler is really stupid and goofy in *Batman Forever*. Jim Carrey tells how Tommy Lee Jones despised him, not the Riddler, but Jim Carrey and his career in general, and made acting across from him awkward. Carrey quotes Jones as once telling him: "I cannot sanction your buffoonery." I'm sure Jim Carrey laughed about that one all the way to the bank.

One of the producers of *Batman Forever* had an inside track to calling up Tommy Lee Jones, having worked with him in the past. Jones would accept the role of Two-Face, but initially did not understand the film's script or why anyone would want to make such a movie. The producer says that he convinced Jones to take the role because of said producer's help in getting Jones an Oscar award for *The Fugitive*. Tommy Lee Jones says that he only took the role because his eleven-year-old son liked comic books and it would entertain his son.

In Tim Burton's *Batman,* Harvey Dent, the character that transforms into Two-Face, was played by Billy Dee Williams also known as Lando Calrissian from the *Star Wars* franchise. One of the reasons Billy Dee Williams accepted the Harvey Dent role was perhaps in hopes of eventually getting to play the villain Two-Face. Rumors that Williams had such a stipulation in his *Batman* contract have been dispelled by the actor, the studio did not break contract with him, he signed on the dotted line for only the single Batman flick.

Nicole Kidman plays Dr. Chase Meridian in *Batman Forever.* The character is a psychologist obsessed with the dual nature of things, an issue playing out for the hero Bruce Wayne the Batman, but also the villains within the film, I guess as a "beat you over the head with it" attempt at exploring a theme. Learnin' for kids! Dr. Chase Meridian is pretty terrible at her job with her interests seeming to be more personal stimulation for sexual desires than anything professional. She is more or less in the movie to be the love interest and damsel in distress. Nicole Kidman has reflected on the movie in interviews wishing that the role had given her more to be and do, chalking it up as having been "being the girl in a *Batman* movie."

A couple of other girls in *Batman Forever* are Drew Barrymore and Debi Mazar. These actresses were merely arm candy for Two-Face, his dual nature girlfriends, who also assist the Riddler when it comes time to set up devious plots against Batman and what-not. Sure, it was a big movie to appear in, but if you ever want proof that Drew Barrymore's transition from child star to adult star didn't involve some hiccups and her having to work her way back into having real industry respect, being one of two bimbos for a comic book villain seems like an adequate way of showing said struggle and work that she had to suffer through.

And then you have Chris O'Donnell filling the shoes of Robin. The character plays out rather corny in my opinion, with his actions and posturing all being more for the minds of children to understand and find cool rather than an adult watching the movie. Maybe that was the intention though and I should not be so critical for a movie not crafted for me.

Except, I WAS a kid when it came out and I still found it all so shallow and stupid.

Bono, the lead singer of the band U2, tried to get himself cast in the movie. The director and producers toyed with the idea of including him, but eventually they scrapped the role. U2 did get a song featured on the soundtrack of *Batman Forever*, which helped promote the film quite well. *Hold Me, Thrill Me, Kiss Me, Kill Me* was the U2 song from the soundtrack and earned U2 a Grammy nomination.

An even bigger song that helped promote *Batman Forever*, however, was the one performed by the artist known as Seal. His song *Kiss from a Rose* was a smash hit and is still stuck in the heads of every person that has ever heard it. *Batman Forever* director Joel Schumacher directed the music video for Seal's chart topping song. At the 1996 Grammy Awards *Kiss from a Rose* helped Seal win Record of the Year, Song of the Year, and Best Male Pop Vocal Performance.

1. ***Toy Story*** - Directed by John Lasseter, screenplay by Joss Whedon, Andrew Stanton, Joel Cohen, and Alec Sokolow. Domestic Box Office: $191,796,233

Toy Story is the movie that made Pixar the biggest name in family film producing, starting a partnership with Disney that eventually resulted in Disney buying the company. As I write this in 2018, I would consider Pixar animated films to still be the most highly anticipated theatrical releases by those who are fans of the genre. Personally, I never became a fan of *Toy Story* or its sequels. I think they are okay films, but the praise and awe given to the stories and emotional depth are unwarranted hype to me.

The story for *Toy Story* revolves around the toys of a young boy named Andy. The toys come to life when humans are not around and in this specific bedroom the leader of the toys is a pull-string cowboy named Woody. However, a new spaceman toy called Buzz Lightyear soon joins the room and there is some jealousy from Woody as Andy seems to want to play with Buzz more than him. One thing leads to another and Woody and Buzz end up getting out of the house and need to work together to find their way back. There are little subplots, though the biggest one might be the fact that Buzz Lightyear doesn't realize he is a mass-produced toy, instead he thinks that he is a real space ranger. The lead characters of Woody and Buzz are voiced by Tom Hanks and Tim Allen.

This film began life as a deal made to turn a short 1988 film called *Tin Toy* into a feature. *Tin Toy* was also directed by John Lasseter who had dealt with some rejection from Disney before helping found Pixar. The short film won the Best Animated Short Film prize at the Oscars for 1988 films and this gained Disney's attention. Fully computer animated films were still a territory being explored and *Tin Toy* paved the way to success with its award win. *Tin Toy* featured the adventures of

Tinny the one-man band. Obviously a lot changed between the initial deal to make the movie and the actual creating of what would become *Toy Story*.

Disney and some of the folks working on *Toy Story* are said to have butted heads when it came to choosing whether or not to make the film a musical. Musicals are the bread and butter of Disney and they wanted the toy characters to break out into song here and there. John Lasseter stuck to his guns in denying the suggestion that song and dance numbers were needed, however, he did compromise in accepting non-diegetic songs to be added into the film. Non-diegetic songs, if you're just now learning about them, are songs that add to the narrative of what is happening on screen in a movie or sing directly about circumstances that the viewer is watching. Randy Newman composed three songs for the film with *You've Got a Friend in Me* being the signature track. I really do not like that Oscar nominated song or Randy Newman's singing in general. The animated television show *Family Guy* does a good job of making fun of Randy Newman if you want to look up a clip of that.

While nominated for three Oscars and breaking new ground, *Toy Story* did not take home any of the coveted statues. However, John Lasseter did get an Oscar Special Achievement award for "the development and inspired application of techniques that have made possible the first feature-length computer-animated film."

1996

10. *A Time to Kill* - Directed by Joel Schumacher, screenplay by Akiva Goldsman. Domestic Box Office: $108,766,007

A Time to Kill is based on John Grisham's 1989 novel of the same name. Set in Mississippi it follows the trial of a black man who killed two white men because they raped his daughter. Racial tension and the lust for violence abounds. Sandra Bullock, Samuel L. Jackson, Matthew McConaughey, and Kevin Spacey, Oliver Platt, Ashley Judd, Kiefer and Donald Sutherland, Chris Cooper, and Patrick McGoohan fill out the cast who were directed by *Batman Forever* director Joel Schumacher.

You can try to pin Joel Schumacher as a certain type of director with a certain style after seeing his Batman franchise entries, but then he goes and directs things like *A Time to Kill*, *8MM*, or *Tigerland* and his versatility is shown. Of course, with *A Time to Kill* he courted no less controversy as when he approved the addition of nipples on to the batsuit.

The subject matter must have been of topical interest, racial issues tend to be that in America, but I am somewhat surprised to see *A Time to Kill* was one of the top ten earning films of the year. Aside from the exploration of racial issues, America I think has a taste for, well, humans have a taste for violence and enjoy movies where it is delivered in the form of vigilantism. In 1996 I recall the horror movie *Scream* being one of the most exciting theater experiences to be had, however, it only ranked at number thirteen on the year in box office take. The movie that fell one spot below *A Time to Kill* on the top earners list is *The First Wives Club*. *A Time to Kill* is not the only surprise to me on the list for 1996, I would have expected *Space Jam*, *The English Patient*, or some of Arnold Schwarzenegger's films to have ranked higher, if not the *Star Trek* film that was released. Or *Mars Attacks!*! I mean, I don't like *Space Jam*, but it was a pretty big movie in that year from my perspective. 1996 overall seems like it was a good year for the movie industry when you look back and see the success had by what would become "bargain bin" features during the boom of DVD. Ah, digging through the bargain bin of movies at Walmart, a sport that has died.

In France the film *A Time to Kill* was considered controversial. Critics questioned how askew the morals and message of the film were. They added a question mark to the title of the film in France. The original novel did not escape debate either in terms of whether or not it attempted to justify murder.

John Grisham wrote a sequel novel to *A Time to Kill* called *Sycamore Row*. This direct sequel went to print in 2013.

9. *The Birdcage* - Directed by Mike Nichols, screenplay by Elaine May. Domestic Box Office: $124,060,553

The Birdcage is a remake of a 1978 Franco-Italian film which itself was an adaptation of a 1973 play. Therefore, while Elaine May nabs screenwriting credit for the American film, other writers have credits for earlier versions of the story. Jean Poiret wrote the play and on the script for the original movie. Francis Veber, Edouard Molinaro, and Marcello Danon also contributed to the 1978 film screenplay.

The plot of *The Birdcage* centers around Armand, a gay cabaret owner, and his drag queen companion, Albert, who agree to pretend they are heterosexual when being introduced to the parents of Armond's son's fiancée. Robin Williams and Nathan Lane headline as the gay couple with Gene Hackman, Dianne Wiest, Dan Futterman, Calista Flockhart, Hank Azaria, Christine Baranski, and more filling out the rest of the cast.

This film has been celebrated by many for showing a homosexual couple in a loving manner, something that may be refreshing to see when considering there was a lot of humor at the expense of gay people being slung around in the 90s without too much thought put into the emotional harm it might be causing.

Originally Steve Martin was going to lead the cast as the character Armand with Robin Williams being offered the drag queen part of Albert. However, Robin Williams did not have interest in Albert's part due to having already spent a good deal of time in drag for the movie *Mrs. Doubtfire*. Steve Martin ended up dropping out of the production due to the often used excuse of "scheduling conflicts" and Robin Williams got to take the part he preferred.

The Birdcage was nominated for a single Oscar: Best Set Decoration, which it did not win. Mike Nichols, the director of *The Birdcage,* however, won an Oscar for Best Director for directing the 1967 movie *The Graduate.* He was nominated in that same category for his films *Who's Afraid of Virginia Woolf?*, *Silkwood*, and *Working Girl.* Mike Nichols died of a heart attack in 2014 with his final film directed having been the 2007 Tom Hanks starring feature *Charlie Wilson's War.*

8. *The Nutty Professor* - Directed by Tom Shadyac, screenplay by David Sheffield, Barry W. Blaustein, Tom Shadyac, and Steve Oedekerk. Domestic Box Office: $128,814,019

The original 1963 film *The Nutty Professor* starred Jerry Lewis as an accident-prone professor with physical looks not generally considered attractive. As somewhat a parody of the story *Strange Case of Dr. Jekyll and Mr. Hyde* the plot of the movie follows the professor on a comedic journey of transformation and self-acceptance after he develops a formula that makes him a better looking, more confident, and all around socially "cooler" fellow called Buddy Love. The 1996 rendition has Eddie Murphy in the title role as a fat professor who after drinking the formula slims down into Buddy Love. The 1996 movie may be of great study value to you if you are looking for a single film source to gather fat jokes from.

One of the major selling points for *The Nutty Professor* was how much mileage the production was getting out of Eddie Murphy's star power. He did not just play the title role, but also put on costumes to play many other roles within the movie, filling the big butts of the Klump family and basically having conversations with himself in the different voices of different obese people. The extensive makeup work on the film won the Oscar for Best Makeup. Whenever I think of the dinner table scene with Eddie Murphy portraying all of the different characters I always think of how the movie *Tropic Thunder* would make fun of that scene many years later with Jack Black spoofing Murphy's one-man show gimmick.

I would talk more about other cast members in *The Nutty Professor*, but, did they matter? This is an Eddie Murphy show, the spotlight never really meant to enhance the supporting cast. They're props. I'm not saying they didn't do a good job, but I do think the product should have taken Eddie Murphy to the next level and had him play his own love interest in the film instead of Jada Pinkett, later known as Jada Pinkett Smith after she married actor Will Smith.

The Nutty Professor did well at the box office and critics were generally in a good mood around the time of release as well. The balance of heartwarming sentiment and lowbrow humor were generally accepted and the sequel to the film had its destiny set. It took some years to get Eddie Murphy back on to the big screen in a fat suit, but *Nutty Professor II: The Klumps* released in the year 2000.

Tom Shayac had directed *Ace Ventura: Pet Detective* prior to *The Nutty Professor* and afterward directed films such as *Liar Liar*, *Patch Adams*, and *Bruce Almighty*. However, his break from comedic films and Hollywood, the inspiration for his 2010 documentary *I Am*, may be a far more interesting story to some than those films. After recovering from a head injury in 2007, Tom Shayac choose to sell off most of his possessions, donate his money to several causes, and move from a mansion into a trailer park. Thus began a spiritual journey for the man that many questioned as being irrational and under the influence of his head injury still. He had knocked his noggin in a bicycle accident.

Tom Shayac is back to working in the film industry and his words for those that questioned whether or not the bicycle accident was the sole reason he took his break from the industry are: " I was already reevaluating the dissonance between making all this money and being on the set with people, the crew, many of whom couldn't afford the basic needs of their families. It didn't seem fair to me. So I don't think the concussion did it although it was definitely a crisis and crisis will often trigger things like this. I didn't give up everything to be happy. In fact, I'm not even sure what happiness is. Happiness comes from the word "happenstance" which relates to things going on outside of you. What was happening to me was definitely on the inside. But after I gave up everything I felt a lot more joy in my life. A lot more contentment."

7. *The Rock* - Directed by Michael Bay, screenplay by David Weisberg, Douglas Cook, and Mark Rosner. Domestic Box Office: $134,069,511

In the Michael Bay directed action feature *The Rock*, Nicolas Cage plays a chemist paired up with the only convict, a role played by Sean Connery, to ever escape the infamous prison turned tourist site Alcatraz. Together they must break into the former prison which has been taken over by angry former military men, led by a character being portrayed by Ed Harris, who have hostages and demands. Oh, and some chemical weapons that need to be disarmed.

I do not have any memories of having seen *The Rock* at the movie theater, but I sure did rent it a lot on VHS. The entire movie was fun as far as action movies go, but I recall specifically being fascinated with the scene in which Nicolas Cage's character, Stanley Goodspeed becomes exposed to the chemical nerve agent and plunges a large needle into his own heart to stave off death and save the day. Some people may recall a certain needle into the chest scene from the movie *Pulp Fiction* and with the rumor that Quentin Tarantino did some uncredited rewrites on the script for *The Rock*, I wonder if he might have gone to the creative well of needles more than once and contributed that moment.

Aside from Tarantino not getting a writing credit on *The Rock*, Jonathan Hensleigh and Aaron Sorkin are two other notable names that are said to have worked on the script. The original spec script was created by David Weisberg and Douglas Cook before going through a virtual carousel of writers. There was some dispute over final film credits involving the screenplay and specifically some, including Michael Bay, felt that the Writer's Guild should have given the screenplay credit to Jonathan Hensleigh.

In news of the horrible and quirky involving *The Rock* vs. reality, apparently an intel source feeding the British Intelligence agency at one point is considered to have used the movie to make up descriptions of chemical weapons he had supposedly seen in Iraq. Considering the coalition did not find the vast stores of chemical weapons that they expected after invading Iraq, one would hope that this source of information was not a key figure in the final war decision making process. It is reported that the British source described seeing chemical weapons with the deadly components stored in glass spheres. This description caused concern because in reality chemical weapons are not constructed in the same manner as Hollywood portrays them. The theory that the informant may have seen the movie *The Rock* and based his description off of that movie soon became born. How far along he strung some people with his information is not clear to me, but it has to have been embarrassing to have been dealing with the informant just to find out he probably wasn't reliable and had just seen too many entertaining action flicks.

Now-a-days if you talk about *The Rock* I bet most people will at first assume you are speaking about actor Dwayne Johnson and his wrestling alter ego called The Rock. It sure does seem like The Rock is in a new movie every month! I'm surprised that Hollywood has not already done a reboot or sequel to *The Rock* starring The Rock.

6. *101 Dalmatians* - Directed by Stephen Herek, screenplay by John Hughes. Domestic Box Office: $136,189,294

Animal hoarders pornography?

The 1996 Disney movie *101 Dalmatians* is a live-action film based off of the 1961 Disney animated film *One Hundred and One Dalmatians*, which itself was based off of a 1956 novel written by Dodie Smith called *The Hundred and One Dalmatians*. I have seen the 1995 film, but my memories of the tale are mostly crafted from having seen the original cartoon as a child.

101 Dalmatians is about a loving couple, Roger and Anita, who were brought together by their loving dalmatian dogs, Pongo and Perdy, and both the humans and the dogs are going to add to the family by having children/ puppies. Anita works for an evil fashion designer named Cruella de Vil who decides that she wants to make a fur coat out of dalmatians. Cruella steals the fifteen puppies born to Pongo and Perdy and then also eighty-four other dalmatians from other parents and places. A great dalmatian rescue adventure gets underway.

Glenn Close stars in the film as Cruell de Vil with Jeff Daniels and Joely Richardson being the couple of Roger and Anita. I've always found it amusing to notice Hugh Laurie is in the movie as one of Cruella's henchmen. He went on to fame after becoming a doctor who breaks the rules on the hit television show *House*. I had a step-parent that was a big fan of *House*, so, I saw a lot of Hugh Laurie working on medical mysteries when I was at their home. Also, perhaps it is of special interest to me because my last name is also Laurie. Yo, Hugh, hook a Laurie up with some big industry connections!

Another amusing fact about *101 Dalmatians* is that the screenplay credit went to John Hughes. Yes, it is THE John Hughes. I doubt many people think of this dog filled Disney movie when they think about John Hughes movies. Or maybe they do and it's just me that finds it amusing. John Hughes is known more for his 80s teen features such as *Sixteen Candles, The Breakfast Club, Pretty in Pink, Ferris Bueller's Day Off, Weird Science,* and *Some Kind of Wonderful*. However, he also is to blame for the goodness of *Planes, Trains, & Automobiles*, *Uncle Buck*, and *Home Alone*.

What is more amusing than knowing that John Hughes wrote the screenplay? Director Stephen Herek made his feature film directorial debut with one of my favorite movies: *Critters*! The 1986 movie *Critters* is about some space alien furballs that want to eat everyone on Earth. It was a great movie when I saw it as a kid and it remains great when I watch it as an adult. Other movies directed by Stephen Herek that I watched more than a few times as a kid include *Bill & Ted's Excellent Adventure*, *Don't Tell Mom the Babysitter's Dead*, and *The Mighty Ducks*. I don't think I ever really enjoyed *Don't Tell Mom the Babysitter's Dead* that much, but the basic premise and cover art for the movie were too much fun to not at least pretend to like it for a few rentals. It did help that the film starred Christina Applegate who had young teens wooed playing Kelly Bundy on *Married with Children*, the slightly too-adult comedy television show that we rarely got to see, thus making it all the more enticing.

The country of Croatia is considered to be the origin point for the breed of dog known as Dalmatians. They were known as coach dogs, guarding horses and carriages, but throughout history were utilized to guard other things before eventually becoming a mascot for firefighters.

5. *Ransom* - Directed by Ron Howard, screenplay by Richard Price and Alexander Ignon. Domestic Box Office: $136,492,681

Ransom is a thriller involving a kidnapping for ransom, however, the father of the stolen child decides to go the controversial route of publicly offering the ransom money as a reward for turning in the kidnappers instead of giving it to said kidnappers for his child back.

The basic attitude behind the premise as portrayed in the trailer for the film, coupled with the charismatic star power of a pre-drunken public rants Mel Gibson must have sold audiences nice and hard (that sounds sexual) because *Ransom* is another movie that I never would have guessed to have made a top ten box office earner list. Perhaps the allure of a parent making a risky choice with their kid's life on the line was a strong fantasy for the mas and pas of 1996?

Mel Gibson leads the cast of the film as the father wanting to get his son back. His wife is played by Rene Russo, who also happened to portray Gibson's love interest in the later *Lethal Weapon* movies. Their son is portrayed by Brawley Nolte, son of actor Nick Nolte. Gary Sinise, Delroy Lindo, Lili Taylor, Liev Schreiber, and Donnie Wahlberg are some of the other cast members of the film.

Mel Gibson can always recall the time period around filming *Ransom* I bet due to the filming got stalled at one point for his appendectomy.

I recall that the movie *Ransom* surprised me with how bloody it got. The movie became a point of contention between my divorced parents when we saw it during a weekend visit to our father's house. My mother would every now and then decide that movies with a restricted rating were not for her children, a stance that she really waffled on, not sure why she would sometimes go on moral crusades that she did not believe in for very long. Anyway, I recall *Ransom* specifically being a movie that had a bloody scene in it that when described as something we saw to my mother led to some overall negative vibes between the households we were going back and forth between.

Aside from those details and my own weaving in of some "child of divorce woes," I don't personally think of *Ransom* as a memorable film. It is listed in history as a high earning film, and I never thought it was completely awful, but neither have I ever been caring one way or another about the film with regard to recommending it to others to watch. Ron Howard is an elite director in the film industry, but not every movie a person directs, regardless of their success, is going to win complete adoration. I wish my projects that don't win adoration would rake in enough cash to place sixth in a yearly theatrical box office race.

4. *Jerry Maguire* - Directed by Cameron Crowe, screenplay by Cameron Crowe. Domestic Box Office: $153,952,592

The Cameron Crowe film *Jerry Maguire* is the story of a sports agent that in a world obsessed with money has a moral epiphany about how his business should be treating their clients as people. He is promptly fired and then sets off to start his own agency following his new philosophy. Tom Cruise stars as Jerry Maguire and Renee Zellweger stars as Dorothy Body the secretary that leaves the company with and falls in love with him. Cuba Gooding Jr. stars as Rod Tidwell the sole client that Jerry is able to keep.

The year 1996 at the movies was one in which Tom Cruise diverted from his regular movie star formula and showed some versatility by appearing in a project such as *Jerry Maguire*. Tom Cruise is someone that reached movie star status, however, the blockbuster action stars are not generally also considered grand masters of the acting craft, they craft a brand based on steady, repetitive performances, and get by on their special X factor appeal. The movie *Jerry Maguire* is an example that shows that one can take a movie star such as Tom Cruise, and still find a place for their style of acting within a different style of movie and make it not only work but make sense with the talent.

As of this date, Tom Cruise has been nominated for three Oscar acting awards, all for lead roles. The movies that garnered him nominations are: *Born on the Fourth of July*, *Jerry Maguire*, and *Magnolia*. Is Tom Cruise great in those roles? I honestly still see the "movie star" and not an Oscar candidate, however, just the attempt at versatility is enough in some cases to surprise people and give them something that feels fresh.

The big question I have with regard to Tom Cruise is: where is the backlash over his exalted status within Scientology? There has been enough horrible information about that "religion" to convince most that it is a cult, yet even with the documentaries and revealed shady dealings of the business running beneath the religious front, the poster children for Scientology are still powers in Hollywood: Tom Cruise and John Travolta. John Travolta may have missed some religious payments along the line, but the career of Tom Cruise has really just continued on an upward climb.

While Tom Cruise and other nominated folks, *Jerry Maguire* netted five Oscar nominations, failed to bring home golden statues, Cuba Gooding Jr. did win for Best Supporting Actor. His Oscar acceptance speech is one that is often featured in clips featuring "best" Oscar moments.

According to the director, the inspiration for *Jerry Maguire* was born out of his disappointment in how his previous film *Singles* was received. After the release of that film and the hurdles it did not successfully leap clear in the opinions of some, he noticed what friends left him and what friends stuck by his side, subject matter that is explored in the moment *Jerry Maguire*'s title character Jerry Maguire departs from his offices only to find only one other person is willing to march out the door with him on a new venture.

Something that was meant to be explored in *Jerry Maguire* was product placement by Reebok. The company paid, in the form of "merchandise and marketing services," to have a commercial featured in the film only to see that not only was their product placement not in the final product, but a character actually says something negative about Reebok. I'm not sure how the issue got smoothed out in the end, but the Reebok material was placed into the film for television airings of the movie as well as becoming a special feature on the DVD release.

The Aimee Mann song *Wise Up* was written specifically for the movie *Jerry Maguire*. However, the song did not get used in the film. Cameron Crowe liked the song and it did get placed on to the musical album soundtrack for the film. Fast forward to the 1999 Paul Thomas Anderson film *Magnolia*, another film for which Tom Cruise received an Oscar nomination, and one will find that the Aimee Mann song *Wise Up* is in the film, sung at parts by Tom Cruise, and has overall become a song generally associated with *Magnolia* instead of *Jerry Maguire*. Iddint dat a fun fact! Yeppo!

Yeppo is Korean for pretty. I just looked that up after typing it.

3. *Mission: Impossible* - Directed by Brian De Palma, screenplay by David Koepp and Robert Towne. Domestic Box Office: $180,981,856

Tom Cruise struck again! Was it because of the alien powers tapped into by the Scientologists?

Tom Cruise got into some major film producing with the formation of Cruise/ Wagner Productions in 1993. The first film to be produced with the help of his company: *Mission: Impossible*. As a fan of the original television series *Mission: Impossible*, Cruise chose the project as something to star in and the producer side of him probably dangled the movie star side of him in front of Paramount, the rights holders for the show, in order to get them to play ball on funding the movie.

An action spy film that has spawned numerous sequels, I don't think I need to get into the plot details of *Mission: Impossible* for you to already understand what it is about: stunts. Tom Cruise has become a crazy stunt man on the *Mission: Impossible* sets and the first film of the series starring him pushed the special effects envelope with a scene involving him dangling down from the ceiling and then also a helicopter into a train tunnel scenario. Perhaps you thought it was all computer created effects, but the truth is Tom Cruise died in the helicopter filming *Mission: Impossible* and one of the Scientologist lizard-people replaced him to further his career.

I enjoyed *Mission: Impossible* when it was released. I have enjoyed all of the sequels as well in terms of they provide bang for your buck at the theater; they make for a good big screen experience. When the first movie released, some of the original cast members of the television show were said to have not approved of the movie. Actor Greg Morris is rumored to have walked out of a screening before it was over because of how badly the movie was pooping on the legacy that had been created by the television show. I did not grow up as a fan of the show. I was aware of it, but it was a "before my time" show that did not happen to get programmed into the classic rerun blocks of shows UHF channel twenty-five offered me on the ole black and white television. If it had been an action version of *Little House on The Prairie* maybe I would better understand the protecting of the original show vision as embraced by and put up on a pedestal by audiences. Then again, *Little House on the Prairie* remade as a Tom Cruise action movie probably would have gotten a thumbs up from me too in 1996.

Director Brian De Palma is not the director I would guess if I were playing the guess the director of *Mission: Impossible* game. When I think of Brian De Palma I think of *Scarface*, *The Untouchables*, *Carlito's Way*, and then *The Black Dahlia* which in my mind stalled his career, though his prior two films *Mission to Mars* and *Femme Fatale* weren't exactly golden nuggets of cinema either. I did see a good documentary about the filmmaker's career called *De Palma*, created by Noah Baumbach, therefore, I should have more knowledge ready about why Brian De Palma seemingly fell out of

Hollywood favor at some point, but only so much fits in my brain and I've been playing a lot of *Grand Theft Auto Online* since that viewing.

If I recall correctly *Mission to Mars* was a turning point for Brian De Palma in terms of him getting tired of working within the big Hollywood studios and all of the arguments over money. He felt unfulfilled and that the work was suffering. Of course, when working in the movie industry I am sure there are many "turning points" of misery, screws grinding under your skin, screwed there by all of the people with the job of trying to screw you. It is said that Brian De Palma and Tom Cruise did not get along during the filming of *Mission: Impossible*.

The legacy of *Mission: Impossible* as an entertainment product now belongs to Tom Cruise. When you see something involving the franchise you see Tom Cruise. You could probably take away the title of the movie and just put Tom Cruise on the poster and people will understand what it is. By 2018 Tom Cruise has starred in six blockbuster *Mission: Impossible* movies and each one ratchets up the stunt work and spectacle; popcorn fun. I'm not sure if they are rotating lizard-people in and out of the Tom Cruise skin to act in the movies, or if it has been the same lizard since the first *Mission: Impossible*.

2. *Twister* - Directed by Jan de Bont, screenplay by Michael Crichton, and Anne-Marie Martin. Domestic Box Office: $241,721,524

Twister is a movie based on that game where you unfold a mat with colored dots all over it and then spin a spinner thing that tells you what body part must touch what color of dot, eventually twisting your body all up in an erotic pretzel with anyone that dared play with you. Obviously that is not true, but I would not be surprised if such a movie is on its way to take its place in film history next to *Battleship*.

Nominated for two Oscar awards, Best Sound and Best Visual Effects, *Twister* is about storm chasers chasing after tornadoes. The storm chasers are trying to be the first to use some technology and gather some information before a rival team of chasers does so. Also, there is a love story about former lovers holding grudges now being forced to work together again, being blown back together by the wind and such.

Bill Paxton and Helen Hunt are the lead stars of the film with supporting character work from Cary Elwes, Jami Gertz, Philip Seymour Hoffman, Alan Ruck, Lois Smith, Sean Whalen, Scott Thomson, and Todd Field. I always think of Philip Seymour Hoffman when I think of the cast for *Twister* as this was a role where upon seeing it I don't think you'd ever guess that he'd become a four time Oscar nominee in acting categories. Hoffman won a Best Actor statue in 2006 for *Capote*. Also, every time I watch *The Lost Boys*, one of my favorite movies, I always think of *Twister* due to Jami Gertz being in both films. Thirdly, morbidly, *Twister* is a movie that when I think about how some of them are dead already.

The movie *Twister* may not have been the smartest movie, but we loved it when it came out. The tornado special effects were awesome to us. Oh, look, a flying cow! Again and again we watched to see that cow. And look out! A house! They just drove through a house in a tornado!

Bill Paxton was an actor that the producers of the film *American Romance* were supposedly considering when casting. I wrote early drafts of the script for that film. I think Bill Paxton's career got a second wind at around that same time with his television work on *Hatfields & McCoys* putting him out of financial reach for the Indie project. John Savage ended up taking the role.

Steven Spielberg's company Amblin Entertainment produced *Twister* with financial backing from both Warner Brothers and Universal Pictures. The screenplay credits went to the originally hired duo of Michael Crichton and his wife Anne-Marie Martin, but it is another Hollywood tale of many a writer being brought in to change things around. Joss Whedon, Steve Zaillian, and Jeff Nathanson all contributed to the script, with some of the writing still going on during the shooting of the movie. One can only assume that they were trying to nail down the twister's motivation.

Director Jan de Bont was meant to go from the success of his gig *Speed* to directing a Godzilla movie. However, creative differences with the producers on that project, probably involving money, had him jumping free into the wind to direct a movie about hard blowing wind if he so chose. He chose. And then he ran off his crew: mutiny! Lots of crew members on the production of *Twister* quit because they could not stand working with Jan de Bont and his choices. At times the actors weren't too happy either as their injuries began piling up during production.

The rock band Van Halen made a song to headline the *Twister* soundtrack. The song called *Humans Being* is not very good. The tile is laughable in my opinion. When I was a teen soundtracks to movies were a big deal, lyrical song based not the orchestral, and I had a large collection from records, to cassette tapes, to CDs, but I cannot say that I ever owned the soundtrack to *Twister*. In fact, I had never even heard of the song *Humans Being* until I looked up information about the soundtrack to write this paragraph.

1. *Independence Day* - Directed by Roland Emmerich, screenplay by Roland Emmerich and Dean Devlin. Domestic Box Office: $306,169,268

Aliens arrive to destroy Earth and humans decide to fight back, thus is the basic premise of the movie *Independence Day*. And that's all I needed to be interested. Dinosaurs and aliens grew up as a big fan of stories involving those, along with serial killers and paranormal happenings, and as an avid book reader I picked up a copy of *Independence Day* the book before checking out the film. Never read the book before the movie if you want to enjoy the movie. After I saw *Independence Day* at the theater my excitement turned to disappointment and it was all because I had read the book first and the events were all either too familiar or off. Over the years I would forget the spell that the book cast over me, however, and enjoy the movie much more.

The concept for the film is said to have originated between director Roland Emmerich and writer Dean Devlin after they worked together on the 1994 released film *Stargate*. In fact, a fun story is that the idea may have been birthed during an interview while promoting Stargate, with talk of alien existence coming up and Emmerich pondering what it might be like to wake up one day to see massive spaceships taking over the sky. He then is said to have turned to Dean Devlin at his side and said, "I think I've got the idea for our next movie."

Independence Day is the movie that truly took actor Will Smith from television actor, *The Fresh Prince of Bel-Air*, to A-list Hollywood superstar. The action film *Bad Boys* had already been released and enjoyed by many of us in the previous year, but the hero that Smith got to play while fighting the aliens in *Independence Day* is the rocket fuel that launched him fully. He stood out in the ensemble.

Bill Pullman plays the president of the United States giving the key inspirational speech, overdone, yet tasty and impactful, of the film. One of the screenwriters, Dean Devlin, was friends with actor Kevin Spacey and actually wrote the role for him. The movie studio balked at casting Spacey in the role, deeming him not leading man material.

The cast of *Independence Day* is packed full of recognizable names and faces, and I will commence with listing some names now: Jeff Goldblum, Mary McDonnell, Judd Hirsch, Robert Loggia, Randy Quaid, James Rebhorn, Harvey Fierstein, James Duval, Vivica A. Fox, Mae Whitman, Harry Connick Jr., and many more that I shall not type out. I will draw some extra attention to the name James Duvall for the purpose of pointing out that he acted in the movie *American Romance* that I originally wrote and originally mentioned in a paragraph in this book about *Twister*. The character that James Duvall played in *American Romance* was a critical component of the script, yet when the movie exited post-production they completely edited him out. I don't know why. I wasn't invited to take part in the shooting of the film or to visit the set. In all honesty, when I watched the finished version of *American Romance* I was confused as to what the heck was even going on.

As a film representing the era of the 90s I feel like *Independence Day* does a strong job. I recently watched it before embarking on this book journey and felt like it has stood the test of time for what it was probably meant to be. They took too long to make the sequel *Independence Day*: *Resurgence*, released in 2016, and it is not as good a movie. However, after watching the sequel and its predecessor I could not help but think about how if they had put the sequel out right after the original with the 2016 special effects capabilities, good grief: our teenage minds would have been blown. The sequel would have been awesome in the 90s, just wasn't awesome in the not-90s.

Independence Day won the Oscar Award for Best Visual Effects in 1997. Another major award for the film was the Grammy that David Arnold took home for Best Instrumental Composition Written for a Motion Picture or for Television.

1997

10. *Tomorrow Never Dies* - Directed by Roger Spottiswoode, screenplay by Bruce Feirstein. Domestic Box Office: $125,304,276

Ugh. More James Bond. The James Bond franchise just doesn't interest me. The Bond movies of the 90s were possibly propped up by the nostalgia of people with original Bond film collections that had already been wooed by his return in *Goldeneye*, but mostly at the theater I'm thinking the advertised stunt set pieces were what justified the ticket prices and packed the seats. Currently superhero movies are the main box office draw in America and one could say James Bond was a superhero of the 90s. A British superhero it seems relevant to point out.

I saw *Tomorrow Never Dies*, probably even saw it at the movie theater, but I do not remember a single thing from the movie nor do I feel compelled to watch it again. The most interesting thing about the James Bond movies to me is the title song that they release for each one. On *Tomorrow Never Dies* that song was *Tomorrow Never Dies* performed by Sheryl Crow.

A part of the reason I feel compelled to point out my disinterest in James Bond films is because I know that the series has a large following and James Bond fans deserve a better write up about one of the entries in said films. The films carved out a section in history for themselves and I'm not going to say it was not earned or that people who enjoy the films are any less viable when it comes to opinions or comparing entertainment tastes.

The plot for *Tomorrow Never Dies* was an original one written for the film, not based off of a James Bond book. The writing process is said to have been a never ending one with lots of folks taking a crack at it and having disagreements all the way through the actual shooting of the film. I guess after all of the thoughts were whirled together it was decided that an evil media mogul trying to start World War 3 made the most sense. Now bring out the sexy ladies and explosions!

Some of the sexy lady duties of the film fell to actress Teri Hatcher. She was actually three months pregnant during filming. Now you can go back and see the seduction with that in mind. Ooo, a steamy bun in the oven scene.

Actress Michelle Yeoh was the lead "Bond Girl" for *Tomorrow Never Dies*, a solid casting choice, as she is not really the damsel in distress type, more of a "butt-kicking wants to do her own stunts" type of actor, not that I am trying to typecast her. The birth name of Michelle Yeoh was Yang Zi Qiong.

The video game version of *Tomorrow Never Dies* did not receive the acclaim that *Goldeneye* did.

9. *My Best Friend's Wedding* - Directed by P.J. Hogan, screenplay by Ronald Bass. Domestic Box Office: $127,120,029

My Best Friend's Wedding, starring Julia Roberts, Cameron Diaz, Dermot Mulroney, and Rupert Everett, is a romantic comedy that manages to appeal to those that enjoy the general formula of such features, yet tweaks the formula at the same time. If you have not seen it I am perhaps ruining the movie for you right here and now by pointing out that the leading lady does not get exactly what she is after in the movie and more than not is technically the antagonist not the protagonist, but all of the happy life lessons and crap are still there to swallow in the end.

The plot is about a woman that realizes that she is in love with her male friend. He is getting married and she needs to break up the wedding so that they can be together because naturally they are the ones really meant to be together. Romantic musings and comedy ensue, and Julia Roberts was still flashing her big smile for the box office gold in 1997.

James Newton Howard was nominated for Best Original Musical or Comedy Score for his work on *My Best Friend's Wedding*. He has been nominated for Oscars a total of eight times with the other seven nominations coming from musical work on: *The Prince of Tides*, *The Fugitive*, *Junior*, *One Fine Day*, *The Village*, *Michael Clayton*, and *Defiance*. The nominations for *Junior* and *One Fine Day* were in the Best Original Song category not for the overall film scores.

The screenwriter for *My Best Friend's Wedding*, Ronald Bass also has screenwriting credit on the films *Rain Man*, *Sleeping with the Enemy*, *Dangerous Minds*, *How Stella Got Her Groove Back*, and many more. Looking at the IMDb page of Ronald Bass right now there appears to be an announced, though not yet realized, television movie event surrounding the *My Best Friend's Wedding* property. It is listed as a "follow up."

Director P.J. Hogan directed *Muriel's Wedding* prior to *My Best Friend's Wedding* and it is possible he wanted a break from weddings after that. In 2003 he directed *Peter Pan* and in 2009 *Confessions of a Shopaholic*. *Confessions of a Shopaholic* was not well received upon release in part due to the financial crisis in America weighing heavy on everyone's minds, but the film, starring Isla Fisher, is funny and worth a watch in my opinion.

8. *Star Wars (Special Edition)* - Directed by George Lucas, screenplay by George Lucas. Domestic Box Office: $138,257,865

In movie history the *Star Wars* science fiction franchise is one of the most epic with the first film releasing in 1977. George Lucas decided to go back and tinker with his old films applying new technologies. Thus, *Star Wars: Episode IV - A New Hope* also known as *Star Wars* was released into theaters after the tinkering as *Star Wars (Special Edition.)*

The cost to rework shots and to rework the sound on the original *Star Wars* is said to have cost in the ballpark of ten million dollars. Therefore, the retouching ended up costing near the same amount of money as it cost to shoot the entire original film to begin with. If you had made *Star Wars*, already an epic revenue generating success, would you spend ten million bucks tinkering with it some more or maybe buy something else to play with?

When I was a child I liked the original *Star Wars* trilogy and as an adult I have seen both the originals and the Special Edition versions, and I'm not really a fan of any of them. Old *Star Wars*, new *Star Wars*, they're all kind of boring to me. And while I'm at it, I'm not a *Star Trek* fan either.

The process to make *Star Wars* a Special Edition involved digitally re-mastering the image and sound with extensive clean-up and restoration work. George Lucas also made a number of changes to the film to, as he stated: "finish the film the way it was meant to be." One of the main goals was to freshen up the elder films so that they could be viewed by a younger audience about to be presented with a whole new trilogy. George Lucas wanted the old films to look as good as the next ones coming out.

The original 1977 version of *Star Wars* was selected for preservation in the National Film Registry of the United States Library of Congress in 1989. In 2014, the National Film Registry still did not have a copy of the 1977 film and it is said that George Lucas refused to submit a copy, stating that he no longer authorized the release of the theatrical version. He offered them the altered 1997 Special Edition release, but the Registry refused it as the first published version must be accepted. The Library of Congress itself probably has a copy of the film, however, as a copy was said to have been obtained when George Lucas initiated a copyright deposit on it back in the 70s.

The character Han Solo in the original Star Wars shoots and kills a character called Greedo. Fans of the film used to debate whether Solo or Greedo fired the first shot in their confrontation. George Lucas altered that famous scene in the 1997 version of the movie making it clear that Greedo initiated the shooting. Diehard fans of the original film were not pleased with the answer given by way of Lucas digitally altering history and perhaps he caved in to the complaints because in the 2004 DVD release of the film the scene was altered yet again, showing both men firing at the same time. So, now you've got several different versions of the movie out there with different things happening in the same scene, what a confusing mess, count me in with anyone that thinks George Lucas should have left the movie alone in the first place. Let your art speak for itself for all of time. If you want to freshen up the movie jump on the Hollywood reboot train!

I won't go on talking about the many other changes to Star Wars for the Special Edition. I think that it is all silly. Sending the film back into theaters so that a new audience can experience the original and the old audience can enjoy some nostalgia makes sense and sound interesting to me but nitpicking at it after it has already cemented its legacy: waste of money.

The original *Star Wars* film received ten Oscar award nominations and won six Oscars. A special achievement Oscar was also given out to Ben Burtt for his work in the industry and on *Star Wars* as a creator of sounds: lightsabers, Yoda's voice, and Chewbacca's voice, oh my!

7. *Good Will Hunting* - Directed by Gus Van Sant, screenplay by Matt Damon and Ben Affleck. Domestic Box Office: $138,433,435

Good Will Hunting, directed by Gus Van Sant, stars Robin Williams, Matt Damon, Ben Affleck, Minnie Driver, and Stellan Skarsgård. Affleck and Damon wrote the script.

The film follows Will Hunting, a blue-collar worker kind of guy, a Boston tough kind of guy, an unrecognized genius kind of guy, who as part of a deferred prosecution agreement after assaulting a police officer, becomes the client of a therapist and studies advanced mathematics with a renowned professor. During his therapy sessions Will re-evaluates his relationships with friends, his girlfriend, and himself, confronting his past and facing his future.

At one point in the movie they say the line: "How do you like them apples?" The line is delivered with a strong Boston accent and after the film became popular that line was being quoted by people all across America with varying degrees of success in capturing the accent. When I was a kid popular movie quotes were a seriously annoying thing. I don't seem to come across people spewing quotes on repeat in my adulthood as much.

Out of a total of nine nominations two Oscar awards were won by people involved with the film. The award for Best Supporting Actor went to Robin Williams while Ben Affleck and Matt Damon got the honor of Best Screenplay Written Directly for the Screen. The script also won the Golden Globe for Best Script in that same year.

Matt Damon and Ben Affleck didn't just spin out a script and "nail it" the first time with regard to *Good Will Hunting*. They got some mentor style help from various other folks in the industry and reworked the material to make it the drama that it became. At one point the script was written as a thriller involving Will Hunting trying to outsmart government entities trying to recruit him into working for them. A rumor, denied by writer William Goldman, is that writer William Goldman either rewrote the script or wrote the entire thing himself to begin with. Goldman says that he looked at the script and only consulted with some opinion and advice, did not do any of the writing.

Castle Rock originally bought the script in order to produce it, however, Damon and Affleck did not see eye to eye with the company and Castle Rock sold the project on over to Miramax. The deal with Miramax was said to have been helped along by director Kevin Smith who declined to take on the directing duties himself.

While *Good Will Hunting* is strong on Boston aspects and did do some filming in Boston, there was a large chunk of the movie actually shot in Canada.

The music of Elliot Smith is featured predominantly throughout the soundtrack of the film, with the actual musical score itself being the work of Danny Elfman. Smith's song *Miss Misery* was nominated for the Best Original Song Oscar losing out to the song *My Heart Will Go On* from the movie *Titanic*. Elliot Smith is a musical artist with the distinct legacy of not only making music that people to this day still adore, but for also having stabbed himself to death. He died in 2003 at the age of thirty-four from two apparently self-inflicted stab wounds to his chest. Conspiracy theories do swirl around the death as the released autopsy report did not officially rule out homicide. Elliot Smith had been arguing with his girlfriend and she was in the home at the time of his death.

6. *As Good as It Gets* - Directed by James L. Brooks, screenplay by Mark Andrus and James L. Brooks. Domestic Box Office: $148,478,011

A slow burn in terms of earning at the box office, *As Good as It Gets* did not open at theaters earning a crazy sum, but audiences did begin to find it and that helped empower it for competition in the Academy Awards the following year.

As a dramatic character piece, something rare to find studios giving much of a budget to these days, the film gave the actors the framework within to show off their craft and the results were golden statues for the two leads. Best Actress in a Leading Role went to Helen Hunt and Best Actor in a Leading Role went to Jack Nicholson, a rare feat in that the two leads from the same film won the main acting trophies of the night. Greg Kinnear also stars in the film and was nominated for the Best Actor in a Supporting Role award, losing out to Robin Williams from *Good Will Hunting*.

Some other cast members of note include Cuba Gooding Jr., Skeet Ulrich, Shirley Knight, and Yeardley Smith with appearances also made by Missi Pyle, Jamie Kennedy, Maya Rudolph, and Julie Benz. Also of fun note is that you can find some name directors appearing in the film, Lawrence Kasdan, Harold Ramis, Todd Solondz, Shane Black all made appearances.

As Good as It Gets is about a misanthropic and obsessive-compulsive novelist, a waitress with an ill son, and a homosexual artist that has been robbed and needs the novelist, his neighbor, to care for his dog, and these three characters and the dog interact and touch one another in the life lessons sort of way that people in movies do.

I did not see *As Good as It Gets* at the movie theater. However, I did own the movie on VHS. We lived in a small town but would sometimes travel half an hour to forty-five minutes away to a bigger city for some grocery shopping. In the bigger city they had a Blockbuster store and I would peruse the discounted, former rental VHS tape section any time that I had some money. *As Good as It Gets* is one of the movies I picked up for a few bucks. I watched it many times, but as I think about the movie today, I have no inkling why other than I happened to own it. There isn't any one aspect of the movie that sticks with me in terms of having been a dramatic inspiration in any way. Maybe I was just ogling Helen Hunt's butt crack over and over again? Because when I think about *As Good as It Gets* for some reason her scene where she shows off her butt crack is the first thing that pops into mind. Sorry female readers for having once again transported you into the lustful, movie consuming mind of a teenage male.

5. *Air Force One* - Directed by Wolfgang Petersen, screenplay by Andrew W. Marlowe. Domestic Box Office: $172,956,409

Terrorists hijack air force one, the personal jet of the U.S. President, thus the title *Air Force One*, and the President onboard fights back. A strong earner at the box office some people point to *Air Force*

One as one of the best action movies of the 90s. As an action movie fan growing up through the 80s and 90s I could have cared less about the movie.

Harrison Ford stars as the President in *Air Force One*. The actor, when he tells the tale of how he landed the role, thanks Mr. Kevin Costner. The script was apparently supposed to be made into a movie starring Costner, but Costner's schedule was too busy, and he suggested that Harrison Ford should be the man to lead the free world and fight the terrorists.

Harrison Ford and *Air Force One* made headlines in America while Donald Trump was campaigning to become President. Donald Trump stated that the President portrayed by Harrison Ford in the movie was one of his favorites for being so heroic. When asked about the praise from Trump Harrison Ford quipped back in the press with something along the lines of, "It was a movie. It's not like that in real life, but how would you know?" And then I guess Donald Trump got the last laugh and actually became the President of the United States of America. Now, let's imagine a movie in which Donald Trump fights off terrorists that have hijacked his jet. Does this movie make you want to laugh or cry?

Glenn Close plays the Vice President in *Air Force One* and while her character did not get to kick butt on the flight, she made sure that her character was not weak. A scene in the script called for the Vice President to cry and Glenn Close refused to weep as she not only felt it demeaning to the strength of the character, but to women in general.

Gary Oldman portrays the lead bad guy in *Air Force One* and the role got him nominated as Best Villain at the MTV movie awards. He was also nominated at that same awards show, along with Harrison Ford, for Best Fight. Mike Myers took home the Best Villain award for his work in *Austin Powers: International Man of Mystery* and the Best Fight award went to Will Smith vs Cockroach in *Men in Black*.

There weren't any acting nominations for the cast when it came Academy Award time, however, the film *Air Force One* was represented with nominations in the categories of Best Sound and Best Film Editing.

Director Wolfgang Peterson also helmed the films *Troy, In the Line of Fire, The Perfect Storm, Enemy Mine* and *Das Boot*; *Das Boot* earned him two Oscar nominations. My favorite film thus far directed by Wolfgang Peterson would have to be the 1984 fantasy film *The NeverEnding Story*.

4. *Liar Liar* - Directed by Tom Shadyac, screenplay by Paul Guay and Stephen Mazur. Domestic Box Office: $181,410,615

After his son makes a birthday wish a lawyer that lies constantly finds that for twenty-four hours it is impossible for him to tell a lie, this is the premise of *Liar Liar* starring Jim Carrey.

Considering how wacky Jim Carrey and director Tom Shadyac got when they had worked together previously on *Ace Ventura: Pet Detective* and then apart they were doing things such as *Dumb and Dumber* and the fat jokes of *The Nutty Professor*, many saw *Liar Liar* as the duo coming back together to make something more grounded, more family palatable. Jim Carrey still pulled his crazy faces, made funny voices, and in my opinion the movie was still pretty darn wacky. However, I can agree with the opinion that there was something to the formula that made *Liar Liar* a bit more middle-lane commercial. The movie seemed like a safer sort of comedy and while I did watch the movie several times and like it well enough, the creative zing was not exactly as flavorful to me. The movie did not become one of my favorites by any means, however, I am sure that Jim Carrey thinks of it fondly considering he made upwards of $20,000,000 for starring in it.

Maura Tierney plays the estranged wife to Jim Carrey's lead in *Liar Liar*. Even though she has a film career as an actor, Maura Tierney is probably more well-known from her work on television shows such as *NewsRadio*, *ER*, and *The Affair*. As of this time she has been nominated for two Emmys in her career and in 2016 won a Golden Globe Award for her supporting role work on *The Affair*.

Jim Carrey is daddy, Fletcher Reede, Maura Tierney is mommy, Audrey Reede, and their wish making son in the film, Max Reede, is played by Justin Cooper. Cooper was making his way through the industry as a child actor on television before *Liar Liar* came along and made him a child actor in a major motion picture. After his feature debut in *Liar Liar* it doesn't look like Justin got a whole lot of major movie work. He did land a big lead as Dennis the Menace in the direct to video *Dennis the Menace Strikes Again* in 1998. Other than that it appears his acting mostly went back to television and then slowed to a halt by 2003. As of this writing the latest news I see on him has him working as a producer on a sports radio program.

Cary Elwes of *The Princess Bride* fame is also in *Liar Liar*, but if I'm being honest I'm really just writing little blurbs about the cast in order to get down the list to Jennifer Tilly who plays the role of Samantha Cole. She seems interesting, I want to learn about her.

Born Jennifer Ellen Chan with a father of Chinese descent and mother of Irish and various other descents that are probably inappropriate for me to brush over in importance, but I'm going CliffsNotes on this biography. I mean CliffsNotes as slang as opposed to officially being sponsored by CliffsNotes. The people at the company Cliff notes do not sponsor nor have any affiliation with my discussion of Jennifer Tilly. CliffsNotes, if you aren't familiar, are study guides that abbreviate things for students to help them better understand or skip out on the dense reading assignment they were actually supposed to do. Jennifer Tilly as far as I know is not affiliated with or a sponsor of CliffsNotes. However, CliffsNotes, maybe you should consider an advertising campaign starring Jennifer Tilly? Oh, man, the length of this paragraph is not very CliffsNotes style at all by this point. Then again, I've never actually used or read a CliffsNotes product and can't vouch for their style of information delivering. Where was I? Yes, so, Jennifer Ellen Chan was born in America, but after her parents' divorce spent a good deal of time being raised in Canada.

Jennifer Tilly has siblings, one younger sibling is Meg Tilly, a Golden Globe winning, and Oscar nominated actress; those awards were for her work in 1985's *Agnes of God*. Jennifer Tilly is no slouch in the awards department herself. She was Oscar nominated for her role in the 1994 Woody Allen movie *Bullets Over Broadway*.

When I think of Jennifer Tilly in movies the first film that comes to mind is the 1996 film *Bound*. *Bound* was the feature directorial debut of the Wachowski Brothers, who over time went through a transition from male entities into females now known as Lana Wachowski and Lilly Wachowski.

After *Bound*, the next film series to flicker into my head is the sequels to *Child's Play* that Jennifer Tilly starred in. She voices Tiffany the evil doll bride of Chucky.

Before any movie roles come to mind, however, the first association I have when you mention Jennifer Tilly is her distinctive voice. Her voice is unique, a voice that can balance between being "cartoon character sounding" and seductive. If you want sexy you watch her in *Bound*. If you want the cartoon you can hear her voicing the character Bonnie in the popular show *Family Guy* or she also did voice work in the Pixar hit *Monsters, Inc*. But, then you've got *Bride of Chucky* and her voice coming out of a doll and perhaps that just best captured both sides to her special voice.

Some fans of Jennifer Tilly may not even be fans of her due to her acting career because she has also made a name for herself as a professional poker player. Televised poker events are watched by some folks just like a sport. I've never watched poker, but from what I understand in reading about it, Tilly is not just an entertaining persona to have sit at the table, she competes and wins.

So, there you have it, Jennifer Tilly was the fourth highest earning film of 1997.

3. *The Lost World: Jurassic Park* - Directed by Steven Spielberg, screenplay by David Koepp. Domestic Box Office: $229,086,679

After the success of the first *Jurassic Park* movie it was pretty much decided that a sequel would be made. Sure, they took a little bit of time to get around to it, but rich people don't have to rush things if they don't want to they've got to spend some time lounging around their pools to justify them as purchases. The author of the original film's book source material, Michael Crichton, is said to have not been keen on writing a sequel to *Jurassic Park*, however, with the film going to go forth, Crichton indeed came up with an idea and published a book. *The Lost World: Jurassic Park* film, however, differs from the book in many ways and Crichton was not involved in the screenplay process this time around.

When *The Lost World: Jurassic Park* released I was excited. After sitting through it at the theater I thought the film was "okay," but my opinion of it only got worse after seeing it a few more times. As of 2018 and having seen all of the *Jurassic Park* films, the first one remains a magical thing in my mind and the rest of them I can do without. *Jurassic World* is a decent watch, just not "magical."

The Lost World: Jurassic Park makes Jeff Goldblum's Ian Malcolm the lead character with Julianne Moore as Sarah Harding joining him in misadventure. The dinosaur action starts out on a jungle island, but by the end a T-Rex gets to run loose in San Diego (many of the shots in that section of the movie were actually shot in Burbank not San Diego.) The film is not without some cool cinematic "moments," but overall just wasn't compelling to me I guess.

Director Steven Spielberg took a break from directing before returning to the craft for this film, but in later interviews would himself talk about how "disenchanted" he was with *The Lost World: Jurassic Park* while on the set. He doesn't seem to have found the movie all that interesting either.

2. *Men in Black* - Directed by Barry Sonnenfeld, screenplay by Ed Solomon. Domestic Box Office: $250,690,539

Maybe dinosaurs did not come through for me in 1997, but aliens were there to pick up the slack. The first *Men in Black* film entertained me and was fun enough that I made sure to own a VHS copy later on.

The concept of "men in black" was familiar to me prior to the movie being released. I had a creepy book about alien abductions in my collection that spoke of weird men dressed in black showing up under bizarre circumstances. The "men in black" were considered quite sinister in those tales, not government agents protecting the universe. Tales of "men in black" getting involved with people that saw UFOs or aliens may have also been featured on the television show *Unsolved Mysteries*. I recall some spooky show that discussed them and considering I watched that show frequently as a kid, I'm betting it was *Unsolved Mysteries* that helped enhance the "men in black" nightmares I had. Specifically, I recall, not sure whether from book or television program, one story about "men in black" arriving after a UFO sighting and the men were potentially not human with visible wires running below the flesh into their necks; that mental picture always stuck with me. The feature film did a good job of making "men in black" less scary.

As of this writing there have been two sequels made and I know I saw the second film, but actually cannot remember if I have watched the third one. The second film did not connect with me in the same way as the first. A cartoon series based off of the comics and movie ran for four seasons, but I never tuned in to that. A fourth film is in production and perhaps already finished and showing at a theater near you as you read this. Why are you reading books?! Go to the movies!

Men in Black stars Will Smith and Tommy Lee Jones as agents that monitor the secret world of alien activity on Earth and try to stop any activities that might put people, planets, or galaxies in danger. The film is a science fiction adventure meets buddy action and comedy formula. Linda Fiorentino, Vincent D'Onofrio, Rip Torn, and Tony Shalhoub also star in the film. The original source material that the film is based off of is the comic book *The Men in Black* created and written by Lowell Cunningham with art by Sandy Carruthers.

Men in Black was nominated for three Academy Awards and won for Best Makeup. Best Art-Set Decoration was one of the categories where it lost, as well as in the Best Original Musical or Comedy

Score where Danny Elfman's score lost out to Anne Dudley's score for *The Fully Monty*.

1. *Titanic* - Directed by James Cameron, screenplay by James Cameron. Domestic Box Office: $600,788,188

James Cameron makes BIG movies and with 1997's *Titanic* he stayed afloat at the top of Hollywood's echelon of power. At the 1998 Academy Awards Titanic took home the top prize of Best Picture along with Best Director, Best Cinematographer, Best Dramatic Score, Best Original Song, and six other golden trophies for a grand total of eleven Oscar wins. None of the Oscars went to any of the actors, though Kate Winslet and Gloria Stuart were nominated.

Titanic follows a young man played by Leonardo DiCaprio, Jack, as he rides on the ill-fated ship of movie title name. Kate Winslet plays Rose the young aristocrat that falls in love with Jack during the voyage all to the dismay of the fellow named Cal that is played by Billy Zane. Jack and Rose are a classic pair of lovers mismatched with regard to social standings, she from the upper crust, he from the less-wealthy wrong side of the tracks. I'll assume that you paid attention in history class and the following is not a spoiler: the ship sinks. The grand sweeping romance goes right down into the dark, cold sea with disaster film grandeur.

The story in *Titanic* does not just give you a window into a past of historical fiction, but also jumps forward in time as the tale is told in order to feature some people that are exploring the wreckage of the ship. It is in these sections of the film that Bill Paxton and Gloria Stuart do their acting work.

North Americans were not the only audiences in love with *Titanic*. The movie conquered all movies on Earth in earnings despite its lengthy run time of around one-hundred and ninety-four minutes. Personally, my butt fell asleep in the theater. I only got swept up in Titanic mania in order to be "in the know" in terms of pop culture and the world around me. I did not actually swoon over the film, however, and do not count myself an avid fan of it. Heck, at the age I was during its height of popularity I'm sure I did my best to rebel against its popularity and talk the movie down. Cool special effects? Nah, I saw the wires. Rated Pg-13? Someone bribed the ratings board, I seen Kate Winslet getting her portrait painted in the buff! Darn, ratings board bribers shouldn't be rewarded. I'm sure that I also debated with anyone paying attention, no one was, over a certain death near the end of the movie where one person was floating on some wood, a door turned raft if I recall, and could have scooted on over to let someone else up on it thereby saving them from freezing to death in the water. If you know what I'm talking about, James Cameron wants everyone know that it was logical, and he tested it himself that the door could not have held a second person and stayed afloat. Sure, sure.

The television show Mythbusters did agree with Cameron about the buoyancy of the door not being able to support two people. However, they also point out that the person on the door could have used their life jacket, tied said jacket to the bottom of the door, and possibly rigged said door to be more seaworthy for a second passenger.

Dives down to the real wreckage of the *Titanic* were budgeted into the film, footage James Cameron insisted would be much needed and cheaper than building models. It really seems that the director's inspiration for making the movie came from his desire to go explore the actual wreckage with the voyage paid for by a movie studio.

Celine Dion sang the Oscar winning song *My Heart Will Go On* for the film. The song, like the movie, would rule over charts of success around the world. The music for the song was composed by the composer of the film's score, James Horner. The lyrics for the song were written by Will Jennings. My *Heart Will Go On* won Record of the Year at the Grammy Awards, as well as Song of the Year, and Best Song Written Specifically for a Motion Picture or Television. Celine Dion won the Grammy for Best Female Pop Vocal Performance for belting out the tune. The song also took home Best Original Song at the Golden Globes.

Aside from Celine Dion singing her lungs out, another key thing that people always think of when they think of Titanic is the moment when Jack exclaims "I'm king of the world!" Supposedly Leonardo DiCaprio made up that line himself in the moment. Fans should celebrate him for it, critics should curse him.

Titanic, with re-releases to theaters over the years, has grossed over two billion dollars worldwide.

1998

10. *Patch Adams* - Directed by Tom Shadyac, screenplay by Steve Oedekerk. Domestic Box Office: $135,026,902

By 1998 I was too dour a teenager to let the yammering Robin Williams entertain me like in the olden days of *Mrs. Doubtfire*. I did what I could to avoid the movie *Patch Adams*, not caring about a guy trying to become a doctor with his bedside manner involving wearing a clown nose and his insistence that laughter is the best medicine.

Once again Tom Shadyac directed a movie that won out at the box office. Critics were not very kind to *Patch Adams*, yet, voyaging into dramatic territory with comedic elements, without Jim Carrey, Tom Shadyac crafted a film that in my opinion worked for the average joe type of movie fan. Kids my age in rural Missouri were touched by the heart of the film and it was indeed popular and spoken of by many, regardless of my own pre-judgment and refusal to buy a ticket, the world of movies once again proved not to revolve around my tastes and opinions.

Patch Adams is a semi-biographical film based in part on the book *Gesundheit: Good Health is a Laughing Matter* by Patch Adams and Maureen Mylander. Mr. Patch Adams himself disapproved of the film and the liberties it took with his story. Real life was altered to make the movie more commercial with story events and characters being fabricated to induce either drama or laughs. Over the years the real doctor has spoken out against the film and how it failed to fund clinics as someone may have promised him. In speeches Patch Adams has spoken of the large paychecks given out in Hollywood, specifically calling out Robin Williams at one point for receiving $20 million to play him, yet not donating the money like the true Patch Adams would. Patch Adams outlived Robin Williams and after the comedian's death did express gratitude toward the actor for portraying him, speaking only kind words about the type of person Robin Williams was and how the influence of the movie did actually help his work in the medical field. So, I guess the movie was a blessing and a curse to the real guy it is based on? I don't know. Personally, I don't think a person can trust the opinion of a suicidal doctor that bounces into the room dressed like a clown. Ha!

Marc Shaiman received an Oscar nomination, the sole nomination for the film, for the musical score of *Patch Adams*. He did not win. Stephen Warbeck took home the award for his work on the score of *Shakespeare in Love*.

Monica Potter played the fictional friend and love interest of Patch Adams in *Patch Adams*. Whenever I think of Monica Potter two roles come to mind, neither one being Cairn from Patch Adams. First, she goes down as being a part of the legendary action film *Con Air*. She was Tricia Poe, lady love of Nicolas Cage's Cameron Poe. Secondly I remember her being in the lackluster thriller *Along Came a Spider* alongside Morgan Freeman. The previous thriller with Morgan Freeman starring as Alex Cross, *Kiss the Girls*, was the superior film in my opinion.

Philip Seymour Hoffman is also featured in the movie *Patch Adams*. He would go on to die in February of 2014, the same year that Robin Williams took his own life. Robin Williams was a summer death, dying in August 2014.

9. *Godzilla* - Directed by Roland Emmerich, screenplay by Dean Devlin and Roland Emmerich. Domestic Box Office: $136,314,294

Puff Daddy and the soundtrack for *Godzilla* were all over MTV to promote the movie. The music became unavoidable in my life with my music television consuming habits of the time, however, I avoided going to see *Godzilla* at the movie theater quite easily. One would think that the concept would appeal to someone with a love for dinosaurs, but, I guess giant lizard monster and dinosaur just did not compute in my brain as being one in the same. Also, the lead of the movie was Matthew Broderick and I did not find myself drawn into wanting to go see Matthew Broderick movies.

The rights to make a *Godzilla* film in America came about due to someone going to a meeting with Sony executives in order to try and get a live-action Mr. Magoo movie made. I want to poke fun at the fact that someone wanted to make a movie based off of the blind, bumbling slapstick antics of the cartoon *Mr. Magoo*, but not only did someone want to make such a movie: they did. Leslie Nielsen starred as Mr. Magoo in the 1997 released film *Mr. Magoo.*

Anyway, legend has it that *Mr. Magoo* is what got the fellow in the door and he sold them on *Godzilla*. Logically, to me, it seems like *Godzilla* should have been the lead into the meeting and then in order to get *Godzilla* you also have to make the movie *Mr. Magoo*. It seems that Hollywood studios were actually passing on *Godzilla*, including TriStar pictures which is a division of Sony. The pitch got presented higher up in the ranks of Sony executives, however, and Sony then bought the rights and set the picture up for the naysaying TriStar to handle.

The soundtrack to *Godzilla*, though I mentioned Puff Daddy, also known as Sean "Diddy" Combs or Sean John Combs or P. Diddy or Diddy or Puffy or the artist formerly known as Puff Daddy or Diddy or whatever, was mostly fueled by alternative rock music. The Puff Daddy track that hit the music video scene as a strong single, *Come with Me*, combined Puffy with rock legend Jimmy Page. Some of the other bands featured on the soundtrack: Foo Fighters, Green Day, Rage Against the Machine, Silverchair, Fuel, Days of the New, Jamiroquai, The Wallflowers, Ben Folds Five, and Fuzzbubble. Fuzzbubble? They were one of the rare rock bands signed to Bad Boy Records run by the aforementioned Mr. Puff n Stuff.

At one point director Jan de Bont, whose 1996 film *Twister* came in second place at the North American box office behind Roland Emmerich's *Independence Day*, was hired to helm *Godzilla*. The script and vision that Jan de Bont presented, however, never moved the production into the shooting phase and a new approach was sought. Roland Emmerich, winner of the box office crown in 1996, took over and helped craft a new approach and script. Roland has said that he wasn't a real fan of the original *Godzilla* and set out to reinvent the creature in an attempt to not be as campy.

In the end, Emmerich directed something that brought in box office dollars, but did not impress his usual critics. The director was prepared for the critical assessment of his work, however, going so far as to include some characters in the movie that made fun of the most famous movie critic duo of the 90s: Siskel and Ebert. In *Godzilla* there is a character called Mayor Ebert who squabbles with his assistant Gene. Siskel and Ebert were not impressed with the film or amused by the jab at them, giving the movie two thumbs down.

8. *Deep Impact* - Directed by Mimi Leder, screenplay by Bruce Joel Rubin and Michael Tolkin. Domestic Box Office: $140,464,664

Disaster movies were in style and *Deep Impact* was the inferior "space object crashing into Earth" movie of 1998 in my opinion. It was another film that failed to capture my attention with regard to wooing me into buying a ticket for a big screen presentation.

In *Deep Impact* a comet is in route to hit Earth and unless humans can destroy it first death and destruction are imminent. The movie follows an ensemble cast of characters as they deal with impending doom. Actors featured in the film include Tèa Leoni, Robert Duvall, Elijah Wood, Vanessa Redgrave, Morgan Freeman, Maximilian Schell, James Cromwell, Jon Favreau, Ron Eldard, Blair Underwood, Leelee Sobieski, and Dougray Scott.

In 1998 *Deep Impact* released before the movie *Armageddon* and even had higher earnings on opening weekend. Yet, I think history shows that audiences preferred *Armageddon* in the long run. I know I did. I got excited to go see *Armageddon*, I did not care about *Deep Impact* at all. The reason for the differences in success is probably due to the vastly different tones of the films. *Armageddon* came out guns blazing with an action movie pedigree and to an Aerosmith soundtrack while *Deep Impact* tried pairing a more dense, emotional soap opera with its disaster plot. The cast members are also a big difference between the films in terms of who is who and who do people have interest in going to watch at the theater. I have watched both films in 2018 and I still enjoy *Armageddon*, but not *Deep Impact*.

Prior to *Deep Impact*, director Mimi Leder's film *The Peacemaker* was released. *The Peacemaker* is an action/ thriller that along with *Batman and Robin* in 1997 helped push along George Clooney's transition from being best-known as a doctor character on the television show *ER* to being a cinema star. After *Deep Impact*, Mimi Leder directed the sappy drama *Pay It Forward* which she would go on to describe as a movie that put her out of favor with the Hollywood powers of the time due to it not being a massive success.

Steven Spielberg almost directed *Deep Impact*. The project is said to have its roots going all the way back to the 70s with some producers trying to remake the 1951 film *When World's Collide*. The project never got off of the ground, but the will to keep trying was strong and in the 90s Spielberg was approached. Initially Spielberg declined because he had the rights to the book *The Hammer of God* by Arthur C. Clarke and was developing it into a movie that he felt would be too similar of a concept. However, a meeting of the minds ended up having Spielberg mash his *The Hammer of God* in with the *When World's Collide* folks to make a movie together. Eventually the concepts were developed into *Deep Impact* without any of the original source material that inspired the process being credited for the end product. Spielberg ended up not directing the film due to having committed to working on the film *Amistad* and some people believe he bowed out of the responsibility due to it not being a secret that the competition film *Armageddon* would be aiming to

278

release in the same year. Steven Spielberg has an executive producer credit on *Deep Impact*.

In some not really related to this discussion, yet I'm going to force it in information. *When World's Collide* is also the name of a fun Powerman 5000 song that I suggest you go listen to.

E.L.E., as the movie *Deep Impact* taught us, stands for Extinction Level Event. If you ever come across any classified government papers discussing an impending E.L.E. you may want to start building a rocket or digging a deep bunker.

7. *Rush Hour* - Directed by Brett Ratner, screenplay by Jim Kouf and Ross LaManna. Domestic Box Office: $141,186,864

A buddy action comedy, *Rush Hour* stars Jackie Chan and Chris Tucker as mismatched personalities that have to team up in order to rescue the kidnapped daughter of a Chinese diplomat.

As soon as I hear the title *Rush Hour* in my head I hear the high-pitched voice of Chris Tucker yelling at Jackie Chan: "Do you understand the words that are coming out of my mouth?" The movie was a smashing success that spawned sequels, but I did not get fully onboard with the series and enjoy the ride. I found the humor of the films more annoying than not. I preferred Chris Tucker's loud personality in the movie *Friday* over his loud personality in *Rush Hour*.

As with the movie *Godzilla*, I found the soundtrack more entertaining than the film. The soundtrack to *Rush Hour* featured the song *"Can I Get A..."* performed by Jay-Z, Amil, and Ja Rule. If you seek out the song I suggest trying both the censored and uncensored versions of the track to decide which version is going to be your "jam." The song has a lot of fun bounce to it. Honestly, that's the only song on the soundtrack that I really thought was cool, but if you gave me the choice of getting to own the music video to that song or the full movie of *Rush Hour* for my entertainment media collection, I would probably choose the music video and song over the movie.

In 2016 *Rush Hour* became the basis of a television series starring Justin Hires and Jon Foo. It was canceled after one season.

6. *Dr. Dolittle* - Directed by Betty Thomas, screenplay by Nat Maudlin and Larry Levin. Domestic Box Office: $144,156,605

Dr. Dolittle is a comedy film starring Eddie Murphy as a doctor that can speak with animals. In 1967 there was a *Dr. Dolittle* film made starring Rex Harrison in the title role. Both films are inspired by a children's book series created by Hugh Lofting. The first book of the series was *The Story of Doctor Dolittle* published in 1920.

When I think *Dr. Dolittle* I immediately think of *The Nutty Professor*. Obviously both films star Eddie

Murphy and were popular within the 90s, but I think it also has to do with the red lettering and white backdrops used in some of the posters for both films. I feel like there was an attempt to bounce off of *The Nutty Professor*'s success as much as possible. It seems to have worked. The financial gains of the first film kept producers interested enough to generate four sequels, with more probably on the way. Eddie Murphy starred in the first two movies.

Betty Thomas, director of *Dr. Dolittle*, directed an interesting film released the previous year in the form of *Private Parts*. *Private Parts* is a biographical film about Howard Stern starring Howard Stern as Howard Stern. My friends and I did not rush to see *Dr. Dolittle*, but we watched *Private Parts* as soon as possible due to knowing it would contain naughty scenes involving female nudity. Nudity and sexual content aside, *Private Parts* is a solid movie. I mention *Private Parts*, not just to recommend another movie, but because it is interesting to see that Betty Thomas went from a film such as that to directing a family film. She followed up *Dr. Dolittle* with the Sandra Bullock film *28 Days* chronicling a women's experience at a drug and alcohol rehab facility.

Betty Thomas did not return to the director's chair for the *Dr. Dolittle* sequels. However, she did work with Eddie Murphy again in 2002 as she directed the action comedy *I Spy*. Owen Wilson co-starred with Eddie Murphy in that film and it has a few chuckle-worthy moments in it. *I Spy* was originally a television show in the 60s starring Robert Culp and Bill Cosby.

Directing movies isn't the only Hollywood skill of Betty Thomas. Aside from director and producer credits, she also has had success as an actress. For seven years in a row in the 80s she was nominated for a Best Supporting Actress Emmy due to her part as Lucille Bates in the show *Hill Street Blues*. She won for that role in 1985. She also won an Emmy in 1990 for her directing work on an episode of the show *Dream On*.

Eddie Murphy has a directing career also. Err, I mean, a directing credit. He wrote and directed the 1989 movie *Harlem Nights* starring himself and Richard Pryor. Eddie Murphy was nominated for Worst Screenplay and Worst Director at the 1990 Razzie Awards. He won for Worst Screenplay. *Harlem Nights* did get an Oscar nomination for Best Costume Design. Phyllis Dalton won that golden statue, however, for the costumes in *Henry V*. The only Academy Award nomination that Eddie Murphy has thus far received in acting came in 2007 for his supporting role in *Dreamgirls*. He did not win, but Jennifer Hudson from *Dreamgirls* went from being a contestant that lost *American Idol* to being an Oscar winner for Best Supporting Actress.

The musical soundtrack released for Dr. Dolittle had a lot of R & B tracks on it. Personally I liked the single "*Are You That Somebody?*" recorded by the artist Aaliyah. Aaliyah tragically died in a plane crash in 2001. She was only twenty-two years old.

5. *The Waterboy* - Directed by Frank Coraci, screenplay by Tim Herlihy and Adam Sandler. Domestic Box Office: $161,491,646

Adam Sandler movies have not been appearing on these lists of successful movies from the 90s, but I would say that among kids of my generation his movies were just as big, if not bigger, than those of Jim Carrey. The rise of Sandler as a theatrical comedy superstar was helped out by his exposure as a cast member on *Saturday Night Live* for a chunk of the 90s. Here are the movies, aside from *The Waterboy*, that were very popular with the teens to young adults of my class thru the 90s: *Airheads*, *Billy Madison*, *Happy Gilmore*, *Bulletproof*, *The Wedding Singer*, *Big Daddy*, and then *Little Nicky* landed in 2000, but I would still consider it a part of the group.

The work of Adam Sandler for me was "hit and miss," but I did indeed see *The Waterboy* at the theater and left energized and smiling. The blend of goofy comedy with hard hitting football action was a winner in my books. Um, book. This book. It's a winner. This book? Winner. Winning. Nobel Prize in literature right here.

The Waterboy is about a stuttering, socially awkward man who works as the waterboy for a college football team. When it turns out that his rage empowers him with the ability to tackle anyone he wants with authority he lands a spot on the football team. His tackling abilities are helped along by his obsession with WWF style wrestling and admiration for body slams. The Waterboy's mamma doesn't like that, wants to shelter her son, so you've got a man making his way in the world tale mixed with sports action, zany comedy, and the exploration of a relationship between a mother and her son. If that sounds stupid to you, well, it kind of is, but it's kind of the good stupid if you're in the mood for stupid. One common complaint from people that hate the movie is that they can't sit through the entire thing listening to the annoying voice Adam Sandler makes his character speak with. I even find Adam Sandler's weird voices annoying, yet, I kind of grew up hearing them and can give them a pass when I find something else about a movie of his to enjoy. *The Waterboy* showed a guy hitting back against the world and what young person doesn't relate to that? Bam! Pow!

Kathy Bates stars in *The Waterboy* as Adam Sandler's mother. An Oscar winner in 1991 for her leading role in the 1990 release *Misery* and also having been featured in the previous year's blockbuster chart topper *Titanic* as the character Molly Brown, some may have wondered what Kathy Bates was doing in a silly Adam Sandler comedy. It is rumored that she took the role because a niece was an Adam Sandler fan, but being a working actress and if one looks at her career, I think the role choice just shows that Kathy Bates may have a decent sense of humor, she has not shied away from other projects deemed by critics as "silly."

Another interesting actress that appears in *The Waterboy* is Fairuza Balk. She played the role of Vicki Vallencourt the edgy romantic interest of Sandler's character. Her name is badass looking and in terms of appearance, Balk is a unique beauty with regard to if you put her in a Hollywood lineup of actors she would stand out.

The feature film acting debut of Fairuza Balk was in 1985's *Return to Oz* in which she played Dorothy. If you've never watched this follow up to the classic *Wizard of Oz* and like weird things, I suggest you check it out. I somehow went through childhood and into adulthood without even knowing of the film's existence. *Return to Oz* was nominated for an Oscar in the category of Best Visual Effects.

Aside from *The Waterboy*, I would say Fairuza Balk's other memorable roles are her appearances in *American History X* and *The Craft*. I enjoyed both of those movies when they were released. The 1990s is the era in which I always see this actress, the decade that I just automatically associate with her name, even though she has continued acting since then. In looking her up it appears that she has also been working in the music industry. She has made music under the artist name of Armed Love Militia.

Jerry Reed, known as a musician and as an actor, probably best known for his role of Cledus in *Smokey and the Bandit*, played Coach Red Beaulieu in *The Waterboy*. He was the antagonist coach of the team opposing Adam Sandler's team, which was coached by actor Henry Winkler. *The Waterboy* was Jerry Reed's final feature film acting performance. Jerry Reed did not die until 2008, but, perhaps he thought he reached the pinnacle of the acting craft by being in *The Waterboy.*

Jerry Reed's music had some impact on my life with regard to being music that I grew up with. We had a Jerry Reed compilation cassette tape that I would listen to over and over again in my youth, mostly drawn to it by the comedic tracks such as *The Bird* and *She Got The Goldmine.*

4. A *Bug's Life* - Directed by John Lasseter and Andrew Stanton, screenplay by Andrew Stanton, Bob Shaw, and Don McEnery. Domestic Box Office: $162,798,565

A Bug's Life is a Pixar movie about an ant trying to save his colony from menacing grasshoppers. His quest for some help gets him hooked up with a group of bug circus performers, insert some words about the fun of adventure and a protagonist rising to the challenge of being a hero here.

In the same year that *A Bug's Life* was released another animated film about an ant came out with the title of *Antz*. When it comes to my memory and those dueling bug movies, for some reason *Antz* is the one I recall seeing the most, not *A Bug's Life*. My guess is that at the time I was drawn more to *Antz* because the advertising let it be known that action star Sylvester Stallone provided an ant voice.

The cast of voices for *Antz* overall is a bigger name affair in terms of my familiarity in 1998 as well; Woody Allen, Christopher Walken, Jennifer Lopez, Dan Aykroyd, Sharon Stone, Gene Hackman, Anne Bancroft, and Danny Glover.

The cast of *A Bug's Life*, competing for bug cartoon of the year against *Antz*, featured Dave Foley, Kevin Spacey, Julia-Louis-Dreyfus, Richard Kind, Phyllis Diller, Denis Leary, David Hyde Poerce, Brad Garrett, Bonnie Hunt, and Hayden Panettiere.

Did I like the movie *Antz* better than *A Bug's Life*? No. I didn't care about either one of them after seeing them. But, there's something about Mary, let's talk about that!

3. *There's Something About Mary* - Directed by Bobby Farrelly and Peter Farrelly, screenplay by Ed Decter, John J. Strauss, Bobby Farrelly, and Peter Farrelly. Domestic Box Office: $176,484,651

There's Something About Mary is full of profane and juvenile humor, but it is not all just a series of gags, the actors involved brought a lot of life into the character's helping the story achieve some depth beyond the slapstick and low-brow jokes. The Farrelly Brothers had already released two comedy movies with no care for being P.C. and *There's Something About Mary* really brought that style of humor back to the forefront of mainstream tastes, or distaste if you prefer, becoming one of the most talked about movies of the year whether a person was offended by it or giggling at it.

I think the movie did a solid job of being a "date" movie as well, appealing to people across the gender identification board not just "guy" humor, though I have heard people lump it into that category before. It's really a romantic comedy? Many mainstream critics embraced the film alongside audiences, a semi-rare occurrence for the style of movie that it is.

The plot for the movie centers around a man named Ted played by Ben Stiller. He's not content in his life and decides that he wants to track down Mary, played by Cameron Diaz, the girl he fell in love with as a teen, to see if maybe the feelings he still holds for her mean that they are meant to be together as adults. There is something special about Mary, something that makes most men that come in contact with her become obsessed with her. Ted finds himself in some weird circumstances and competing against some weird fellows in trying to woo Mary. Matt Dillion takes on a key role as the private eye hired by Ted, who also becomes infatuated by Mary. Chris Elliot, Lee Evans, Lin Shaye, Jeffrey Tambor, Keith David, Markie Post, Sarah Silverman, Richard Jenkins, Brett Favre, and Harland Williams are some of the many other names that showed up to play with the Farrelly Brothers.

The "hair gel" scene from *There's Something About Mary* was one of the most popular moments discussed by viewers after the movie released. It remains an infamous scene in movie history and if you have not seen the movie don't read on because in this very sentence I am going to tell you that it is a scene where Mary mistakes semen hanging off of Ted's ear for hair gel, grabs it, and smears it into her hair causing her hair to stick up funny.

Behind the scene of that specific scene Cameron Diaz is said to have had some reservations about pretending to put jizz in her hair. However, she is said to have been won over, trusting the directors and after seeing what they were going to do to her hair realizing that perhaps it would indeed be a funny moment as opposed to being career ending smut.

The Farrelly Brothers themselves questioned their own scene not wanting to shock people or gross them out, not looking to "push the limits" as many assume they try to do. It took the laughter in test screenings to settle their nerves as to whether or not the scene was too over-the-top or worth keeping for the laughter.

Meanwhile, Ben Stiller supposedly had his own reservations about that scene with regard to the glob of spunk dangling off of his ear. He is said to have argued that a person would feel it hanging there and that they should write something in the script about his character not having good feeling in his ears to explain why he doesn't notice it before Mary does. A story like this is a good one for showing people how the creative process during a shoot works. People will analyze every little detail and it is a skill to know when you are over-thinking something and understand when to go with the flow. This is where the director earns part of their paycheck, directing the vision and tone of the film, gaining and holding the trust of the actors so that the vision can be realized as intended. If that specific scene had bombed as shot, I don't think many would have blamed the actors, the Farrelly Brothers would have gotten the critical stoning. The scene is funny in part due to the fact that, yes, common sense says he should have felt it hanging off of his ear, but, he didn't.

W. Earl Brown, whom I did not mention in the list of cast names earlier, plays the role of Warren in *There's Something About Mary*. Warren is Mary's special needs brother. It can be easy for the P.C. police to try and argue that people with mental disabilities should not be featured within such a comedy because it is concerning to think that people might laugh at them for being different. However, the Farrelly Brothers have made a point of mentioning that they are aware of preconceived notions involving jokes in which a handicapped person is involved and from their perspective the character of Warren was not made handicapped for laughs, rather, having grown up around handicapped people, they felt like incorporating one into the story organically as any other person. There are handicapped people in life, therefore, there should be handicapped people in movies, even movies that skew toward insensitive humor at times.

The character of Warren is actually based off of a neighbor and friend of the Farrelly Brothers and said friend even has a cameo in the film. Mary's step-father, played by Keith David, is also based off of a real person, the Farrelly's own father. Also, the early scene of Ted zipping himself up into the zipper of his pants, ouch, yep, a supposed real event that happened to a kid visiting their house when the Farrelly's were younger.

2. *Armageddon* - Directed by Michael Bay, screenplay by Jonathan Hensleigh and J.J. Abrams. Domestic Box Office: $201,578,182

There is a lot of critical hate for the works of director Michael Bay. When I was a teenager my friends and I were not critical about the director's technical approach. His films to us felt like a new energy had landed on the scene. *Armageddon* is considered by many to be a terrible and silly film. I thought it was cool and I still enjoy it now. It is a blend of dramatic, heroic soap opera drama within a science fiction disaster premise, spun out with the fast tempo of an action movie, and at a smidge over two and a half hours long it can sometimes actually feel rushed.

Is my admiration driven in part by nostalgia? Probably. It is popular for people to look back on the film and criticize it, even many of the people involved with the production have been known to do that. I can understand people not liking the way the film is edited together in a rapid flow of clips. All of the rotating camera shots, I can understand someone thinking the movie tries too hard with tricks, style over substance, there are many valid arguments against liking the film. All of that style, however, took action movies to another level and my developing, action movie fan mind embraced the adrenaline produced back in the 90s. My defending of the work is not just nostalgia, or a brain washed by early exposure, because I have found many Michael Bay movies to be entertaining: *Bad Boys*, *Bad Boys 2*, *The Rock*, *The Island*, *Pain & Gain*, and *13 Hours* were all worth the ticket price to me. Wait, maybe I was brainwashed as a teen. How would I know? Maybe I should join the revolt against Michael Bay movies. I've never liked the *Transformers* movie series directed by him.

The plot for the film *Armageddon* is about oil drillers being sent into space to land on an asteroid so that they can drill into it and place a nuclear bomb inside. The need to do this is brought on by the fact that the asteroid is on a collision course with Earth, an end to all life on the planet event. Some of the creators of the movie *Deep Impact* have claimed that someone from *Armageddon* sat in on their meetings and wrote down all that they could in order to purposefully make a competing movie of similar ilk. The production teams did have a public feud going back and forth with insults flying in the press.

"It happened before. It will happen again."

The opening narrator of the movie delivers an ominous warning that not only sets the mood for *Armageddon*, but if you think about it sets up the potential for a sequel. I mean, when I think of Armageddon the word, I think: the end. However, with the opening showing the planet being hit by an asteroid during the time of the dinosaurs, and the narrator's warning paired with it, I get fixated on "it can happen again," and think *Armageddon* 2: *The End of the World All Over Again*.

Critics may have taken this movie too seriously. Throw science out the window folks! There is an early scene in which Billy Bob Thornton is demanding solutions from his NASA team with regard to stopping the asteroid. After a few suggestions he yells: "Come on guys we've got to come up with something realistic here!" And the smartest guy in the world helps develop a plan to send roughneck oil drillers into space to defeat the asteroid. The scenario is so not realistic that the line of dialog delivered by Billy Bob Thornton to me helps wipe away any complaints people may have over logic. It's meant to be entertainment, fun, not realistic. Sometimes I am guilty of not being able to check my brain and reality at the door when it comes to picking a movie apart over realism, but I've never had that problem with *Armageddon*.

If I were going to complain about the logic of the film I might start with the usage of time. There are many moments in the film where in one section X

293

amount of time is supposed to have passed, yet the film cuts to another part where Y amount of time seems to have passed, even though the parts are supposed to be occurring synchronized with one another.

The cast of *Armageddon* is packed with familiar names and faces. Bruce Willis, Ben Affleck, Billy Bob Thornton, and Liv Tyler are probably considered the leads, with Bruce Willis and Ben Affleck really being the main leads. Their star power is surrounded by supporting star power, the real special ingredient to the movie perhaps, with the likes of Steve Buscemi, Will Patton, Owen Wilson, Michael Clarke Duncan, and Peter Stormare filling the shoes of some quirky characters. William Fichtner, Jason Isaacs, Keith David, and many more make the most of their screen time bringing solid presence as well.

The movie looks like a lot of money was put into it for sure. Even with advances in technology the special effects for *Armageddon* don't look too bad as I watch it in 2018. You can see some weak edges around some of the effects, specifically during the space shuttles taking off from Earth section. Best Sound, Best Special Effects Editing, and Best Visual Effects were three of the four categories for which the film received Oscar nominations.

The fourth Oscar nomination that *Armageddon* received was for Best Original Song. The song *I Don't Want To Miss A Thing*, written by Diane

Warren and performed by Aerosmith, lost out to *When You Believe* from the animated feature *The Prince of Egypt*. The music video for the song became the second most popular video aired on MTV in 1998, beat out in airplay by only the Brandy and Monica video for *The Boy is Mine*.

1. *Saving Private Ryan* - Directed by Steven Spielberg, screenplay by Robert Rodat. Domestic Box Office: $216,540,909

Saving Private Ryan is an epic WW2 movie that follows a group of soldiers with the special mission of finding Private Ryan. They are meant to extract Ryan from the battlefield due to all of his brothers having been killed and the U.S. government deciding that the Ryan family had sacrificed enough, they did not wish to see the future of an entire family wiped out. This film is considered by many to be the greatest war film ever made. As of this writing I can't really think of any other war film off the top of my head that has been able to capture the violence and drama in such a gritty fashion. The film won five Oscars: Best Director, Best Cinematography, Best Sound, Best Film Editing, and Best Sound Effects Editing. It somehow lost the Best Picture category to the film *Shakespeare in Love*.

Robert Rodat wrote the screenplay for Saving Private Ryan. He is said to have been inspired by the true life tale of the Niland brothers. Three of the brothers were thought to be dead and the sole survivor sent back to the United States to serve his country outside of the combat zones. In real life, though not in the inspired film, one of the thought to be dead brothers turned up alive having been a prisoner in a Japanese POW camp.

The screenplay for *Saving Private Ryan* did get Robert Rodat an Oscar nomination, but he lost out to Marc Norman and Tom Stoppard who wrote *Shakespeare in Love*. Other screenplay credits earned by Robert Radot include: *Tall Tale*, *Fly Away Home*, *The Patriot*, and *Thor: The Dark World*. He also created the television series *Falling Skies*.

Saving Private Ryan brought in the most box office dollars within the North American market, but *Armageddon* actually went on to make more money worldwide. The top five in worldwide box office results of 1998 were in this order: *Armageddon*, *Saving Private Ryan*, *Godzilla*, *There's Something About Mary*, and *A Bug's Life*.

1999

10. *The Blair Witch Project* - Directed by Daniel Myrick and Eduardo Sanchez, screenplay by Daniel Myrick and Eduardo Sanchez. Domestic Box Office: $140,539,099

In 1998 I went to the theater to see *The Blair Witch Project* due to it being an "everyone is talking about it" phenomenon. I went into the movie knowing that it was a movie. After watching it I was confused as to why everyone loved it. I think it was less about the movie actually being all that interesting and more about the fact that people thought it was real. I had arguments with classmates over whether or not the footage in the movie was real found footage. Perhaps my never being suckered into the fakery of the film's marketing was in part due to the fact that we did not have the Internet in my household at that time, from what I understand the perpetrating of the hoax was strong on the world wide web.

I want to say that another film could never fool people in the same vein as *The Blair Witch Project* but considering how often people fall for fake news still, I'm sure something will come along.

Basically the movie is about a group of people that wander around a forest where a witch has set up shop for haunting. The movie is comprised of "found footage" supposedly discovered after the disappearance of the people seen in the footage.

The Blair Witch Project's success helped get the sequel made: *Book of Shadows: Blair Witch 2*. The sequel released in 2000 without trying to pretend it was "found footage." I actually watched the sequel at the theater as well. The thing I remember most about the sequel is that the Marilyn Manson song *Disposable Teens* was featured on the soundtrack.

Aside from the soundtrack to *Book of Shadows: Blair Witch 2* the Manson song *Disposable Teens* appeared on his album that was also released in 2000: *Holy Wood (In the Shadow of the Valley of Death.)* The album is considered by some to be a rather dark piece of art. At a factory that I once worked at, I was playing Marilyn Manson's Cd and I recall being told that I would have to turn the volume down because I was making the other employees want to slit their wrists.

Over the years there have been books, comic books, and video games created based off of *The Blair Witch*. In 2015 a documentary about the making of the film was released with the title *The Woods Movie*. In 2016 the series got another entry in the form of the film *Blair Witch*. As I write this a television series is supposedly in the works. People in the future can tell me about that if it comes to fruition because I doubt I watch it.

9. *Runaway Bride* - Directed by Garry Marshall, screenplay by Josann McGibbon and Sara Parriott. Domestic Box Office: $152,257,509

Runaway Bride is a romantic comedy about a woman that leaves men at the altar on their wedding days. She earns the nickname the "runaway bride" and a reporter is sent to research her for a story as she prepares for yet another wedding that she may or may not run from. The film was directed by Garry Marshall, the same man that helmed *Pretty Woman*, and stars Julia Roberts, the same woman that starred in *Pretty Woman*, along with Richard Gere, the same man that starred in *Pretty Woman*.

In 2005 a woman in real life got dubbed the "Runaway Bride." Jennifer Wilbanks vanished just days before her wedding. Three days later she returned with a story about having been kidnapped and sexually assaulted by a couple that nabbed her when she was out for a run. However, she soon came clean that she had hopped on a bus and went into hiding due to "personal issues." Wilbanks ended up going to court instead of to the chapel, getting a couple of years of probation along with some community service, hefty fines, and some appointments to have her mental health checked up on.

8. *The Mummy* - Directed by Stephen Sommers, screenplay by Stephen Sommers. Domestic Box Office: $155,385,488

Pauly Shore happened in the 90s. His movies are not showing up on these lists, but when I was a kid I'd say that we rented far more Pauly Shore movies than we did Adam Sandler or Jim Carrey movies. When you're younger I think you're more likely to watch movies over and over again and that is why I say Pauly Shore movies were more popular to us, they were released when I was younger, Sandler and Carrey hit their pop culture stride at the older end of my teens. I bring up Pauly Shore because of his movie *Encino Man*. When I think of actor Brendan Fraser, star of the 1999 movie *The Mummy*, I always think of him first as Link, the caveman from *Encino Man*.

Brendan Fraser had other early roles, but much of his exposure in pop culture, prior to being the leading adventurer in *The Mummy,* came *via Encino Man, Airheads, and then George of the Jungle. By the time The Mummy came out in 1999 Fraser was possibly typecast in my mind as someone meant to play goofy, somewhat dumb characters. I personally did not have any interest in seeing George of the Jungle facing off against a mummy. My perspective was from the consumer viewpoint of a late teen. As I've aged and worked in the movie industry, seeing the uphill struggle of what it is not only to start, but to maintain an acting career, I can see the frustration that is experienced, even by a successful actor, at what they are pinned down as at any given time in terms of being a "product." It sort of makes me want to go back in time and root for Brenda Fraser in his battle against the mummy or at least critically dislike it for less shallow reasons than I saw the facial expressions of a certain caveman and a jungle man every time I looked at him. I liked Encino Man and Airheads, by the way, as a kid. George of the Jungle, which I could have lived without seeing, is probably to blame for my not taking interest in Brendan Fraser starring films in my older teens. Of course, my not caring about the mummy movies and his career didn't sink any ships: The Mummy was the sixth highest grossing film in North America on the year and spawned sequels and spinoff movies, not many actors can say that got to star in something like that.*

The Mummy is heavy on CGI. I can vaguely recall that aspect being a strike against the film in my teen mind as well. I'm not sure why, guess it was just released in a window of time where I was too cool for CGI. Or perhaps I just did not like the results that they were showing off in the trailers. There is no point in trying to decode or understand the whims of the teenage mind in full. It's not like I turned my nose up at all CGI offerings. It's not like I didn't give a thumbs up of approval to a movie in the previous year about an oil drill team flying into space to blow up an asteroid with a nuke.

There are some cool "what might have been" stories about the creative process that went into bringing about *The Mummy*. It is said that at one point the studio was looking into doing a low-budget mummy film with Clive Barker. Clive Barker is a book author, painter, and the filmmaker behind *Hellraiser*, *Nightbreed*, and *Lord of Illusions*. The tone of his movies have a way of creeping under a person's skin and his imagination in presenting new demons or creatures is unparalleled. I've always enjoyed the rich detail within his books and it is impressive how well he has been able to translate

302

his creations from written word into moving pictures. If Clive Barker had been given *The Mummy* duties there is no question that I would have been lined up to see it on opening day.

Joe Dante, Wes Craven, George A. Romero, and Mick Garris are other names that supposedly put in some thought at Universal over how to reignite the classic monster character. Eventually Stephen Sommers came along with his passion for the material and is said to have talked the studio into expanding their thinking and opening up the company wallet to produce a summer blockbuster to be released in May. Sommers would go on to direct the sequel *The Mummy Returns* and then moved on to *Van Helsing* and then *G.I. Joe: The Rise of Cobra*.

7. *Big Daddy* - Directed by Dennis Dugan, screenplay by Steve Franks, Tim Herlihy, and Adam Sandler. Domestic Box Office: $163,479,795

Big Daddy stars Adam Sandler as a thirty-something bachelor, Sonny, who despite having a law degree, coasts through life in a manner that his girlfriend labels as both lazy and immature. In a twist of fate a five year old boy, a supposed offspring of Sonny's out of town roommate, is left at the apartment and Sonny schemes a way to impress girls by passing the kid off as his own foster child. He decides to be the cool type of dad and let the kid make up his own rules which result in some comedic bits, but ultimately the story is a heartfelt coming of age drama about understanding responsibility and caring for others beyond yourself.

The film is still a comedy with plenty of silliness explored, however, it did mark a bit of a change for Sandler compared to the even more low-brow efforts he was known for previously. I wouldn't say it was a complete transition out of his brand of comedy, but there was a new tone of seriousness struck within the film. I think the 1998 film *The Wedding Singer* actually had some of that element as well, but the concept and presentation of *Big Daddy* overall realized that vision more, showing off how versatile Sandler's acting could be.

Big Daddy was the first film that Adam Sandler did for Sony's production company. It also marks the last film before Sandler embarked on his own production adventures forming his company Happy Madison Productions. The Sony connection stayed intact with Happy Madison keeping some production offices on the Sony Pictures Studio lot. The first film created by Happy Madison was *Deuce Bigalow: Male Gigolo* starring Rob Schneider. I saw that movie at the theater and my friends and I thought it was quite funny.

Dennis Dugan had directed Adam Sandler prior to *Big Daddy* and has directed films starring him since. Some of the work that Dugan and Sandler have done together include: *Happy Gilmore, I Now Pronounce You Chuck and Larry, You Don't Mess with the Zohan, Grown Ups, Grown Ups 2, Just Go with It,* and *Jack and Jill.*

The child character in the film *Big Daddy* wasn't portrayed by a single actor, twin brothers Cole and Dylan Sprouse took on the role. The Sprouse brothers continued acting becoming the title characters of Zack and Cody in the Disney television show *The Suite Life of Zack and Cody.* When he got older Cole Sprouse landed the role of Jughead Jones on the popular show *Riverdale* which re-imagined the Archie comic book characters as a teen/ young adult television program.

In 1999 Limp Bizkit's second album *Significant Other* was one that I listened to a lot. It came out in the same month as *Big Daddy* the movie came out into theaters. *Big Daddy* featured the Limp Bizkit song *Just Like This* from *Significant Other,* helping the movie capture even more cool factor in the moment.

6. *Tarzan* - Directed by Chris Buck and Kevin Lima, screenplay by Tab Murphy, Bob Tzudiker, and Noni White. Domestic Box Office: $171,091,819

In 1999 my interest in Disney animated films was low and my interest in an animated *Tarzan* movie was at zero percent. Perhaps if it had been about an animated woman in a loincloth my seventeen year old hormones may have at least considered watching the movie. As it stands, I've never sat through the entire *Tarzan* cartoon of 1999. I've only seen bits and pieces of the movie as it played on a television that my younger siblings were watching. Tarzan stories were never something that caught on with me.

This Disney version of *Tarzan* lays claim to the fame of being the very first animated version of the Tarzan story. Tarzan, of course, is a character that ended up in the jungle as a human child and was raised by apes into a vine swinging hero.

This film did not follow the general Disney musical formula in that the characters in the film did not break out into song and dance numbers. They did not slouch with regard to adding music into the movie though. Phil Collins was brought on board to create and sing the music featured in the film. He won an Oscar the following year for the *Tarzan* song *You'll Be In My Heart*.

Tony Goldwyn providing the speaking voice for the adult Tarzan in the film. He was the villain in the 1990 Patrick Swayze movie *Ghost*. Tony Goldwyn is said to have had a hard time trying to do Tarzan's signature "yell," and that vocal aspect of the character was provided by Brian Blessed who also provided the voice of the character Clayton in the film.

Minnie Driver, who was nominated for an Oscar for her role in *Good Will Hunting*, provided the voice for Jane in Disney's Tarzan. Some of the other actors involved were Glenn Close, Rosie O'Donnell, Lance Henriksen, and Nigel Hawthorne.

An animated television series called *The Legend of Tarzan* picked up where the film left off and aired from 2001 to 2003. There were also two direct to video animated sequels for the film: *Tarzan and Jane* in 2002 and then *Tarzan 2* in 2005. Disney also produced a *Tarzan* Broadway show which lasted a little over a year in 2006 to 2007.

5. *The Matrix* - Directed by The Wachowski Brothers, screenplay by The Wachowski Brothers. Domestic Box Office: $171,479,930

Something kept me from seeing *The Matrix* when it played in theaters. Word of mouth spread about the film and I know I had the desire to see it and did so as soon as it was released on home video for rental. Now I have a mystery on my hands. I won't bother you with the investigation, I won't drag you down into the dark pit that is my memory, won't get you lost as I am apt to get lost, but why did a young man, an avid buyer of tickets to theatrical movie releases, not get to see *The Matrix* in its theatrical release? It may never be solved.

I sure did think the movie was cool when I saw it though. The Academy of Motion Picture Arts and Sciences liked what they saw and heard too. *The Matrix* won four Oscar awards: Best Visual Effects, Best Film Editing, Best Sound, and Best Sound Effects Editing.

The movie made technological advances in stunt work and special effects while blending action and science fiction without compromising the integrity of either film genre. It ended up seeming like a smarter than usual action film, an intellectual's action movie if you will. I enjoyed the workout that the science fiction concept gave my brain while the violence hit hard. Seventeen year old American boys love their violence and porn.

The slow motion "bullet time" effects were created for *The Matrix*, inspiring many films afterward, but whenever I think of the action of the movie for some reason my mind flashes immediately to the lobby shootout where the bullets blow apart the pillars. While there is obviously a lot of computer assisted sequences in the film, many of the locations for action sequences were sets built specifically for the movie, which allowed total destruction with practical effects.

The Wachowski Brothers, as they were known at the time, did not have an easy path to getting studio backing for *The Matrix*. The budget needed meant a lot of risk and the duo were not known as directors. It's kind of crazy to see that they were able to make something as astounding as *The Matrix* as only their second Hollywood film.

The Wachowskis, after some transitions now known as Lilly and Lana, started their film credits as writers. They wrote the screenplay for the 1995 action film *Assassins* in which Sylvester Stallone and Antonio Banderas compete against one another. The duo then moved into directors chairs for the movie *Bound*, which they also wrote, released in 1996. *Bound* must have impressed the right people because *The Matrix* was their next project to get backed. As a part of the process of selling Warner Brothers on funding the movie a "comic book" was created, basically a 600 page storyboard, shot for shot showing off of what the movie would be.

Keanu Reeves stars as the lead in *The Matrix*. As the story goes, however, actor Will Smith was first offered the part and turned it down to instead star in the film *Wild Wild West*. I did see *Wild Wild West* at the theater and yuck. It's fun to imagine what sort of song or music video Will Smith might have released to pair with *The Matrix* had he taken that role.

When *The Matrix* sequel was released in 2003, *The Matrix Reloaded,* I was excited and made sure to see it on the big screen. It disappointed me and when the third film, *The Matrix Revolutions*, came out I waited for it to be a rental before watching. The first time I tried watching *The Matrix Revolutions* I recall getting bored and turning it off. Neither sequel to *The Matrix* won me over.

4. *Austin Powers: The Spy Who Shagged Me* - Directed by Jay Roach, screenplay by Mike Myers and Michael McCullers. Domestic Box Office: $206,040,086

The sequel to *the 1997 film Austin Powers: International Man of Mystery, Austin Powers: The*

Spy Who Shagged Me follows the spy that in the original film was cryogenically frozen in the 60s only to be thawed out in the 90s as he now travels back in time to the 60s from the 90s. Once again Austin Powers is up against his foe Dr. Evil, who has used time travel to go back and steal his mojo. Mike Myers stars as both Austin Powers and Dr. Evil.

The Austin Powers movies spoof a lot of different movies. It seems that slapstick and over-the-top goofy comedies come around in cycles with every now and then one of them striking the funny bone of audiences and becoming a pop culture hit. Kids at my school seemed obsessed with Austin Powers reciting lines and bad accents in the hallways. This sequel made more money in its opening weekend than the first film made in its original theatrical run altogether. As with many trendy things, I never fully embraced the series, did not really care about the movies.

The character of Austin Powers is a blend of British influences, but mainly Mike Myers has said that he created the character as a tribute to his father who introduced him to a lot of British pop culture such as James Bond and The Beatles. As for Dr. Evil, there is some controversy surrounding that character. Dana Carvey, Garth from *Wayne's World* and a Mike Myers colleague on *Saturday Night Live*, believed the nuances of the character were stolen from his own impression of *SNL* head honcho Lorne Michaels.

Aside from the leading spy and villain, I can recall the favorite characters of those around me seemed to be Mini-Me as played by Verne Troy and then Fat Bastard which was Mike Myers in a fat suit and heavy makeup. *Austin Powers: The Spy Who Shagged Me* actually got an Oscar nomination for Best Makeup, so, Fat Bastard may have been responsible for that.

The soundtrack for the film was led by the Madonna single *Beautiful Stranger*. In 2000 the song won a Grammy for Best Song Written for a Motion Picture, Television or Other Visual Media. The music video was directed by Brett Rattner and promoted the film with Austin Powers appearing in it. Another strong single off of the *Austin Powers: The Spy Who Shagged Me* soundtrack, one that I recall getting a lot of MTV attention, was the Lenny Kravitz cover of *American Woman.* I am known to sing out a line of that song from time to time, the guitar riff is permanently stuck on my brain, but with the lyrics changed to "American Wesley, stay away from me." It makes sense, feel free to sing that version too.

Aside from directing three Austin Powers movies, Jay Roach is also known for directing the first two films of another comedy series. He directed the 2000 release *Meet the Parents* as well as its sequel *Meet the Fockers*.

3. *Toy Story 2* - Directed by John Lasseter, Ash Brannon, and Lee Unkrich, screenplay by Andrew Stanton, Rita Hsiao, Doug Chamberlin, and Chris Webb. Domestic Box Office: $245,852,179

The story for *Toy Story 2* involves toys again. Woody the toy cowboy is stolen by a toy collector and the other toys, including Buzz Lightyear, set off to rescue him. Tom Hanks and Tim Allen returned for the leading cowboy and spaceman voice work.

Audiences are known to find the *Toy Story* films to be touching, heartfelt, warm. The business behind the scenes of a film production is usually not those things and rumor has it that Disney wanted *Toy Story 2* quicker than the production team was moving on it, leading to some grumpiness and some firings during the process. At one point the aim for *Toy Story 2* is said to have been the direct to video market, not another theatrical release. Yet, release to theaters it did and a success it was.

One specific horror story from behind the scenes of *Toy Story 2* involves an animator doing some routine file deletion. The animator accidentally chose the root folder for Toy Story 2 to be deleted and two years of work vanished. When the mistake was discovered they checked their backup servers for the material only to find that their backup servers had failed previously and not stored the work. Luckily a technical director had been doing work from home and had backups of the work on her home computer. The production ended up losing only a few days' worth of work instead of having to start over from scratch.

The club store Costco has its own *Toy Story 2* horror story; Toy Terrors from Retail! When the film was released on home video they did an "Ultimate Toy Box" box set edition. It is estimated that 1,000 copies of the movie that were shipped to Costco featured a technical goof. In the middle of the movie dismayed parents found that a scene from the R rated John Cusack film *High Fidelity* suddenly appeared with all of its salty language included. The product was recalled, but if you're a collector of Disney products I'm sure you'd like to have that there "unrated" cut. John Cusack's sister Joan Cusack does happen to provide the voice for Jessie the Yodeling Cowgirl in *Toy Story 2*.

Randy Newman returned to provide music for this sequel. His song *When She Loved Me* was nominated for an Oscar but lost out to the Phil Collins song *You'll Be in My Heart* from *Tarzan*.

2. *The Sixth Sense* - Directed by M. Night Shyamalan, screenplay by M. Night Shyamalan. Domestic Box Office: $293,506,292

If you have not seen *The Sixth Sense* and want to I advise you not to read this section because I am going to spoil the ending.

M. Night Shyamalan's movie *The Sixth Sense* came to theaters with a lot of hype about a shocking, twist ending. My friend and I went to see the film at the theater to discover what all of the fuss was about. Even though I did not have the Internet and spoilers were not a thing, just knowing that there was going to be a twist ending primed my brain for solving the puzzle. After the opening scene of the movie played, I turned to my friend and whispered: "that's the twist, Bruce Willis is dead." I was right. Well, Bruce Willis didn't die, but the fictional character he was playing did.

The Sixth Sense is about a psychologist, played by Bruce Willis, trying to help a young boy, played by Haley Joel Osment, who thinks that he can see dead people. He can. And Bruce Willis is one of the dead people.

The movie did not have much impact on me due to my guessing the ending and then sitting through the entire movie only to be proven right. I have seen it several times and don't hate it by any means, but it's not the ground-breaking event to me that it was for a slice of time at the tail end of the 90s.

The film was nominated for six Oscars, winning none. Bruce Willis did not get nominated for his lead, but Haley Joel Osment and Toni Collette, who played the mother to the child, both received Best Supporting Actor nominations. The film did land in the major categories of Best Picture, Best Director, and Best Screenplay, but the winners of the year in those three categories went to: *American Beauty*, *American Beauty*, and *American Beauty*. Heck, if

I've ruined *The Sixth Sense* for you, perhaps you'd be interested in watching a little something called *American Beauty*.

Riding on the wave of popularity from *The Sixth Sense*, M. Night Shyamalan went to work trying to repeat his formula of a "twist" ending movie. His next films *Unbreakable* and *Signs* both did well from what I can recall, but then he did *The Village* and it was fairly lame. He followed that up with *Lady in the Water* and *The Happening* and at that point I think his career in terms of people getting excited for an M. Night Shyamalan movie fell off the wave and got soggy. After his next three movies, *The Last Airbender*, *After Earth*, and then *The Visit*, he directed *Split* in 2016 and that film seemed to get him back in the good graces of audiences once again. I mean, before *Split* came out and people enjoyed it, I would often hear the question: "who keeps giving M. Night Shyamalan money to make movies?"

The Sixth Sense came to home video in March of 2000. It became the top selling DVD for the year 2000.

1. *Star Wars: Episode One - The Phantom Menace* - Directed by George Lucas, screenplay by George Lucas. Domestic Box Office: $431,088,295

My butt fell asleep while watching *Star Wars: Episode One - The Phantom Menace* at the theater.

Yawn. I judge a movie by how good my butt feels while watching it.

This was the film that started *Star Wars* back up for a new generation, the first in a new trilogy, and I saw all three of the films at the theater not because I actually wanted to, but because my friend wanted to and going to the movies, a forty-five minute drive, is one of the only things you can do for entertainment when living in a tiny rural town, if you're not into doing meth or heroin that is. If you're into those drugs then you probably don't have the time or money for movies, though, maybe you do drive to the theater parking lot to break into cars for items you might sell for more meth and heroin. Who am I kidding? Even crackheads bought a ticket to the *Phantom Menace*. It was an event indeed.

The Phantom Menace stayed at theaters for forever it seemed like to me. It opened in May but was still playing when my friend and I went to see *American Pie* in July. I recall that day well because I was already old enough to buy a ticket to an R rated movie, but he was some months shy of seventeen and needed to sneak in. He bought a ticket to *The Phantom Menace* and then walked into *American Pie* instead. One problem with that plan was that he and I were the only two people in the theater at that time watching *American Pie*. We spent a part of watching that movie wondering if theater staff would catch on and boot him out. They did not. I liked *American Pie* way more than *The Phantom Menace*.

The *Star Wars* films are such an epic undertaking with regard to writing about them. There is a ton of information out there, and products to buy, for fans to debate and dissect, I wouldn't be doing the film any justice yammering on any farther about it. I'm not lazy! But, my butt is falling asleep and I want to get out of my office chair.

Made in United States
North Haven, CT
04 April 2024